THE
GOOD GARDENER'S
ENCYCLOPEDIA

THE
GOOD GARDENER'S
ENCYCLOPEDIA

month by month in the garden

STANLEY B. WHITEHEAD

SPRING BOOKS • LONDON

Uniform with this volume

THE GOOD COOK'S ENCYCLOPEDIA
THE GOOD HANDYMAN'S ENCYCLOPEDIA
THE GOOD HOUSEWIFE'S ENCYCLOPEDIA

© Stanley B. Whitehead 1964

PUBLISHED BY SPRING BOOKS

WESTBOOK HOUSE • FULHAM BROADWAY • LONDON

Printed in Czechoslovakia by Tisk, Brno

T 1352

Contents

Gardener's Calendar

*To every thing there is a season, and a time to
every purpose under the heaven: A time to be
born, and a time to die; a time to plant, and
a time to pluck up that which is planted.'*

ECCLESIASTES

AS THE preacher reminds us, life in all its forms has its cycle
and rhythm of growth and decline. In the largest sense,
the clock by which they are regulated is that of the universe
by which the planets, stars and other bodies of space are set
and maintained in their courses and movements. Narrowed
down from the macrocosm of the universe to the microcosm
of our own world, and still further to that of our own garden,
the forces that determine the cycle of plant growth are those
of climate and their influence upon the immediate environment
of plants.

Although these forces vary from day to day, from week to
week, from month to month, and from year to year in their
incidence and timing, they do have a certain and sure progression. The seasons follow one another in due sequence,
with plant life quickening and flourishing as the light and

7

heat rays of the sun strengthen in duration and intensity, and declining as they weaken.

It is this fact that makes it possible for the gardener to plan and carry out his work within the somewhat arbitrary order and framework of a calendar. But such a calendar is made for the gardener rather than for the plant. It cannot lay down hard and fast rules as to the precise timing of what must be done, since no two years in a temperate clime are alike. It is, therefore, a guide as to what may be done when weather and soil conditions are suitable.

The hints and suggestions given in this encyclopedia, therefore, must be interpreted in the light of the climatic and environmental conditions prevailing in your own garden; while the general weather conditions of your locality have an important say in how your garden grows, they are subject to modification within the garden itself, depending on its position in relation to surrounding ground and country, and its own plant population.

Obviously, a garden situated on the southern side of a hill will tend to be warmer, especially in spring, late autumn and winter, than one on the northern, although only a few hundred yards may separate them physically. The effects of air currents and wind are greatly modified by hedges and sheltered lees of fences, buildings or plants. Within a garden, some parts will be found to sponsor earlier growth than others.

Nevertheless, the timing of gardening operations and planting is of fundamental importance. Both from the angle of growing plants with the maximum of success and ease, and of conserving gardening time and energy, it is vital to do the right thing at the right time. What is done must fit in with the rhythm of plant life at that particular time. No use planting potatoes during the height of summer, for potato growth and tuber formation depend on the length of the day. But the best time to plant potatoes for optimum yields may vary by three, four or more weeks according to the individual garden.

In practice, it is the climatic and environmental conditions within your own garden that count, and these are primarily affected by the following six factors.

Latitude. Broadly, the farther north your garden is, the less warmth and the less light you can count on from the sun. The cooler your range of temperatures, the hardier your plants need to be. Spring arrives later, and plant growth is that much delayed; while autumn comes sooner, with earlier maturity and harvest among plants.

Nearness to the sea. Proximity to the sea modifies the full effect of latitude in that slightly warmer conditions tend to prevail during the colder months of the year, particularly on southern and western coasts, especially where the Gulf Stream exerts its influence. This often means that a slightly earlier start to growth occurs in spring, and less hardy plants have a better chance than in the same latitude inland. On eastern and northern coasts, however, the effect of the sea's proximity is often offset by cold drying winds of continental or arctic origin, especially in spring.

Altitude. The higher your garden, the colder and more exposed it will be, which will make for a late spring and an early autumn, though the full effect of altitude may be modified by the lie or aspect of the land, and its height relative to surrounding land. Light intensity tends to increase with latitude, making for good and rapid growth when temperatures are in step.

Aspect. If your garden faces south to south-west, it receives much sun, both daily and seasonally, which makes for extended growth. The garden is well warmed, and so can be cultivated early in the spring, and autumn tends to come late. With a northerly or easterly aspect, the daily duration of sun is shortened at the approach of sunset, and light duration and intensity diminished. This delays warming-up of the soil in spring, and fosters greater susceptibility to low temperatures.

Height relative to surrounding land. This is important because of its effect on air currents. If your garden lies in a depression of ground, cold air will tend to gravitate to it. It will then be susceptible to spring, autumn and winter frosts to a greater degree than the higher surrounding land. The same effect also results when cold air flowing from higher ground is trapped by walls, fences, buildings or hedges placed across the slope, so that it cannot escape to lower ground.

Soil. The readiness with which a soil absorbs and retains sun heat has a profound effect upon seed germination, root activity and subsequent growth. This is chiefly affected by two things—porosity and colour. The more porous a soil, the more freely air circulates through it, and the more quickly it reacts to sun heat and atmospheric temperatures. Thus light, sandy, gravelly or chalky soils of open texture warm up relatively quickly in spring, permitting an earlier start to be made with sowings, plantings and croppings. The heavier and more clayey the soil, the more moisture it contains, and the longer it takes to warm. The gardener with a heavy, moist soil may therefore find himself one to three weeks behind his fellow on a light, porous soil.

Colour affects soil temperatures in that the darker the colour, the more completely it absorbs the sun's heat rays, and the more slowly it loses their warmth. A dark-coloured soil not only absorbs sun heat quickly in the early spring, but also retains it to lengthen the autumn growing period. Ideally, the best soils are those which are porous and dark by reason of the presence of decomposing, humus-forming matter. Since the latter also contributes to a better soil structure and more openness, most soils can be ameliorated by its addition in the form of regular organic manuring.

And having taken all these weighty matters into account, there is still the garden's own micro-climate to be considered. As your garden evolves and becomes planted with its permanent inhabitants, it acquires a climate of its own. A screen or a hedge here will give shelter and slightly raised temperatures in its lee, permitting the earlier planting or cropping of certain plants. Some parts will get more sun than others. Alterations in levels and aspects bring changes, and with observation you come to know the fuller possibilities of all parts of your domain. In the shelter of hardy plants, less hardy subjects may be attempted. As you come to know your garden better, the timing of your garden operations will be more precisely influenced by your knowledge of its modified and localised climate, and your garden calendar arranged to meet the needs of your plants for their best performance.

January

As the day lengthens, the cold strengthens.
17TH CENTURY ENGLISH PROVERB

FROST is an excellent soil conditioner, especially where soils contain much clay, pushing soil particles apart in clods on freezing so that they break up into smaller crumbs, which can be easily worked after thawing into a fine surface tilth for sowing. So push on with soil preparations, digging or bastard-trenching in mild weather.

Work in organic manure where needed in the vegetable plot, in new flower borders and shrub planting stations; but do not lime at the same time—wait at least three weeks. Lime coming into contact with fresh manure reacts chemically with a resultant loss of plant nutrients, such as nitrogen.

Keep off the soil on days when it is wet and sticks to your boots. Clay, compressed when wet, becomes brick-like when it dries, and is hard to break down to good crumb structure.

The gardener's New Year resolution should be to order

13

seeds early. Evergreens and conifers for spring planting, plants and roses for late winter planting, should be ordered without further delay.

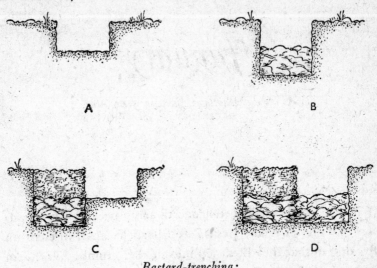

Bastard-trenching:
a. Trench of top-soil with one spit removed.
b. Subsoil forked over and broken up.
c. Top-soil turned over on to the broken subsoil.
d. Subsoil of second trench forked over.

Overhaul tools and implements. Rust can be cleared with modern rust-removing solutions; then oil bright steel parts with a thin machine oil. Have lawnmower and all cutting tools resharpened, if necessary.

Overhaul power machinery—motor mower, cultivator, etc.,—and see that engines are decarbonised and tuned. The hours of use determine the necessity for this.

Wooden handles of spades, forks, etc., need sand-papering

14

when the factory finish wears off, and should then be wiped with a rag soaked in boiled linseed oil.

On a wet or cold day, clean and repaint wooden labels with white lead or aluminium paint; clean and treat stakes, supports and wooden-work for plants with a wood-preservative, preferably of the organic solvent type; never creosote for use with plants, as both solution and fumes are toxic to them.

Flowers: Expect few to be in bloom this month, although the first flowers of the large snowdrop, *Galanthus elwesii*, will begin in a sheltered spot.

Protect growing tips of bulbs and corms just breaking the soil from slugs and snails by putting down metaldehyde bait pellets in mild, damp spells.

Weed borders, especially of perennial weeds such as dandelions, docks, couch grass, etc. A two-pronged fork is most useful for working in among border plants.

Dust greened, mossy soil with calcium cyanamide, and then top with an inch-thick mulch of sawdust, chopped straw, or peat.

Dress lily-of-the-valley *(Convallaria majalis)* plantings with rotted manure or good vegetable compost.

Go round over-wintering biennials such as wallflowers, stocks and sweet williams during frosty weather, and refirm the soil if it has lifted. No need to wait until a thaw, when the soil will only puddle.

Clear paeony crowns of dead stems and foliage, and cover with an inch of peat or sawdust, through which the new growth can break clean in spring—this helps to prevent infection of blooms with botrytis disease.

Safest fertiliser for the herbaceous border is bone-meal, 3 to 4 oz. per sq. yd., under a mulch of organic matter.

Make or remake flower borders and beds. Bastard-trenching or deep digging pays on heavy soils or soils with hard subsoils.

Paths: Make and remake paths when weather conditions permit. Paths intended for foot traffic only may be laid direct on the soil, but it is wiser to lay paving on a bed of ashes or sand. To take heavy traffic, as in driveways, a foundation of 'hard-core'—packed broken stone, brickbats or coarse clinker—is needed under the ashes or sand. Gravel paths are best laid on a layer of fine rock sand, from the same quarry or pit as the gravel.

Freedom from perennial weeds on new paths calls for dressing the ground with a total weed-killer before laying: raw creosote is effective for a year or two; arsenical weed-killers for three to five years, but they must be used with due appreciation of their toxic character, and children and animal pets kept away from them.

Stone flags and paving, made green and slimy with algae and moss growth, should be swabbed down with a solution of ordinary household domestic bleach on a dry day.

Destroy moss on paths by applying a mercurised moss eradicant (normally made for lawns) or by spraying with a 1:8 solution of tar oil emulsion and water.

Hedges: Hedges of deciduous shrubs and trees may be planted in mild weather, given workable soil. Quick or hawthorn

(Crataegus monogyna), growing well on all soils; beech *(Fagus sylvaticus)*, on well-drained and limy soils; or hornbeam *(Carpinus betulinus)*, on damp soils, make the best boundary hedges. Handsome dividing hedges can be made from *Berberis thunbergii atropurpurea*, the purple-red leafing barberry; spring-flowering *Prunus cistena* 'Crimson Dwarf', or the golden-leafed privet, *Ligustrum ovalifolium aureum*. Bastard-trench along the hedging line, work in bone-meal or basic slag to the top spit, plant firm, and top-mulch with rotted organic matter. Prune plants back to half their stature after planting, to ensure a well-branched hedge, filled with growth to the bottom.

Rake out the bottoms of established hedges to expose over-wintering insect grubs and parasites to birds.

Destroy coarse grasses with a dalapon grass herbicide.

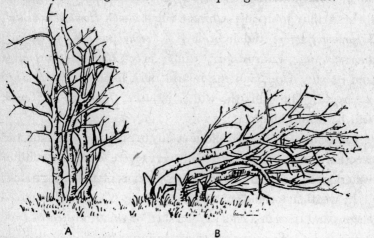

Laying a thorn hedge:
a. Hedge before laying.
b. Hedge laid; note cuts at base of stems.

17

Destroy brambles and tough, broad-leaved perennial weeds with a 2,4,5-T herbicide, but confine the solution carefully to the weeds; and use only where the hedge is well established.

Prune and trim overgrown deciduous hedges, as opportunity affords, before the end of March. Beech and hornbeam can be cut fairly hard back; quick can be improved by layering — a process of severely thinning out older growth, cutting through main stems about three-quarters way near their base, and laying at an acute angle, held in place by stakes and interwoven branches, to regenerate.

Shrubs and Trees: Likely to be in flower—heaths such as *Erica carnea* vars. 'King George', 'Springwood White', 'Springwood Pink' and 'Winter Beauty'; *Erica* x *darleyensis* and its form 'Arthur Johnson'; Chinese witch hazel, *Hamamelis mollis*; *Viburnum fragrans* and hybrids *V.* x *bodnantense*, *V.* x 'Dawn'; *Viburnum tinus*, Laurustinus; winter sweet, *Chimonanthus praecox* and its var. *luteus*, and the hybrid bush honeysuckle, *Lonicera* x *purpusii*. On walls the winter jasmine, *Jasminum nudiflorum*, will be in full bloom.

Continue planting of deciduous shrubs and trees when soil and weather conditions permit. Only very severe frost or snowfall or waterlogged soil need stop you. (See November for planting notes.)

In weather too inclement for planting, place newly arrived shrubs and trees in a cool garden shed or cellar, protected from actual frost. As wrapped, they are quite safe for up to three weeks, and should not be disturbed. Before planting, dip roots in a tub containing a creamy 'soup' of soil and water.

18

Protect newly planted shrubs and trees from hard frost by top mulch of organic litter (bracken, straw, compost, leaves, etc.). Tread lifted soil down again after a night of frost; no need to wait for thaw.

Clear weeds around established shrubs, lightly fork over the top inch or two of soil to facilitate the penetration of winter rains.

Top-dress, after heavy rain, rhododendrons, azaleas, enkianthus, pieris, erica, and other plants loving a lime-free, acid soil with a mulch of autumn's rotting leaves, twigs, etc., gathered for this purpose.

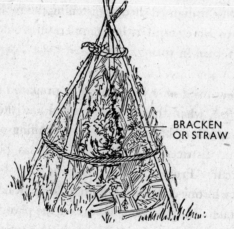

BRACKEN
OR STRAW

One way of giving winter protection to tender conifers and shrubs.

Protect shrubs whose hardiness is doubtful against hard weather by enclosing in a 'stook' of bracken or straw, in a loose airy tent of sheet polythene, a wrapping of hessian or sacking, or a wigwam of leafy evergreen boughs.

Conifers are particularly vulnerable to a combination of dry cold and wind. Place temporary wind-screens of hurdles, heavy coir netting, pea-stick fences or sheet polythene on exposed side of plants. Bind branches of upright-growing conifers such as cypresses with twine to prevent snow weighing them down and breaking them. Syringe or spray conifer and evergreen plants with water during dry weather, when low temperatures may prevent them raising enough moisture from the soil to keep their leaves turgid and alive.

Do not attempt to plant conifers or evergreen shrubs in cold weather, even if their roots are in a ball of soil. Keep them in the greenhouse or lighted shed, moistening the roots and foliage from time to time, until rising temperatures and better soil conditions return in spring.

Roses: New roses may be planted in prepared soil (see November notes), when the weather is open and the soil friable.

There is much to be said for winter pruning of bush roses, especially in districts where diseases such as blackspot and mildew occur. Prune growths carrying late buds or hips, cutting back by one-half their length at least. Rake up all fallen foliage, detach old, off-colour leaves on the plants, and burn.

Spray bush roses while dormant with a copper sulphate solution ($\frac{1}{2}$ oz. per gallon of water, plus a wetting agent) to help in the control of black spot by destroying over-wintering spores.

Give a top-dressing of rotted organic matter (manure, compost, hop manure, or moist peat) to rose beds, leaving to be weathered in.

Lawn: Wet weather may reveal poor drainage and water-logging. Mark the areas concerned for attention under drier conditions. Hopelessly wet areas call for subsoil drainage. Others may improve if (*a*) opened up by deep hollow-tine forking to remove cores of soil; and (*b*) top-dressed with coarse sand or grit.

Hard frost and dry, cold wind can do much damage to lawns and impair their recovery. On new lawns, it is worth covering with polythene sheeting. On older lawns, set up screens of hurdles or coir netting to deflect the wind, and give a top-dressing of screened loam and sand.

Snow does no harm. If no fertiliser has been given in autumn, apply fine bone-meal (2 oz. per sq. yd) and let the snow take it down when it melts.

Carry out levelling in mild weather, by lifting turf thinly, adding or subtracting soil underneath as necessary, and replacing the turf. Roll very lightly.

This is a good time to insert plastic or aluminium lawn edging, to give firm 'shoulders' to your turf and save time and labour in edge-trimming.

Rock Garden: Weed hard when weather permits. Apply a 2,4,5-T brushwood-killer to blackberry brambles and woody weeds, and leave for four weeks to do its work. Paint it on to avoid any weed-killer affecting an alpine plant. For coarse grasses, use a dalapon herbicide. Where weeds such as oxalis and celandine are rampant, lift the entire plants carefully with roots and soil, and burn.

21

Top-dress or mulch alpines with a broad collar of stone chippings—granite for the lime-intolerant, limestone or dolomite for the others—to promote good surface drainage.

Cover hairy or woolly-leaved alpines with plastic caps or small pieces of glass on wire clips to prevent rain over-wetting them and causing rot.

Protect choice alpines from the attentions of slugs and snails in mild spells of weather by scattering metaldehyde bait pellets about them.

Water Garden: Place one or two large pieces of cork, floating foam plastic, a rubber tyre or balls, or some wood in the pool before freezing weather. It absorbs some of the expansion of the water when it freezes and prevents damage to the pool walls.

Break the ice on a pond daily, when it forms, but where there are fish do it gently with a drill, not a hammer or by a sudden blow. Otherwise, fish are likely to be killed by the vibration and concussion.

Keep garden pools well-filled. A minimum depth of 18 in. is essential to avoid a pool being frozen solid; plants might survive but fish would not.

Keep any ice on the pool clear of snow, since lack of sufficient light may result in oxygenating plants dying, and the water failing to support the fish. A tent of transparent polythene or PVC sheeting on a simple framework could be arranged over small pools, preventing or delaying their freeze-up, and easing the problem of snow removal.

Fruit: Although it is technically possible to plant fruit trees from November to March, it is wise to plant as soon as possible within this period.

Regard this month as the deadline for planting stone fruits — cherry, damson, plum, apricot, nectarine and peach — as they start into growth relatively early in the year. Reasonably well-drained soil, provided with lime and well dug, is needed. On light soils, put a few forkfuls of rotted manure or compost in the base of the planting hole, cover with soil, and plant on top of this. The trees are shallow-rooting, and should be staked at planting time.

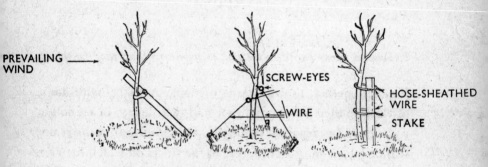

Three ways of staking newly planted trees.

Plant nut trees — Kentish cob, frizzled filbert or 'Pearson's Prolific' — which succeed in most soils.

Complete winter pruning of apples, pears and crab apples as soon as possible, in mild weather, not in frost.

If it is intended to graft older trees with newer varieties in spring, take the scions early this month — young shoots of last year's growth, ten to twelve inches long, about pencil-thick.

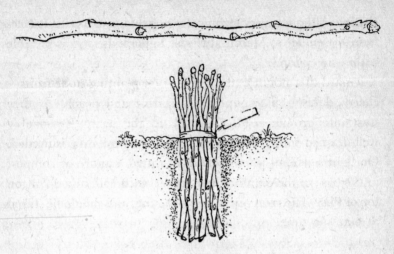

Scions for grafting:
a. Dormant apple shoot, selected as a scion.
b. Selected scions buried in the soil to await grafting time in spring.

Bundle together, tie with raffia or twine and label with name
of variety; then bury upright for half their length in the soil in
a sheltered border until required. This ensures that the scions
will be a little more dormant than the stocks on which they are
subsequently grafted and will unite well. Chosse apple scions
to graft on apple stocks and pear scions to graft on pear stocks
for best results.

Complete winter spraying of fruit trees when the first calm,
mild day comes along, using a tar oil emulsion. This controls
apple sucker, aphids (eggs), and clears trees of moss and lichen.
Spray cherries and plums first; then apples, and pears, gooseberries and currants. Use a $7\frac{1}{2}\%$ concentration for a first
application, a 5% for a routine application, where trees have

24

been winter sprayed in a previous year. If weather prevents winter spraying, precautions will have to be taken in spring spraying (see April notes). An alternative is to use a di-nitro-ortho-cresol (DNOC) petroleum oil preparation, which can be used at similar concentrations, up to four to six weeks later, with similar effects. It also controls the red spider mite.

Clean up orchard floor of dead and fallen leaves after spraying, for burning with prunings.

Clean and weed the strawberry bed, detaching old, discoloured leaves from the base of plants, and removing old runner stems and weak runners attempting to root. Apply organic matter—manure, compost, peat, deep litter poultry manure, etc.—liberally between plants, and lightly fork in with top 2 in. of soil.

Weed raspberries, and apply organic matter liberally between the rows as for strawberries.

Tip-prune over-tall canes of established raspberries, or weave the tip growth along the top wire of supports.

Examine last year's shoots of black currants towards the end of the month for abnormally swollen buds—indicative of infestation by the big bud mite—and prune out when found, burning the prunings.

Vegetables: Prepare a cropping plan for outdoor vegetable plot. Arrange things so that neither the same vegetable is grown on the same ground for two years running, nor vegetables of the same family follow one another immediately. The chief exceptions are onions, which can be grown on the same ground for year after year provided the crop remains healthy, pest- and disease-free; perennial vegetables such as rhubarb, globe artichokes, horse-radish, and perennial herbs.

On small plots, strip-crop, growing different kinds of vege- tables in narrow strips or rows, instead of beds. This minimises spread of any infection or pest infestation, and takes an even toll of soil fertility. Every third year, change the direction of the rows.

On larger plots, practice rotation. For a four-year rotation, divide vegetables into four main groups:

(1) Early potatoes, and maincrop potatoes.

(2) Peas, beans, French beans, runner beans, onions, leeks, celery.

(3) Roots—carrots, parsley, parsnip, beet, turnips and swede.

(4) Brassicas—cabbage, cauliflower, Brussels sprouts, kale, savoy, and saladings—lettuce, radish, etc.

Plant one fourth of your plot with each group; then each succeeding year, rotate the vegetable groups to occupy the ground previously occupied by the preceding group. Thus, in second year, group 2 follows group 1, group 3 follows group 2, and group 4 follows group 3. This also simplifies manuring and liming.

Separate the application of organic manures, especially farmyard, stable, pig, and poultry, from that of lime in any of its forms. If mixed together before or immediately after application, chemical reactions result in a loss of nitrogen in the form of gaseous ammonia. Let at least two te three weeks lapse between manuring and liming; then both can be inte- grated with the soil without nutrient loos.

Use fresh or green manure on ground to be cropped with potatoes, and reserve rotted manure or compost, or prepared manures such as hop manure, for other crops—brassicas, saladings, onions, leeks and celery. Peas, beans, French beans and runner beans may be grown on ground organically manured for a previous crop, and root vegetables normally need no organic manuring.

Lime according to the needs of the crop to be grown (see February notes, pages 38-40).

Lime for brassicas (cabbage, cauliflower, Brussels sprouts, savoy, kale), peas, beans, runner beans, French beans, onions, leeks, celery, lettuce, radish, swede, turnips and saladings, when pH is below 6·0, but only sufficiently to raise this to within the pH 6·0 - 6·5 levels.

Lime for potatoes and roots only if pH is below 5·5. No vegetable crop needs an alkaline soil, and too much liming can prevent the best yields.

Use a soil thermometer as a guide to early sowings out of doors. Germination is poor and slow in cold soil, and seedlings are vulnerable to pests, diseases and weather.

Try a first sowing of broad beans on well-drained, sheltered soil with a south aspect when soil temperature registers 50°F., (10°C.), at a depth of 2 - 3 in. Be prepared to protect seedlings with cloches if a hard, keen, frosty spell develops.

Make a first sowing of peas, under a similar soil temperature test, towards the end of the month, using a round-seeded variety, such as 'Early Superb', 'Meteor', 'Feltham First', 'Pilot', 'Foremost', or 'British Lion'.

27

Plant shallots, if you have a light to medium soil well drained and organically manured for a previous crop, setting the bulbs, buried to half their depth, in the soil with a trowel; avoid forcing or pushing them in, which only consolidates the soil under them and makes rooting more difficult. Dress soil freely with soot, or cover with nylon net to deter birds and cats.

Lift rhubarb roots for forcing, expose to frost on the top of the soil for a week or two, and then take indoors. Roots need to be at least three years old for forcing, and are discarded afterwards. Force under greenhouse staging, cellar or shed, with temperature of at least 45° - 55°F. (7° - 13°C.) and let stalks develop in the dark.

Continue to bring in chicory plants for forcing (see December notes), but remember a temperature of 55° - 60°F. (13° to 15·5°C.) is needed.

Split clumps of chives before they start new growth, replanting the best bulbs singly, 4 in. apart. Surplus can be dried and used in cooking as minute onions.

Get your seed potato tubers as early as possible, and set to chit or sprout—placing the tubers 'eye-end' or free-end uppermost in shallow trays, stacked in a light, frostproof greenhouse frame, shed or room; good light and a steady temperature of about 40°F. (5°C.) are essential.

Plant mint roots in rich soil in shallow boxes, well firmed, and bring to a warm greenhouse or the window-sill of a warm room for forcing. (See also November notes.)

Protect celery still to be harvested against hard frost by covering with bracken or straw and barn cloches.

A   B

Chitting potato seed tubers:
a. A well-chitted potato seed tuber ready for planting.
b. Seed tubers placed in a wood pulp egg tray for chitting or sprouting.

Inspect stored crops periodically to remove the odd rotting or diseased specimen. Keep potatoes in absolute darkness. Keep roots—carrots, beets, parsnips—cool. Keep onions and garlic dry.

Plants Under Glass: some definitions

Cold frame—low walled structure with top glazed light, chiefly used for growing early crops of hardy vegetables and plants, and raising seedlings; hardening off greenhouse-grown seedlings in spring; sheltering semi-hardy perennial plants through the winter.

Portable frame—low walled box-like structure with top glazed light, chiefly used to protect pricked-off seedlings, pot plants, etc., in early spring and inclement weather, and to harden off greenhouse-grown stock.

Heated frame—a low-wall structure with top glazed light and heat provided by means of a hotbed, hot water or electrical

29

heating, chiefly used for early and out-of-season growing of salad crops and low-growing vegetables, such as early potatoes, melons, cucumbers, etc.

Cloche—portable glass or clear plastic film structure, shaped for placing over growing crops or plants to secure weather protection and slightly higher growing temperatures.

Cold greenhouse—glass-framed structure without heat, chiefly used for summer crops such as tomatoes, and plants, spring seed-raising, and the protection of semi-hardy plants in winter.

Cool greenhouse—a greenhouse where sufficient heat is maintained to keep winter temperatures above 45°F. (7°C.) on the coldest nights.

Warm greenhouse—a greenhouse where winter temperatures are maintained above 55°F. (13°C) in winter.

Hot or stove house—where temperatures are maintained above 60°F. (15°C.) in winter, for the growth of sub-tropical and tropical plants.

Make a hotbed if you have the necessary organic material for decomposition. Traditionally, a mixture of half stable manure and half leaves is used; but at a pinch any mixture of equal parts by bulk animal manure (fresh) and unrotted vegetable refuse (straw, hay, etc.) can be used. Mix, moisten and stack 2 - 3 ft. deep a heap 2 ft. wider on all sides than the frame to be put on top. After two to three weeks turn the heap, top to bottom, sides to middle, with a fork, and restack very firmly. Place portable frame on top; jacket exposed hotbed with sods or soil to retain heat. Cover inside frame with soil (for direct-sowing) *or* sand or ashes if plants are to be raised in boxes or pots. Ready for use when temperature falls to about 75°F. (24°C).

Sow radish ('Saxa', 'Early Scarlet Round', 'Wood's Long Frame' varieties), early carrots ('Perfect Gem', 'Golden Ball', 'Early Horn' varieties) and lettuce ('Attractie', 'Early French Frame', 'May King' and 'Unrivalled' varieties) in heated frame.

Except where stated, the following hints refer to plants grown in the cool greenhouse.

Maintain night temperatures at about 45°F., day 50° - 55°F.

Remember that the Achilles' heel of winter plant growth in Britain's climate is *light*, both in length and intensity. When light is short and weak, growth is slow and plants are less demanding; thus on dull grey days less watering, less warmth, less feeding and less ventilation are needed.

Water moderately and cautiously.

Ventilate briefly, chiefly in the midday. If windy, open ventilators on the lee side only.

Plants you may have in bloom:

In a cold greenhouse—*Camellia japonica* and its varieties, *Daphne odora*, *Erica carnea* and varieties grown in pots.

In a cool greenhouse—above-mentioned shrubs and *Epacris purpurascens*, *Erica caniculata*, *E. hyenalis*, *Gardenia thunbergia*, *Rhododendron javanicum*, *Begonia natalensis*, *Clivia gardenii*, hardy bulbs, such as snowdrops, *Crocus speciosus*, *C. imperati*, etc., *Eranthis* x *tubergiana*, *Iris danfordiae*, *I. histrioides*, *I. bakeriana*, *Narcissus tazetta*, grown in pots. *Abutilon insigne* and *Jasminum primulinum* are good pillar or climbing shrubs.

31

Primula malacoides, *P. obconica* and *P. sinensis* need only cool conditions, moderate watering (when lower leaves sag) and temporary shade from hot shafts of sun in finer weather.

Keep the florist's azaleas, *Azalea indica* vars., truly derived from *Rhododendron simsii*, flourishing in temperatures never above 55°F., and avoid over-watering to prevent bud-dropping.

Keep the florist's cyclamen, varieties of *Cyclamen persicum*, flowering under cool conditions, light shade, and watering by immersion, from below.

Make up standardised seed and potting composts for greenhouse work, using the John Innes formulae for soil composts, or formulae based on the University of California recommendations.

Seed and potting composts

John Innes Seed Compost (J.I.S.)
  2 parts by volume medium loam, preferably sterilised
  1 part   ,,   sedge or sphagnum moss peat
  1 ,,   ,,   coarse sand
  plus, per bushel:
  1½ oz. superphosphate
  ¾ oz. ground chalk, ground limestone or whiting

John Innes Potting Compost (J.I.P. 1)
  7 parts by volume medium loam, preferably sterilised
  3 ,,   ,,   sedge or sphagnum moss peat
  2 ,,   ,,   coarse sand
  plus, per bushel:

4 oz. John Innes Base fertiliser*

¾ oz. ground chalk, ground limestone or whiting

J.I.P. 2 (used for second potting on)
formula as for J.I.P. 1, but with twice the quantities
of J.I.B. fertiliser and ground chalk per bushel

J.I.P. 3 (used for final potting on)
formula of J.I.P. 1, but with three times the amounts
of J.I.B. fertiliser and ground chalk per bushel

U. C. (University of California)

D. 1 MIX†:   Suitable for seeds, cuttings, and seedlings on
pricking off.

3 parts by volume pure sphagnum peat

1 part   ,,   washed silicate quartz sand

plus, per bushel:

1.5 grammes sulphate of potash

1.5   ,,   potassium nitrate

48   ,,   superphosphate

96   ,,   calcium carbonate

120   ,,   ground Dolomite limestone

0.5   ,,   trace element mixture (I.C.I. or
from an horticultural chemist).

---

* John Innes Base fertiliser — 2 parts by weight hoof and horn meal
(13 % N), 2 parts by weight superphosphate (16 - 18 % P_2O_5), 1 part
sulphate of potash (48 % K_2O).

† May be bought ready prepared for use through seedsmen, nurserymen
and horticultural shops.

D. 2 MIX*: as above, plus, per bushel:

      28   grammes hoof and horn meal

This is then suitable for potting on, and for most plants grown in pots.

D. 3 MIX: As for D.I., plus, per bushel:

      56   grammes hoof and horn meal

This is suitable for final potting of strong growing plants.

C. MIX: Suitable for many plants, particularly annuals, tomatoes, cucumbers, and plants under glass.

      Equal parts by volume of pure sphagnum moss peat and washed silicate quartz sand

      plus, per bushel:

56	„	hoof and horn meal
56	„	superphosphate
6	„	nitrate of potash
6	„	sulphate of potash
56	„	calcium carbonate (ground chalk or limestone)
168	„	ground Dolomite limestone

Remember seeds need air, plus moisture, plus sufficient warmth for rapid and successful germination, especially soil warmth for early sowings.

Make tentative first sowings of tender and half-hardy annuals, given bottom heat of 65° - 70°F. (18·3° - 21·1°C.).

---

* May be bought ready prepared for use through seedsmen, nurserymen, and horticultural shops.

Sow seeds of winter cherry, *Solanum capsicastrum* and vars., with bottom heat of 60° - 65°F. (15·5° - 18·3°C.).

Sow seeds of conifers, cypresses such as *Chamaecyparis lawsoniana* and vars., and *Cupressus macrocarpa*, for hedging and screening plants, with bottom heat of 60°F. (15·5°C.).

Make first sowings of tuberous begonias, gloxinias, *Impatiens balsamina*, *Grevillea robusta*, and *Plumbago capensis* towards the end of the month, with bottom heat.

Bring in bulbs for forcing when showing an inch or so of shoot growth, and grow on under cool conditions.

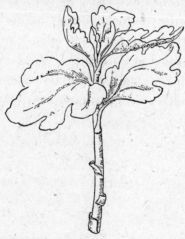

A chrysanthemum cutting prepared for planting.

Take cuttings of chrysanthemums as they are ready. An excellent way of growing these on without check is by means of the peat-wood fibre pots.

Take cuttings of perpetual flowering carnations, inserting

singly in $2\frac{1}{4}$ in. peat-wood fibre pots, and giving slight bottom heat.

Make a sowing of sweet peas in special long pots towards the end of the month, to be transplanted outside eventually.

For peas in spring make sowings of a dwarf early variety, ('Kelvedon Wonder', 'Little Marvel', 'Feltham First') in 9 in. pots, 6 seeds to the pot; or a taller variety ('Foremost', 'Gradus', 'The Pilot') in the border.

Sow onion seeds if large bulbs for exhibition are desired, with bottom heat of 55°F. (12·7°C.); good varieties are 'Ailsa Craig', 'Unwin's Reliance', 'Carter's Flagon'.

Flood vine border thoroughly early in the month in cold and cool greenhouse. If necessary, give top-dressing of an organic fertiliser prior to watering.

Bring in strawberry plants, prepared for forcing (see August notes), and place the potted plants on shelves near to the light.

February

February, fill the dyke
With what thou dost like.
THOMAS TUSSER

DESPITE its reputation, February generally has more dry days than wet. Make good use of these to complete soil cultivations. Any deep digging, trenching or bastard-trenching should be finished this month in order to give the soil time to settle, integrate and become a homogeneous whole before plants begin to make demands on it. Light sandy or stony soils, and soils with a gravel or free-draining subsoil need no more than simple digging.

Organic materials—manure, compost, etc.—added from now on must be fairly well decomposed, otherwise it will temporarily depress fertility by absorbing the energies of nitrogen-releasing bacteria.

On acid, sticky clays use gypsum—horticultural grade, not builder's plaster of Paris—to condition the soil and give a more porous and better structure. Must be worked into the soil and mixed thoroughly with it, not just sprinkled on top. Use 6 - 8 oz. per sq. yd; to subsoil and top-soil, if both are clayey. On strongly acid soils, lime may be needed also. Gypsum (calcium sulphate) works by its calcium salts replacing sodium salts (which cause the stickiness) in the soil, the latter then being leached from the soil and lost in drainage.

Lime the soil if necessary, but lime for the crop or plants to be grown, rather than overall. Remember all garden plants grow best in soil that is on the acid side, and there is no need to induce a state of alkalinity or even neutrality in the soil.

The chief function of lime is to facilitate chemical reactions in the soil whereby mineral salts are made soluble and available as nutrients to plants. Too much can be as inhibiting as too little. Lime also furnishes a nutrient, calcium, and has a beneficial effect on soil condition in the case of clay, by causing flocculation—the aggregation of fine clay particles into tufted larger fragments which leads to better aeration and drainage.

To lime correctly, know your soil's pH value. The pH scale indicates the alkaline-acid balance of the soil solution. On this scale the number 7·0 indicates neutrality. Higher numbers indicate alkalinity, lower numbers acidity, but in geometrical progression. A soil of pH 5·0 is ten times more acid than one of 6·0.

Ascertain your soil's pH by taking small samples at 2 - 4 inches depth, and testing with a simple soil-testing colorimetric outfit, which is accurate enough for practical purposes. Then consult the chart given here which indicates the appropriate range of pH for most plants.

pH Value of soil	Effect on availability of plant nutrients	Effect on plants
8·0	Very rarely encountered in Britain.	
7·6—7·3	Strongly alkaline. Availability of phosphorus, potassium, iron, manganese, boron and sodium reduced.	Stunted, sparse, thin growth. Tendency to chlorosis in green-leaved plants. Tolerated by some flowering shrubs such as buddleia, cistus, forsythia, clematis, cornus, philadelphus, lavender, spiraea, viburnum; trees such as holly, thorn elder and box.
7·2—7·0	Neutral.	Less marked symptoms of chlorosis in some plants. Most plants do reasonably well if soil is well manured.
6·8—6·4	Slight to moderate acidity. Optimum reaction for the majority of garden plants and crops. Maximum availability of all mineral nutrients.	Optimum growth in most plants, except lawn grasses, bramble fruits, and the *Ericaceae* family.
6·0—5·5	Moderate to strong acidity. Declining availability of phosphates, and tendency to loss of calcium, magnesium, and potash by leaching.	Suits lawn grasses, most shrubs, trees, and flowering plants, potatoes, tomatoes, cucumbers and marrows, raspberries, strawberries and blackberries.
5·0—4·5 and below	Very strong acidity. Very poor availability of phosphorus.	Poor top growth, tendency to white marginal scorch, leaf distortion, poorly developed root system. Members of the *Ericaceae* family do well—*Erica* spp. (except *E. carnea* and vars., *E. mediterranea*) azaleas, rhododendrons, kalmia, gaultheria, pieris, stewartia, and camellia, vaccinium, and skimmia.

The amount of lime needed depends on the degree of acidity to be corrected, the type of soil, and the kind of lime used. See table below. A single application of lime lasts for three to four years.

Amount of hydrated lime needed to bring soils to optimum levels of acidity (pH 6.4 to 6.8)

Soil acidity or pH value	Hydrated lime needed per sq. yd.				
	Light sandy soils	Sandy loam or silt soils	Medium loam soil	Clay loam soil	Heavy clay soils
6·0	3 oz.	4½ oz.	6 oz.	7½ oz.	8 - 9 oz.
5·5	4½ ,,	6 ,,	8½ ,,	10 ,,	11 ,,
5·0	5½ ,,	8½ ,,	10½ ,,	11½ ,,	13½ ,,
4·5	6 ,,	9½ ,,	11½ ,,	12½ ,,	14½ ,,

If ground limestone or chalk is used, increase amounts by one-third

In making early sowings in the vegetable and ornamental garden be guided by soil temperatures and the openness of your soil. Broadly, northern gardens will be two to three weeks behind those in the south at this time of the year; and clay soils are slower to warm than sand. Do not be tempted by the odd days of warm sunshine that February often borrows from spring. Use such days to complete alterations and basic garden construction.

Flowers: Coming into bloom—snowdrops *(Galanthus nivalis)* and varieties; *Crocus ancyrensis, C. chrysanthus* and varieties, *C. sieberi, C. sativus* ('Cloth of Gold'); winter aconites—*Eranthis*

cilicica, E. hyemalis; Iris histrioides, I. unguicularis, I. reticulata, I. danfordiae; Narcissus cyclamineus and varieties, particularly 'February Gold'; Christmas rose *(Helleborus niger)* and *Helleborus viridis.*

Place cloches, bell-glasses or hand-lights over early-flowering bulbs and corms likely to be injured by adverse weather. Protect from slugs in damp mild periods by putting down metaldehyde bait pellets.

Lift overcrowded clumps of snowdrops for division and replanting immediately the flowers are over, and while vigorously making leaf. One of the few bulbous plants that are best propagated in this way.

A lily-of-the-valley 'pip' or flowering crown.

Plant lily-of-the-valley *(Convallaria majalis)* 'pips' or crowns in shady moist positions, with growth tips just beneath the

41

soil. 'Fortin's Giant' is a cultivated variety, larger and longer-stalked than the type; *rosea* has rose-tinted flowers, strongly scented.

Sow sweet pea seeds in prepared (deeply dug) ground. Chip black-seeded varieties to ensure good germination, removing a small piece of the seed coat with a penknife or file on the opposite side to the 'eye' of the seed. Brown and mottled coloured seeds do not need chipping, as their seed coats are not so hard and impervious. Lime, phosphates and potash must be adequate for sweet peas. Pre-fertilise with a mixture of 3 parts by weight superphosphate and 1 part sulphate of potash at 2 oz. per sq. yd. A soil of pH 6 or above contains enough lime.

Corms of *Anemone fulgens*, *A.* x 'St. Brigid' and *A.* x 'De Caen' may be planted 2 in. deep, for late spring and early summer flowering.

On days when the soil is drying out, weed and stir the soil among spring flowering bedding plants, such as wallflowers and stocks. A sprinkling of Chilean potash nitrate ($\frac{1}{2}$ oz. per sq. yd) will help flowering if this is given towards the end of the month.

Start tackling overgrown and weedy herbaceous borders. Hardier perennial plants can be lifted, divided and replanted, and a mulch of organic matter over the roots then given to keep out the frost.

Plant the claw-like corms of *Ranunculus asiaticus* in Persian, French, turban and paeony-flowered varieties.

Lift corms of *Gladiolus primulinus* hybrids left in the ground from the previous year for sorting; replant the large new corms on fresh ground, and plant out the 'spawn' or tiny corms in reserve ground to grow on.

Look over primroses, polyanthus, primulas and autumn-planted pansies for slug damage in mild weather. A timely spraying with a metaldehyde emulsion can save threatened plants.

Paths: Complete construction or alterations to paths as quickly as the weather permits.

First-class, quick-draining paths can now be made with cold bitumen-tarred stones: a 3 - 4 in. layer of bitumen coated ¾ - 1 in. stone aggregate well tamped and levelled, covered by ¾ - 1 in. bitumen-tarred fine chippings, again well rolled and firmed, gives a weed-free, long-lasting footing.

Clear cinder, brick dust or fine gravel paths of weeds with the hoe and rake; and then apply a residual weed-killer, based on simazine, to keep weed-free for a year.

Hedges: Deciduous hedge plants can be planted up to the end of March, but it is wise to get flowering hedges of Prunus types planted up as soon as possible this month—*Prunus cerasifera atropurpurea* for a coloured leafing and pink-flowering hedge up to 6 - 8 ft., *Prunus cistena* for a crimson leafing, white-flowered low hedge of up to 3 - 4 ft.

Finish clearing hedge bottoms of weedy growth, fallen leaves and debris. Dust or spray with a gamma BHC/DDT insecticide if there is reason to suspect the presence of flea beetles or other plant parasites.

Shrubs and Trees: Likely to be in flower—all the shrubs mentioned under January notes, plus *Erica carnea* and its varieties 'Queen of Spain', 'Mrs. Samuel Doncaster', 'Prince of Wales', 'Queen Mary', and *vivellii*; *Erica mediterranea* 'Silver Beads', and 'Brightness'; *Hamamelis japonica* and varieties *arborea* and *zuccarinana*; *Stachyurus chinensis*, *S. praecox*; and on walls, *Chaenomeles speciosa* and its varieties. Among trees, the Chinese cherry, *Prunus conradinae*, the Chinese peach, *P. davidiana*, the Cornelian cherry, *Cornus mas* and its varieties, and *Azara microphylla* are in bloom in sheltered gardens. On a warm south wall, *Clematis cirrhosa* can be expected to bloom, and in a sunny wall corner the Californian silver-tassel bush *(Garrya elliptica)* will carry long, silvery-grey catkins, particularly long on the male form.

Little time should be lost in planting deciduous shrubs and trees arriving this month, provided the soil is workable, being neither waterlogged nor frost-bound (see November notes for planting details).

Spray ornamental flowering almonds, peaches, plums and cherries against the leaf curl fungus disease *(Taphrina deformans)* towards the end of the month, when stone fruit trees are sprayed, using a captan or copper or lime-sulphur fungicide.

Prune the yellow winter-flowering Jasmine, *Jasminum nudiflorum*, as the flowers fade, shortening each flowered shoot to within two buds of its base. On old, overgrown plants, some of the older shoots can be severely cut or entirely removed. On walls, train the remaining shoots to cover the space available, rather than allowing growth to become a tangle. Top-dress roots with a moderate application (2 - 3 oz. per sq. yd.) of a complete fertiliser and a mulch of fairly rotten organic matter.

Not ready for planting? If, for any reason, planting stations for newly arrived deciduous shrubs or trees are not ready, plant them up in large 'fyba' pots with ample rooting depth, and stand in a wind-sheltered part of the garden until preparations can be made for their permanent planting. They can remain in such pots for up to a year, being planting out pot-and-all when convenient, even in high summer. They must be kept watered, of course, during dry weather and in the growing season. Alternatively, if planting has to be delayed for up to three or four months, place plants with their roots in well-moistened peat, contained in a trench or wooden bin.

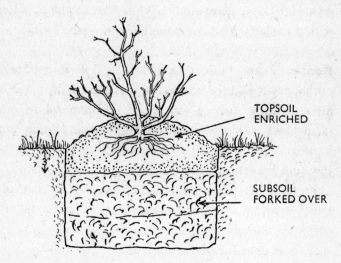

TOPSOIL
ENRICHED

SUBSOIL
FORKED OVER

How to plant shrubs on poor, chalky or wet clay soils.

No attempt should be made to dislodge the peat from the roots on planting, which can be successfully done in late spring or early summer, if plants are well watered after being placed in the garden.

Establish shrubs on heavy, sticky clay, or poor made-up soils, exposed subsoil, or chalk, by planting with roots almost on the surface, and covering with good loam soil mounded over them. The soil itself should be thoroughly well broken and liberally laced with rotted organic matter or moist peat.

You can grow azaleas and rhododendrons and other lime-intolerant shrubs on soils which contain lime, up to pH 6·6, *if* you take out a spit of the soil, dust the basin of the planting station with powdered sulphur ($\frac{1}{2}$ - 1 lb. per sq. yd), replace soil with a mixture of equal parts by volume of sphagnum moss peat and loam, plant shallowly, and treat plants periodically with a chelated iron compound (Sequestrene Iron).

Roses: Prune bush roses, hybrid tea, floribunda and polyantha, newly planted this month and next, fairly hard directly after planting, cutting just above the most robust, outward-facing bud within 6 - 8 in. of the ground. Prune new roses hard in order to get a framework of branches from low down the bush for future years.

Prune newly planted standard roses severely as soon as the weather begins to soften towards the end of the month or in early March, cutting shoots to two or three buds or 'eyes' of their base or point of the graft union.

Prune newly planted climbing H. T. roses by shortening

shoots only by about one-third their length, and train them in to the horizontal. Do not prune the variety 'Mermaid' or the everblooming class such as 'Coral Dawn', 'Royal Gold', 'Marigold', 'Golden Showers', and 'The New Dawn' at all the first year.

Unless you follow the winter pruning system, the main pruning of established H. T., floribunda, polyantha and bush roses can be done in late February in southern mild districts, late March in the Midlands and North, or early April in very cold areas. (See March for detailed notes on rose pruning.)

Buy in or make up your base fertiliser for roses, to be applied and lightly forked in with the remains of the winter mulch. Tonk's formula for roses is readily made up at home— 12 parts by weight superphosphate, 10 parts nitrate of potash, 8 parts calcium sulphate (gypsum), 2 parts magnesium sulphate (Epsom salts), 1 part sulphate of iron—for application at 4 oz. per sq. yd., after pruning. But note: newly planted roses are better off without any fertilisers during their first year, assuming that the soil has been properly prepared. Let them get their roots nicely established, and do not force flower production. They will then do better and live longer.

Lawns: Finish any laying of new turf before the end of this month, especially on light soils, or the turf will not have time to root and knit well with the soil before drying spells of weather or drought comes along. (See November for turfing notes.)

Prepare the seed-bed for new lawns to be sown this spring. On light and well-drained soils it is often sufficient simply to dig over the top spit, work it with cultivator and rake to a firm level. On heavy or clay soils or where the subsoil has been exposed, put down a layer of crushed clinker and ash, 4 in. thick, under the top 3 in. of soil. On soils subject to waterlogging, subsoil drainage by round drainpipes or tiles will be necessary. (See November for drainage notes.)

Lighten heavy topsoils by working in grit, coarse sand or vermiculite. Improve light sands and chalky soils by working in sifted lawn peat and loam to improve moisture retention.

Pre-fertilise all seed-beds for grass with a mixture of 4 parts by weight superphosphate, 2 parts ammonium sulphate and 1 part sulphate of potash, at $1\frac{1}{2}$ - 2 oz. per sq. yd., raked into the top 2 in. of soil, and leave fallow. (See March for sowing notes.)

Mow established lawns showing signs of growth, though not too closely.

Aerate the turf mat by forking or slitting.

Prevent worm casts smothering fine grasses by scattering them with a whippy cane or the back of a spring-toothed rake. If excessive, apply a worm-killer in dull, mild weather when the worms are casting. Powdered lead arsenate at 2 oz. per sq. yd. gives long-term control; but, being highly poisonous, it needs careful handling and keeping in security until used. Mix with an equal bulk of sand, and keep animals and children off the lawn during application and until it has been washed in by rain. Once it is in the soil it is out of harm's way.

Slash the crowns of rough, coarse grasses with a sharp kitchen knife and weed out with roots. They are usually the first to grow. There is no effective selective weed-killer for them which will distinguish between the unwanted coarse grasses and the fine-leaved lawn grasses.

Where moss is prevalent, apply a non-poisonous (to animals, etc.) mercurised moss eradicant to destroy it *in situ*. Raking and scarifying only distributes the fine tendrils and spores to increase infestation. Examine underlying predisposing causes— poor drainage, declining soil fertility, poor competitive power of grasses—to prevent reinvasion of moss.

Treat daisy-infested patches with lawn sand towards the end of the month, when leaf surfaces are dry. On medium to heavy soils use a mixture of 3 parts by weight sulphate of ammonia, 1 part calcined sulphate of iron and 20 parts coarse sand, at 4 oz. per sq. yd. On light, sandy or chalky soils, substitute sifted loam for the sand. Destroys or checks most broad-leaved, rosetted weeds.

Complete any levelling of ridges and hollows that is needed. Ridges can be levelled by cutting the turf thinly and rolling back, removing excess soil and replacing the turf. Apply thin layers of about $\frac{1}{8}$ in. thick of sand and loam to depressions. When the grass grows through, repeat until the hollow is filled.

Rock Garden: Continue to weed intensively. Annual weeds can be quickly scotched by a dab of a paint-brush dipped in a selective 2,4,5-T weed-killer solution, but do not let this touch alpine plants.

Prevent slug and snail injury to choice alpines by putting

down metaldehyde bait pellets the moment the weather turns damp and mild.

Control unwanted growth of algae, lichen and moss on stonework by painting with a 10% solution of tar oil wash.

Building a rock garden? Follow these key principles. Place it in the open, not under trees. Avoid a draughty position or low-lying pocketed site. If possible, let the main axis be east to west, with a good slope to the south in northern areas and where cloud and rain often prevail; but north to south in more southerly gardens, where summer rainfall is often low. Assure good drainage, especially in the topsoil. See soil is free of perennial weed roots before you plant. To get a natural effect, study professionally made rock gardens at shows, or outcrops of rock in nature. The actual thing is a hundred times more informative than descriptions in print.

Water Garden: For general pool maintenance, consult notes given under January.

Excavate for a new garden pool in readiness for planting in April to June. Place it in an unshaded spot, well out of the reach of tree roots, where it will get morning or evening sun. Midday shade from adjacent garden features (walls, buildings, rock garden, hedges, etc.) is, however, useful. Shape is largely a matter of personal preference. Size determines what plants and how many you can grow. A depth of $2\frac{1}{2}$ ft. should be regarded as minimal if fish are to be kept. Small pools can be made by sinking watertight containers—old porcelain baths, galvanised ware, old water cisterns, or halved wooden casks—into the soil, preferably liberally painted with a bitumen paint before filling. Large pools require lining. For an inexpensive pool a lining of heavy (500 gauge) sheet polythene may be used, laid on a base of 2 - 3 in. of sand over the bottom of the excavation, and carried up to overlap the sides at the top, and anchored in position with large stones or a surround of flags. Provided care is used not to puncture the sheeting with a fork or tool, such a lining has a life of about 5 to 7 years, but tends to become brittle and more easily damaged with age.

Prefabricated pools in fibreglass, metal or plastic material only require an excavation into which they can be snugly fitted. For concrete-lined pools, excavations should be at least 4 in. greater at the sides and base than the dimensions of the finished pool.

Fruit: After about the middle of February, apples, and pears which have not yet been winter sprayed with a tar oil emulsion to destroy aphis eggs, etc., should be sprayed with a di-nitro-ortho-cresol (DNOC)-petroleum oil wash, at $7\frac{1}{2}\%$ concentration for a first application, and at 5% concentration for routine application. This spray can be used on apples or pears up to about mid-March, and helps to control red spider as well as aphids.

Spray outdoor nectarines and peaches with lime-sulphur 3% concentration) or a colloidal copper fungicide when the buds are just beginning to open ('bud-burst' is the technical term) to prevent infection by the leaf curl fungus, *Taphrina deformans*. Related ornamental varieties should be sprayed at the same time (see under *Shrubs*).

Protect early flowering wall fruit trees—nectarines, peaches, etc—with hessian sacking, netting or sheet polythene on nights when frost is threatened and may damage the open flowers.

Cut fruited canes of autumn fruiting raspberries ('November Abundance', 'Hailsham', etc.) to within 6 in. of the ground. 'Lloyd George' variety may be induced to later fruiting by similar treatment.

Complete organic manuring of soft fruits—raspberry, strawberry, gooseberry and currants.

Vegetables: Use only fairly well-rotted organic matter, moist peat or prepared hop manure as humus material in preparing ground for vegetables from now on.

Plant garlic in sunny position, on well-drained soil, dressed with a mixture of 3 parts by weight hoof and horn meal, 4 parts bone-meal, at 2 oz. per sq. yd. Place the cloves or separated segments about ½ in. deep, 12 in. apart; harvest when tops begin to yellow in late July.

Sow fresh parsnip seeds in soil organically manured for a previous year's crop. On heavy soils make a deep hole with a dibber or pointed pole, 12 - 24 in. deep; fill each hole with sand or sifted burnt earth; sow two seeds ½ in. deep; remove the weaker seedling when seeds have germinated—gives long, unforked roots.

Make maincrop sowings of broad beans, longpod or Windsor type—the latter usually yield the heavier crops—from mid-

February onwards, on soil well provided with lime (pH 6 - 6·5), and pre-fertilised with bone flour at 2 oz. per sq. yd., or super-phosphate at 1 oz. per sq. yd. Sow seeds 2 in. deep, 8 - 9 in. apart, staggered in double or treble rows.

Sow first early peas, round and wrinkled seeded varieties, on prepared ground well supplied with lime and phosphates, in the south, and on sheltered borders elsewhere. A soil temperature of 50°F. (10°C.) is desirable for good germination. Seedlings can stand several degrees of frost. (For round-seeded varieties see January notes.) Good wrinkled seeded varieties include 'Kelvedon Wonder', 'Peter Pan', 'Hundredfold', 'Little Marvel' and 'Laxton's Progress', which grow 18 - 24 in. tall; and 'Provost', 'Early Morn' and 'Thomas Laxton', growing $3\frac{1}{2}$ ft. tall.

Prepare 'drills'—V-shaped trenches about 12 in. deep—for early potatoes, and dress with a mixture of equal parts by weight powdered copper sulphate and ground limestone, using 1 lb. to 50 linear yd. of drill, to prevent infestation with small black slugs. Do not manure or plant for at least 3 weeks.

Give spring cabbage and coleworts a light dressing of nitro-chalk ($\frac{1}{2}$ oz. per sq. yd.) when weather turns mild, stirring it lightly in over the roots.

Prepare new bed for asparagus as soon as possible, bastard-trenching the area, and taking out all roots of perennial weeds encountered. Fork in farmyard manure, compost, stable manure or seaweed liberally, up to one barrow-load to 2 sq. yd., and then leave until planting time. (See under April for planting notes.)

Plant Jerusalem artichokes. These do well in almost any soil that does not get waterlogged and does not mind shade, so can be used for any odd corner of the garden needing soil improvement. Enrich soil with compost or half-rotted leaves, and a dressing of hydrated lime (4 - 6 oz. per sq. yd.). Plant tubers 4 - 6 in. deep (deeper in light soil), 15 in. apart. Top growth reaches 6 - 8 ft. tall, and can make a useful temporary windbreak by open wire fencing.

Stand seed tubers of maincrop potatoes, 'eye' end up in shallow boxes or cardboard egg-trays, to sprout in light, frostproof shed or room, temperature about 40°F. (5°C.).

Plants Under Glass: Under cloches—make a sowing of early carrots ('Amsterdam Forcing', 'Nantes'), and of radish ('Carters Sixteen Days', 'Saxa', 'Extra Early Scarlet Round').

In heated frame or greenhouse, with bottom heat of 45° to 55°F. (7° - 12°C.), sow seeds of celery, leeks, lettuce, onions and first early cauliflowers ('Forerunner', 'Snowball') in boxes or peat-wood fibre pots, using John Innes Seed Compost or U.C. Soilless Compost (see p. 32), to give plants for transplanting out of doors later.

Standardise your technique for raising plants from seeds. Sow in seed trays (standard size is 14 in. × 8 in., 2 in. deep), or seed pans, or peat-wood fibre 1¾ in. or 2 in. pots or strips, using a standard compost. Water compost prior to sowing, allow to drain, and warm in greenhouse or frame. Sow shallowly roughly twice the diameter of the seed, and thinly. Cover with sifted sand, though very fine seeds may need only pressing into the soil. Cover seed container with sheet of glass and, except in special instances, with opaque paper; and turn sheet of glass daily, wiping free of moisture. Immediately seedlings show green shoot growth remove paper cover, give good light but not direct sun, and, with opening of first seed leaves, remove glass. Seedlings should be advanced to the source of light (i.e. near to the glass of frame or greenhouse) as growth increases, to ensure sturdy development.

Sow tender half-hardy annuals and half-hardy perennials such as *Gesneria* hybrids, *Celosia cristata*, *Gloxinia* hybrids, *Impatiens balsamina* varieties, *Mimosa pudica*, *Streptocarpus* hybrids, *Martynia fragrans*, *Torenia fournieri*, and the climbers *Pharbitis learii*, and *Quamoclit pinnata*, with bottom heat or soil temperature of 60° - 70°F. (15·5° - 21°C.) and air temperature of at least 50° - 55°F. (10° - 13°C.); all to flower in summer, indoors or out.

Sow half-hardy annuals such as antirrhinums, asters, cosmea, nemesia, *Didiscus coeruleus*, *Felicia bergeriana*, lobelia, African marigold, petunia, salpiglossis, and *Begonia semperflorens*, with bottom heat of 55° - 65°F. (13° - 18°C.) and minimum air temperature of 45° - 50°F. (7° - 10°C.) to provide plants for early summer bloom out of doors.

Greenhouse plants you may have in bloom:

In a cold greenhouse—*Camellia japonica* and its varieties, *Camellia sasanqua*; *Abutilon megapotamicum*; *Daphne odora*; *Hamamelis mollis*; *Erica carnea* and vars.; snowdrops (*Galanthus nivalis* and vars.); *Crocus chrysanthus* and vars., *C. susianus*, *C. imperati*, *C. balansae* and Dutch crocus, grown in pots; *Cyclamen coum, C. vernum*; *Iris danfordiae, I. histriodes, I. bakeriana,* and *Narcissus tazetta.*

In a cool greenhouse (minimum night temperatures 45° to 50°F., i.e. 7° - 10°C.)—above mentioned shrubs and bulbs.

Shrubs as for January, plus *Acacia dealbata, A. pulchella, Boronia pinnata, Diosma ericoides, Haemanthus natalensis.*

Shade greenhouse primulas—*Primula malacoides, P. obconica* and *P. sinensis*—from hot sun, and keep cool to maintain in bloom.

Bring in to flower, in succession as growth tips and foliage appear above ground, hardy bulbs such as hyacinths, narcissi and tulips. After flowering, remove flower heads and keep foliage growing to develop and mature the new bulb.

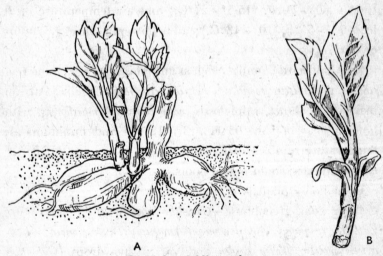

Obtaining dahlia cuttings:
a. Obtaining growth from tubers buried in moist peat.
b. The severed cutting, ready for planting.

Start dahlia tubers into growth in moist peat or vermiculite to yield shoots for cuttings. Detach shoot cuttings at base, insert singly in $2\frac{1}{4}$ in. peat-wood fibre pots, using J.I.P. 1 or U.C. compost.

Start tuberous begonias into growth for late spring or early summer bloom, or to yield cuttings for propagation as suggested for dahlias.

Continue taking cuttings of chrysanthemums.

Divide roots of cannas into convenient pieces and start into growth, in boxes of moist peat, at 60°F. (15·5°C.); when rooting, pot up separately in $4\frac{1}{2}$ in. pots.

Sow tomato seeds about the last week of the month to give plants for summer fruiting in greenhouse, temperature 60°F. (15·5°C.). Transplant seedlings to separate pots immediately seed leaves are big enough to grasp with finger and thumb.

Pot autumn rooted cuttings of zonal pelargoniums (geraniums) and water cautiously, increasing as growth increases.

Start the coral-tree, *Erythrina crista-galli*, into growth with moderate watering; replace top inch or so of old pot soil with fresh compost.

Sow melon seeds for summer fruiting under glass or in frames, singly in pots, temperature 70° - 75°F. (21° - 24°C.).

Cross pollinate open flowers of apricots, nectarines and peaches growing under glass, using a camel-hair brush or a rabbit's scut, carrying pollen from one flower to another.

Sow seeds of cucumber singly in pots, at a temperature of 70° - 75°F. (21° - 24°C.).

March

From Dis's waggon: daffodils
That come before the swallow dares, and take
The winds of March with Beauty.
                                    SHAKESPEARE

A BUSY gardening month, but often a difficult one with spring pressing on winter's heels. Pre-eminently a planting and sowing month, but nature and the weather must call the tune, not the calendar.

Most deciduous shrubs and trees and perennial border plants should be planted as soon as ground conditions permit, if not already installed. Towards the end of the month when daily temperatures begin to rise, make a start planting evergreens and conifers. (See notes under *Shrubs and Trees*, page 71.)

As soon as the frost moves out of the soil, and drying winds tend to raise 'the peck of March dust worth a king's ransom', break down rough-dug soil, forking and raking it to a fine, crumbly tilth, to make a seed-bed.

Choose your time well if you have a clayey, cloddy soil.

Break it down as soon as it is workable when drying. Don't leave it too long or the clods become brick-hard.

Soil temperature and moisture content determine the best time to sow. Latitude, amount of sunshine, and texture and colour of soil, are the critical factors. The farther north you garden, the later you must delay first sowings. With a succession of sunny days the soil heats up remarkably quickly. But the more moisture a soil contains, the slower it warms. This means soils with clay in them are often a week or two behind sandy, light soils in fostering seed germination. Dark soils absorb the heat rays of the sun more readily and retain them better than light soils. But don't go by the atmospheric temperature in assessing soil warmth—use a soil thermometer. When the soil temperature climbs above 55°F. (13°C.), it is time to start the first sowings.

Rake in weathered soot (soot that has stood at least three months under cover) or completely rotted, black organic matter to darken light and chalky soils.

Late starting? Simply dig or fork over the top 6 - 8 in. of soil, working in sifted, rotten compost or manure, moist peat or hop manure, but no fresh unrotted material. Break the soil down as you work; tread it firm by walking on it on your heels, give basic fertiliser and rake level.

New garden? Avoid trying to do too much at once, or planting for permanence in a hurry. Concentrate on getting the soil weed-free, well-drained and in good condition during the first year. Rely largely on annuals for colour and flowers—and material for your compost heap later.

Crop fruit and vegetable areas and even a prospective lawn area with potatoes, plus organic matter.

Some sowing tips: Seeds need a good balance of moisture and air, plus warmth, to germinate freely and strongly. The old adage has it 'sow dry, plant wet', but dryness of the soil in sowing refers to surface only.

Sow neither too shallowly when seeds remain unmoistened, nor too deeply when they suffer from oxygen starvation. A good rule of thumb is to sow at two to three times the broadest diameter of the seed. In sandy, light soils, however, seeds can be placed a little more deeply; in heavy, dense soils a little more shallowly. When it can be easily located, there is some advantage in placing a seed with the hilum or 'eye' uppermost.

On sand, chalk or silty soils, liable to dry out quickly, cover seeds with moist peat or old compost rubbed through a fine riddle. Practise the same trick on soils that form a crust when they dry out after rain.

On clay soils and wet soils, cover seeds with coarse sand or vermiculite, at least when sowing early in the year.

Dress seeds with a suitable combined fungicidal and insecticidal seed dressing. The cost is very trivial, and prevents losses from soil-borne diseases such as damping-off and stem-rot of seedlings, and from insect pests such as wireworms.

Apply base fertilisers, compounded to provide a balance of plant nutrients, at least seven to ten days before sowing or planting in spring.

Know your fertilisers: Remember that the purpose of fertilisers is primarily and overwhelmingly to provide plants with essential nutrients for growth and development. They are concentrated, and may be of inorganic (chemical) or organic (plant or animal) origin. Too much at any one time can do harm, both to soils and plants.

There are 12 to 14 essential mineral nutrients that plants need from the soil, usually divided into *(a)* the major elements— nitrogen, phosphorus, potassium, calcium, magnesium, sulphur and iron; *(b)* the trace elements—manganese, boron, zinc, copper, molybdenum, and possibly sodium and chlorine, according to the relative amounts in which they are required.

In nature the sources of these nutrients are the mineral rock fragments and the organic matter of which soils are formed. They are made available to plant roots by the physical and chemical reactions that take place in the soil and by the activities of certain forms of soil life, particularly soil bacteria and microorganisms, entering the soil moisture in the form of soluble nutrient salts. What is not immediately taken up by plants may be stored in the soil or lost in drainage.

Under cultivation, soils lose their nutrient salts more quickly than they are replaced naturally, both in the plants grown and in the more rapid penetration of rains and loss of soil moisture in drainage. Humus-forming organic matter in the form of manure, plant and animal remains puts back some of the nutrients, but it is even more important as the base of biochemical soil activity and the means by which soluble mineral elements may be retained more strongly in the soil.

Fertilisers are not a substitute or alternative to organic manure or compost, but complementary to it.

Fertilisers are usually designed to provide the nutrient elements most subject to loss and deficiency in soils, particularly the major elements of nitrogen (N), phosphorus (P or P_2O_5) and potassium (K or K_2O). Calcium may be provided in case of need by liming. Sulphur is very rarely deficient, but occurs as a second element in many fertilisers. The need for magnesium and iron arises only occasionally and in special circumstances, and is easily corrected.

Deficiencies in the trace elements can be as disastrous to plant growth and development as those in the major elements, but happily occur seldom in well cultivated and organically manured soils. Care is needed in correcting them as the amounts are small and easily exceeded. Get expert advice when such a deficiency is suspected.

Fertilisers are assessed according to their nutrient content, which determines their effect on plant growth. They are used according to the speed with which they act or their nutrients become available to plant roots. Their end reaction indicates their effect upon the acid-alkaline balance or pH of the soil.

Fertilisers of organic origin are usually held to be of more benign and persistent action.

Fertilisers may provide one or more mineral nutrients. Those providing one nutrient in the main are known as 'straight' fertilisers; others are compound.

The following are the more important fertilisers in common use.

FERTILISERS PROVIDING NITROGEN, needed in all plant growth processes, especially to promote growth of stems and leaves and rich green colour.

Ammonium sulphate (20·6% N): inorganic, quick-acting, acid end reaction. Used chiefly in spring and early summer when plants are growing actively.

Nitrate of soda (16% N): inorganic, very quick-acting, neutral end reaction. Usually used alone as a stimulant to young growing plants.

Nitro-chalk (15·5% N, also contains calcium carbonate): inorganic, quick-acting, alkaline end reaction. Usually used alone as a stimulant to growing plants on acid soils.

Calcium cyanamide (20·6% N, also contains calcium carbide): inorganic, quick-acting, alkaline end reaction. Often used in weed control and as an activator of decomposition.

Urea (46% N): inorganic, very quick-acting, acid end reaction. Chiefly used in preparation of liquid fertilisers.

Dried blood (12 - 13% N): organic, quick-acting, acid end reaction. Used in spring in seed-beds, and to feed growing plants.

Hoof and horn meal (14% N): organic, steady-acting, slightly acid end reaction. Used as a base fertiliser in late winter and in spring.

FERTILISERS PROVIDING PHOSPHORUS, needed in all vital processes of plant growth, particularly to foster root development and the ripening of fruits and seeds. The content of a fertiliser is usually expressed in terms of phosphoric acid (P_2O_5).

Superphosphate $(18\% P_2O_5)$: inorganic, quick-acting, neutral end reaction. Chiefly used in spring and early summer, prior to sowing or transplanting.

Basic slag $(8 - 18\% P_2O_5, 40 - 50\%$ calcium carbonates): inorganic, very slow-acting, alkaline end reaction. Inexpensive, long-term source of phosphorus, for autumn-winter application on moderately acid soils.

Bone-meal $(20 \cdot 5\% P_2O_5, 3 \cdot 7\% N)$: organic, slow-acting, alkaline end reaction. For autumn-winter application, especially for new stock in flower, shrub or fruit borders.

Steamed bone flour $(27 \cdot 5\% P_2O_5)$: organic, steady-acting, alkaline end reaction. For late winter and spring use, especially to seed-beds and for late planted stock.

Mono-ammonium phosphate $(61 \cdot 8\% P_2O_5, 12 \cdot 2\% N)$: inorganic, very quick-acting, acid end reaction. Chiefly used in preparing liquid 'feeds'.

FERTILISERS WHICH PROVIDE POTASSIUM OR
POTASH, needed for sturdy, healthy growth, and healthy development of growing points of plants; for good resistance to
disease, and to promote good colour in flowers. A fertiliser's
content is usually expressed in terms of potassium oxide (K_2O).

Sulphate of potash (48% K_2O): inorganic, quick and steady-
acting, acid end reaction. May be used at any time of the
year, as potash content is not readily lost in leaching.

Muriate of potash (50% K_2O, 15% NaCl): inorganic, quick
and steady-acting; neutral end reaction. May be used instead
of sulphate of potash, but not recommended for clayey soils,
owing to salt content.

Muriate of potash, high grade (60% K_2O, 3% NaCl): inorganic, quick and steady-acting, neutral end reaction. May
be used instead of sulphate of potash; slightly smaller quantities
being required.

Chilean potash nitrate (14 - 15% K_2O, 10 - 15% N): inorganic, quick and steady-acting, acid end reaction. A combination of potash and nitrogen, excellent for spring use, and
as a 'feed' for crops, flowers and fruits, especially on light soils.

Nitrate of potash, or saltpetre (40% K_2O, 12% N): inorganic,
quick and steady-acting, slightly alkaline end reaction. Chiefly
used as ingredient for liquid fertilisers, or for feeding stimulant
of pot plants.

Wood ashes ($2\frac{1}{2}$ - 7% K_2O, 30 - 40% CaO): inorganic, though of organic origin, quick and steady-acting, alkaline end reaction. Potash content variable according to type of wood and burning. May be applied at any time, as available, to lime-tolerant plants.

FERTILISERS OR SALTS WHICH PROVIDE OTHER NUTRIENTS. These are only likely to be required in exceptional instances.

Magnesium sulphate or Epsom Salt ($MgSO_4.7H_2O$): inorganic, quick acting, alkaline end reaction. Pome fruits (apples, pears), crops intensively fed with potash (tomatoes, potatoes and plants under glass), and plants on open sandy soils are most likely to suffer deficiencies.

Sulphate of iron, calcined ($FeSO_4.7H_2O$): inorganic, steady-acting, acid reaction. Largely used on lawns in conjunction with ammonium sulphate. It should be noted that many of the above fertilisers carry other mineral nutrients as 'impurities', such as sulphur, zinc, copper, and manganese in small amounts.

Use compound fertilisers for basic fertilisation of seed-beds of crops and plants this month and in spring. These are usually combinations of straight fertilisers designed to provide nitrogen, phosphorus and potash, sometimes known as the NPK trio, and may be made up as a general fertiliser which can be safely used for most plants, or as compounds to suit the needs of specific soils or crops. Compound fertilisers may be bought ready-mixed, in powder, granular or liquid form. Nutrient analysis is indicated usually by a ratio figure, such as 7:7:7, meaning 7% N or nitrogen, 7% P or phosphoric acid, and 7% K or potash; this is the analysis of a popular Ministry of Agriculture sponsored general granular fertiliser sold under the name of Growmore.

Other compound fertilisers are marketed under brand names. Those described as organically based usually have organic materials—bone-meal, rapemeal, hoof and horn, etc.—as part of their composition. Alternatively, compounds can be made up at home, but attention must be given to their thorough mixing.

A simple approach—mix 2 parts by weight hoof and horn meal, 1 part bone-meal, 1 part superphosphate and 1 part sulphate of potash together thoroughly; use at 4-6 oz. per sq. yd., for base fertilisation. Analysis: 6·3% N: 7·7% P: 9·6% K. Well suited to all vegetables, soft fruits and flowers, especially on poor soils. Supplement by light feeding during growth.

Flowers: Coming into bloom—*Anemone apennina, A. blanda; Chionodoxa luciliae, C. sardensis;* large-flowering crocus; *Narcissus cyclamineus;* early daffodils; water-lily tulips; *Bergenia ligulata, B. delavayi; Helleborus orientalis, H. viridis; Saxifraga oppositifolia;* and in wild garden, heliotrope *(Petasites fragrans).*

Grasp the opportunity on fine days after rain to lift, divide and replant border plants such as delphiniums, *Ourisia coccinea,* heuchera, Michaelmas daisies, armeria, astilbe, hemerocallis (day lily), geum, helenium, coreopsis, *Dicentra spectabilis,* hosta (funkia), erigeron, inula, lychnis, lysimachia, phlox, *Polygonatum officinale*, potentilla, trollius, thalictrum, sedum, scuttellaria, sidalcea, solidago, stachys, rudbeckia, and veronica.

Check first shoots of pernicious weeds such as horse-tails *(Equisetum* spp.), bindweed *(Convolvulus arvensis)*, and ground-elder *(Aegopodium podagraria)* by painting with a 2,4 - D or 2,4,5-T selective weedkiller. Repeat as often as new growth breaks through.

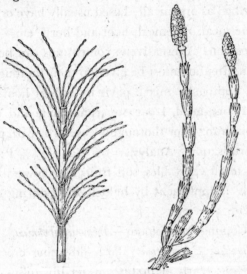

The common horse-tail, Equisetum arvense: *a difficult weed to eradicate.*

Plant out young plants of pyrethrum, sweet william, *Chrysanthemum maxima* 'Read' hybrids, hollyhocks, and biennial and perennial campanulas.

Make first sowings of hardy annuals out of doors, in well-drained, friable soil, enriching soil with superphosphate (1 oz.

per sq. yd.) or steamed bone flour (1½ oz. per sq. yd.), raked in. Sow thinly. Cover fine seed with sifted sand. Spray seed stations with a metaldehyde emulsion to deter slugs, after sowing. Most hardy for early sowings are alyssum, calendula, candytuft, *Chrysanthemum coconarium* and vars., clarkia, collinsia, *Euphorbia marginata*, layia, limnanthes, nemophila, saponaria, viscaria, nasturtiums.

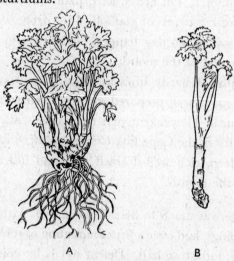

A   B

Propagating delphiniums:
a. A delphinium rootstock lifted in spring for propagation by cuttings.
b. A typical detached delphinium cutting, prepared for planting.

Take young shoot cuttings of delphiniums and lupins which you wish to propagate; insert them in porous sandy loam in cold frame or under cloches on warm border.

Lift and sort montbretia corms, discarding the strings of corms below the largest at the top, and replant the latter early in the month.

Sow seeds of mignonette, Shirley poppies, sweet sultan and larkspur on limy soil.

Plant out sweet pea seedlings raised in peat-wood fibre pots in prepared positions.

Plant bulbs of African spire lily, *Galtonia candicans*, 6 in. deep and 6 in. apart, mid-distance groups in open sunny border, to flower in summer. On heavy soils, plant on base of sand.

Begin planting corms of gladioli, 4 in. deep, 6 in. apart, in deep, rich soil, when day temperatures begin to rise steadily towards the end of the month.

Plant bulbs of hardy lilies as soon as they are available, 4 - 6 in. deep, in well-prepared soil, enriched with leaf-mould and bone-meal. They take a year to become really established.

Plant bulbs of the Cape lily, *Crinum powelli*, 8 in. deep, 9 in. apart, in deep, rich well-drained soil and full sun, towards the end of the month.

Paths: There is much to be said for gravel paths of $\frac{1}{4}$ - $\frac{1}{2}$ in. stone chippings, laid over a firm foundation of rock sand. Such paths often outlast asphalt. Defeat weeds by going over with flame-gun, or spraying with a residual weedkiller based on simazine, this month.

Trim edges of grass paths, and make shoulders firm with metal or plastic lawn edging.

Hedges: Get planting of deciduous hedges completed this month; firm roots well and water thoroughly after planting.

Prune all deciduous hedges, newly planted, hard; remove one-half to two-thirds existing growth, in order to get well furnished bases for the future. During first year after planting, plants are preoccupied in making new roots, and nothing is lost by pruning hard.

In mild districts, planting of evergreen and coniferous hedges and screens may be started towards the end of the month, if the soil is warming up.

Shrubs and Trees: Likely to be in flower—*Erica carnea* and vars. (see February notes); *Erica meditarranea* 'W. T. Rackliff', *E.* x *darleyensis*; *Camellia japonica* and varieties, *C.* x *williamsii* hybrids, *C. sasanqua*; *Chaenomeles alpina, C. speciosa* and varieties; *Cornus mas*; *Corylopsis spicata*; *Daphne mezereum* and vars., *D. odora*; *Mahonia japonica*; *Forsythia giraldiana, F. ovata, F.* x *intermedia* 'Lynwood', *F.* x *intermedia spectabilis, F. suspensa*; *Magnolia stellata*; almond *(Prunus communis)*; *Prunus* x *blireana, P. cerasifera nigra, P. incisa* (Fuji Cherry); *Rhododendron hippophaeoides*; *Ribes sanguineum* and vars. (flowering Currants); *Viburnum tinus; Vinca major, V. minor.*

Complete planting of deciduous shrubs this month, soaking the roots after planting and top-mulching with organic matter, peat or leaves.

Protect newly planted and somewhat tender shrubs such as *Caryopteris* x *clandonensis, Ceanothus* spp., *Hydrangea macrophylla* vars., *Hypericum* spp., *Indigofera gerardiana*, against spring frosts by covering with tents of sacking, sheet polythene, or boxes, in hard weather. They become hardier when once established.

Plant clematis out of pots in deeply dug soil, enriched with limestone grit and bone-meal, placing roots in partial shade

71

when possible, or top-dressing with rotted organic litter; and prune to just above the second or third node from the base. This ensures a vigorous start to new growth and forestalls wilt.

Prune established large-flowering clematis of the Jackmanii and Viticella groups to within 6 in. or so of the base of last year's growth.

Prune winter-flowering heaths (*Erica carnea*, etc.) when the flowers fade and brown; trimming flowered shoots away with shears to speed the work.

Prune other winter-flowering shrubs—*Hamamelis mollis* (witch hazel), winter sweet (*Chimonanthus fragrans*), *Lonicera fragrantissima*, *L.* x *purpusii*—only if it is necessary to promote new branching shoot growth, when flowered shoots may be cut back by one-third to one-half their length.

Prune *Artemisia arborescens* when new growth is seen to be budding low down, cutting out last year's growth to its base.

If the largest flowers on long arching stems are wanted on *Buddleia davidii* and its varieties, prune the growth from the previous year hard back to within a bud or two of its base, preferably towards the end of the month.

Thin the growth on shrubby *Potentilla fruticosa* vars., by cutting out the old spent stems fairly drastically.

Make a start planting evergreen and coniferous shrubs and trees about the third week in the month on light soils and in warm districts; but April and May are better planting months on cold, wet soils and in cold districts.

Roses: Prune established bush and standard roses, not already

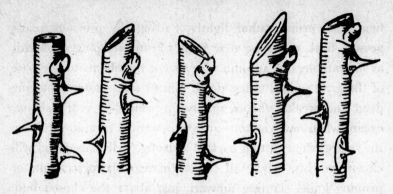

Pruning roses:
a, b, c, d. Incorrect pruning.
e. Pruning correctly done.

tended. First, cut away dead, diseased and frost-injured growth entirely, and cut weak, thin shoots right out or severely back to a strong bud near their base, on all types of bush roses. Then prune according to type and according to subsequent growth required. For strong shoot growth giving large blooms on strong stems, as for exhibition, prune hard; for a greater profusion of roses, as for garden display, prune moderately. Hybrid tea (H.T.) roses—prune shoots to a suitably placed bud, facing the direction in which new growth is desired. Normally, confine pruning to last year's growth. On long-established roses, however, it is permissible to remove one or more of the oldest branches to base. Floribunda and grandiflora roses—prune less severely than H.T.s, thinning out weak growth, and cutting back last year's shoots to well-placed strong buds. As bushes age, remove one or more old branches to foster new growth from the base. Standard roses—after the first year, prune rather lightly, cutting the previous year's growth back to strong new buds. Prune weeping standards as for ramblers in autumn. Never cut out shoots to the base of the graft union, unless dead. Shrub roses—after removing dead and weakly shoots, simply tip-prune last year's shoots, except when new vigorous growth is wanted from lower down the stems, when cutting back to a strong, well-placed bud will encourage this. Make all cuts with razor-sharp secateurs or pruning knife, slanting upward, just above the chosen bud. Burn prunings and fallen leaves, especially if any trouble from black spot disease was experienced last year.

Apply a balanced compound rose fertiliser after pruning (see February notes), and rake lightly in.

See that the point of union where the bush rose was budded is just covered with soil, to keep it moist and able to bud new framework shoots.

After rain, mulch the rose bed with rotted compost, moist peat or moist weathered sawdust, about 1 in. thick, to within 4 in. of the base of the plants.

Lawns: Sow a new lawn on prepared soil (see February notes) as soon as warm growing conditions and rising daily temperatures prevail — in the latter half of the month on sandy or light soils, but postpone till April on heavy clays and in cold districts.

Use the first calm day that comes along for sowing. Lightly rake the surface to leave tiny furrows in it, first in one direction and then at right-angles. Mark off in 6 ft. wide strips, both ways. Seed at 1 oz. per sq. yd., using a modern mixture chiefly of fescues and bents for a fine ornamental lawn. Divide seed into two equal parts, and mix with an equal bulk of sand to aid even distribution. Sow one half of the seed in one direction, the other half at right-angles, broadcasting along a 6 ft. strip at a time. Lightly rake or brush to cover seed, not more than $\frac{1}{4}$ in. deep. May be very lightly rolled with wooden roll when surface-dry. Criss-cross area with black cotton or nylon thread on short sticks to deter birds feeding on the seed or dust-bathing; or cover with sheet polythene for about a week. Apply a pre-emergent weed-killer immediately after sowing, to prevent competition from weed seedlings, especially annuals.

Slit and scarify areas of thinly grassed turf on established lawns, dress with superphosphate (1 oz. per sq. yd.), and over-sow with seeds mixture ($\frac{1}{2}$ oz. per sq. yd., bulked with sand); rake and cover seed lightly with sifted sand or soil.

Apply a well-balanced compound lawn fertiliser at the end of the month to established lawns—2 - 3 oz. per sq. yd., either a proprietary brand, or the formula suggested by the St. Ives (Turf) Research Station: 15 parts by weight sulphate of ammonia, 15 parts dried blood, 40 parts fine bonemeal, 25 parts superphosphate, 5 parts sulphate of potash.

Spot-treat any remaining patches of daisies, pearlwort or rosette-leaved weeds with lawn sand (see February notes for formula); but no selective weed-killers should be used for at least seven days after fertiliser treatment.

Roll lightly to true the lawn surface, after frost, when surface is dry.

Mow regularly, at least weekly, when growth starts, but take a fairly high cut ($\frac{3}{4}$ - 1 in.) during cold or drying windy weather, and let cuttings return to the turf.

Watch for leatherjacket infestation, revealed by loose, dying grasses in browning patches, and the presence near the surface of the greyish-brown to black, tough-skinned grubs of the crane flies. Apply a gamma-BHC (lindane) or DDT insecticide to the area; or flood with water and cover with a tarpaulin or black sheet polythene to bring the grubs to the surface overnight, when they can be swept up. Re-seed later.

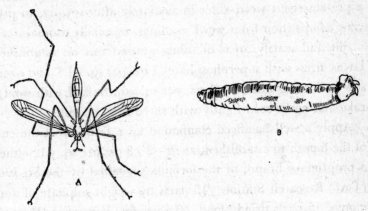

a. The adult 'daddylonglegs' or crane fly, Tipula oleracea.
b. Its larval form or grub, the leatherjacket.

Sow seeds of *Anthemis nobilis* for a chamomile lawn, thinly and shallowly, either in seed boxes or on a prepared nursery bed in a warm sheltered spot out of doors. Transplant seedlings, when large enough to handle, to the prepared lawn area (must be completely free of weeds), 3 - 4 in. apart, to grow and knit together into a sward that only needs occasional cutting and suppression of flower stalks. Suits light and well-drained soils.

Rock Garden: Coming into flower—*Anemone appenina, A. blanda; Chionodoxa luciliae, C. sardensis; Crocus aureus, C. biflorus, C. chrysanthus* and vars., *C. minimus, C. susianus, C. tomasinianus; Cyclamen repandum* (mild districts only); *Eranthis* x *tubergeniana; Iris histrioides, I. danfordiae, I. reticulata* and vars.; *Narcissus asturiensis, N. bulbocodium, N. cyclamineus; Tulipa kaufmanniana, T. praestans; Erica carnea* and vars., 'Winter Beauty', 'Springwood White', 'Springwood Pink', 'Eileen Porter', and *vivellii; Morisia monantha; Saxifraga burseriana* and vars.; *Saxifraga oppositifolia splendens; Primula juliana* hybrids.

Sows seeds of dwarf hardy annuals in seed pans to be raised in cold frames, and to give summer colour. Suggested kinds are *Alyssum* 'Little Dorrit', 'Royal Carpet', 'Pink Heather'; Candytuft 'Fairy Mixed'; *Gilia capitata; Linaria* 'Fairy Bouquet'; *Nemophila insignis; Sanvitalia procumbens; Silene* 'Armeria Rose'; *Tagetes pumila* 'Golden Ring'; and *Lobelia erinus compacta*.

Sow seeds of dwarf alpine perennials in seed pans in cool greenhouse, such as *Achillea tomentosa aurea; Alyssum montanum; Aubrieta* varieties; *Campanula carpatica, C. pulla, C. portenschlagiana Dianthus* x *allwoodii alpinus, D. caesius* and hybrids; *Iberis saxatilis; Papaver alpinum; Thymus serpyllum* and vars.

Sow seeds of *Thymus serpyllum* and vars., *T. hirsutus*, in boxes or pans, to give seedlings for planting up small alpine 'lawns', on well-drained or chalky soil.

Planting up of a new rock garden may go forward now and

during April, with plants ex pots. This is probably the best time to plant in the wetter west of Britain.

Continue weeding, with paint brush and a solution of a selective weed-killer—MCPA, 2,4-D or 2,4,5-T products for broad-leaved weeds; CMPP or mecroprop for clover; dalapon for coarse grasses and twitch. Confine the solution to weed stems and foliage.

Lightly fork in dressings of a gamma-BHC insecticidal dust to the soil where soil pests—wireworms, chafer grubs, etc.—are feared.

Place pellets of a metaldehyde slug bait under broken convex pieces of flower pot, coconut shell or citrus fruit rind to protect plants from slugs and snails.

Water Garden: Let leaking pools empty to where water level remains constant. Examine exposed sides for cracks. Where found, chisel or rake out loose and crumbling concrete, then repair by filling with a waterproofing bitumen paste; finally coat the walls with the same bitumen material in paint form (Ganderbak, Aquaseal, Rito, Synthaprufe, etc.). When dry, pool can be refilled. If the leak is in the base, pool will have to be emptied completely, of plants and soils as well as water, and the whole treated. This is best done in April.

Stop greening of water by algae growth by putting a flat board or two to float in the open spaces until plants make leaf growth. The shading checks algae growth.

Do not be tempted to feed fish until temperatures are rising daily and the fish are active. Then give a little regularly, say early in the morning, at first; small pink and red worms, chopped scrambled egg, left-over oatmeal porridge, woodlice, scraped raw lean meat, dried Daphnia, are suitable—but no more than the fish readily take. A second feed per day can be given later in spring and summer.

Neutralise the alkalinity of freshly constructed concrete and cement-lined or cement-repaired pools either by *(a)* painting, when set, with bitumen paint, before filling; or *(b)* filling with water, staining the water a good port-wine red with potassium permanganate, leaving at least 4 days, emptying and flushing of deposits on base. Either way, the pool is then ready for planting up.

Spring-clean established pools, thinning and pruning plants, removing decaying leaves and stems, but do not remove any bottom silt or mud where there are fish.

Fruit: There is still time to plant apples and pears, but leave them unpruned, and do not let them bear fruit in the first year; there is enough strain on their constitution in getting their roots established.

Prune raspberries planted this month down to soil level so that all growth energies may go into forming the new fruiting canes for next year.

Plant maiden strawberries in well-prepared bed, but de-blossom the first year. They will then build up good fruiting crowns to give a good account of themselves for the following three years.

Prune newly planted currant and gooseberry bushes fairly

severely, shortening shoots to three or four buds from the base. You sacrifice fruit for this year but get strong fruiting shoots for next year, and a framework of good branches.

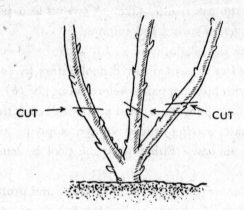

CUT →   ← CUT

A newly planted two-year-old black currant, showing where to prune.

Give no fertilisers to newly planted fruit trees in the first year, but mulch with organic matter—compost, hop manure, dried sewage sludge, etc.—after rain.

Give base fertilisers to established fruit trees and soft fruits this month. Broadly, dessert apples and gooseberries need adequate potash, and equal parts by weight sulphate of ammonia and sulphate of potash at 2 oz. per sq. yd. is useful; while for culinary apples and black currants, 2 parts by weight sulphate of ammonia and 1 part sulphate of potash at 2 oz. per sq. yd. would be more satisfactory.

Give a mixture of 1 part by weight hoof and horn, 1 part sulphate of ammonia, and 1 part sulphate of potash to raspberries and strawberries, at 2 - 3 oz. per sq. yd. Every fourth year add a little magnesium sulphate, say $\frac{1}{4}$ oz. per sq. yd., to these fertilisers. Phosphates (bone-meal) should be given each autumn.

Spread mulching material over roots of fruit trees and bushes later in the month, after rain—left-over compost, spent mushroom compost, dried sewage, straw, etc.

Look for signs of the big bud mite infestation in black currants—abnormally swollen buds on young shoots. The mites migrate from these infested buds when they open in spring and spread infestation. If present, spray the bushes with lime-sulphur (3% concentration) when the flower racemes reach the 'grape bud' stage, or the leaves about the size of a shilling—usually at end of March or early April. If sulphur-shy varieties —'Davison's 8', 'Wellington XXX'—are grown, reduce concentration to 2% lime-sulphur.

Black currants at the 'grape' stage of flower development.

Give first application of a captan fungicide around the end of the month to pears when buds begin to swell (bud-burst stage), if scab disease was serious last year.

Vegetables: Apply balanced compound base fertilisers and break down the soil with fork and rake to form a friable seed-bed tilth.

Sow second early peas such as 'Giant Stride', 'Onward', 'Kelvedon Monarch', 'Phenomenon' and 'Dwarf Defiance' to grow 2 - 2½ ft. tall; and 'Achievement', 'Evergreen', and 'Duke of Albany' to grow 4 - 5 ft. tall.

Make first sowings of brassicas on separate nursery bed when soil temperatures remain above 50°F. (10°C.): Italian green sprouting broccoli; cabbage ('Tender and True','Winnigstadt'); Savoy cabbage ('Dwarf Green Curled', 'Best of All'); Brussels sprouts ('Dwarf Gem', 'Cambridge Special' for early crops); cauliflower ('Early London', 'Early Giant'): and Kohl rabi. All seeds ¼ - ⅜ in. deep.

Sow leeks in nursery bed, thinly, ½ in. deep. Use 'Lyon', 'Musselburgh' or 'Prizetaker' to give winter crops.

Sow lettuce on seed-bed from mid to late March to transplant in late April. Varieties are numerous, and choice will probably depend on individual preferences—smooth-leaved cabbage type ('Attractie', 'Tom Thumb', 'Ideal'); crinkled-leaved cabbage ('Iceberg', 'Holborn Standard', 'Wonderful'), or cos ('Giant White', 'Lobjoit's Green', 'Histon Crispie').

Sow radish in drills ½ in. deep, in moist, rich soil for quick maturity: variety according to personal preference, globe, turnip-shaped, or long; colour red or white, or half and half. Make successional sowings at 2 - 3 week intervals. Can be catch-cropped between peas, beans and brassicas, if pushed for space.

Sow carrots in drills thinly, 9 - 12 in. apart, $\frac{1}{2}$ in. deep—early varieties to give tender roots, maincrops ('Autumn King', 'James Intermediate') for storing—on ground organically manured for the previous year's crop.

Sow turnips in drills 12 in. apart, $\frac{1}{2}$ in. deep, from about mid to late March, as weather warms up—'Snowball', 'Golden Ball', 'Manchester Market' are all good.

Sow onions out of doors in first half of the month if possible, on well-prepared firm seed-bed, $\frac{3}{8}$ inch deep. Use fresh seed for good germination. 'A.1', 'Bedfordshire Champion', 'James Keeping' for storing; 'Ailsa Craig', 'Flagon' for showing.

Sow parsley on good, well-drained soil, thinly, $\frac{3}{8}$ in. deep, for summer picking; thin plants well, up to 9 in. apart.

Sow round spinach on good, humus-rich soil, $\frac{1}{2}$ in. deep, in drills 12 - 15 in. apart. Place seeds—actually capsules of up to 3 seeds—6 - 8 in. apart, and thin to one seedling each later.

Plant seed tubers of early potatoes in later half of the month, about 12 in. apart. Give ample organic manure, and a light dressing of a compound fertiliser. For early maturing of the crop, cover rows with black sheet polythene, cutting a cross-shaped (+) slit for each tuber to grow through. No earting-up needed.

Rake any loose litter from established asparagus beds, weed, and dress with agricultural salt (2 - 3 oz. per sq. yd.) early in the month. Follow with a top-dressing of 3 parts by weight superphosphate, 1 part sulphate of potash, at 2 oz. per sq. yd., a fortnight later, and prick in. Get rid of any couch grass or coarse grass weeds by applying a dalapon herbicide.

Plants Under Glass: Under cloches—a sowing of dwarf French beans may be made towards the end of the month; 'Lightning' or 'Sunrise'. Catch-crop with radishes.

Greenhouse plants you may have in bloom:

In a cold greenhouse—*Camellia japonica* and varieties; *Daphne retusa, D. odora; Enkianthus* spp. (lime-free compost); *Abutilon megapotamicum*; Dutch crocus, hardy narcissi and early tulips, started into growth outdoors and brought in to flower. Pot-grown alpines, such as saxifrages of the Kabschia group, *Saxifraga irvingii, S. burseriana* 'Gloria', *S. b. sulphurea*, etc.; *Primula allionii* and its forms, *P.* x *pubescens*, and young plants of *Pulsatilla vulgaris* and *P. vernalis.*

In a cool greenhouse (minimum night temperatures 45°-50°F. (7°-10°C.)—above shrubs and bulbs, plus: *Acacia decora, A. pulchella, A. retinodes; Anthyllis barba-jovis* (Jupiter's beard); *Epacris impressa, E. purpurescens; Gardenia thunbergia; Gastro-lobium bilobum; Gnidia pinifolia, Macleania speciosissima*, which are shrubs; *Clianthus formosus* (syn. *dampieri*), *Clivia miniata, Crinum moorei; Hymenocallis calathina;* and *Hibbertia dentata.*

Control ventilation according to temperature, increasing as temperatures rise in the daytime, but decreasing ahead of their fall. In spring, it is usually most effective to open ventilators an hour or two before moon, and close an hour before dusk:

the amount of opening depends upon the warmth of the day and wind. Remember wind can extract warm air rapidly. Open ventilators on the lee side when strong winds blow. An extractor fan linked with the thermostatic control of temperature takes the guesswork out of ventilation by working automatically.

Regulate watering according to growth and atmospheric conditions. Naturally, as plants make more active growth, they need more water; but actual growth activity is relative to light intensity and temperature. The sunnier the day the more active the growth, and the more water is used and needed. On cloudy or rainy days, water only moderately. The danger is to over-water, especially young plants.

Use clean water, avoiding water from a stagnant or standing source open to the sky, since it may be contaminated with algae and 'green' your soil.

Spray or syringe plants on those days when the sun shines freely, but always in the early part of the day, so that the plant surfaces are dry by nightfall.

Make main sowings of half-hardy and hardy annuals for planting out in May or early June, with bottom heat of 55° to 65°F. (13 - 18°C.). Small propagating units are excellent for this. Seed in variety for small gardens can be raised by sowing in peat-wood fibre pots. Without bottom heat, wait until the last week of the month, or early April.

Sow seeds of *Primula malacoides* ('Coral Pink', 'Lilac' and 'Orange Scarlet' are lovely new forms), *P. obconica (gigantea* vars. for largest flowers), *P. sinensis*, and *P. stellata*, in J.I. or

U.C. Compost, with gentle bottom heat (about 55°F., 13°C.). Plants will come into bloom for Christmas.

Sow seeds of polyanthus and primrose under like conditions, to be planted out in May. Also easily raised under cool conditions from seed are *Primula bulleyana*, *P. pulverulenta*, *P. japonica*, and *P. sikkimensis*; sow thinly in seed pans, keep in partial shade.

Sow pansies in boxes in frame or greenhouse towards the end of the month, to give summer and autumn bloom.

Sow seeds of hardy perennials, when temperatures of 50° to 55°F. (10° - 13°C.) can be assured, such as *Alyssum saxatile*, *Anchusa italica*, auriculas, aquilegia, *Aster alpinus*, *Coreopsis grandiflora*, erigeron, helenium, heuchera, *Meconopsis betonicifolia*, *potentilla* hybrids, pyrethrum, *Kniphofia* hybrids (red hot poker), and *Veronica spicata*.

Continue to make sowings of *Browallia elata*, *B. viscosa*, *Celosia cristata*, *C. plumosa*, *Gesneria* hybrids, *Gloxinia* hybrids, and *Streptocarpus* hybrids, to give flowering pot plants.

Make a sowing of *Kalanchoë vulkan*, *Kochia childsii*, *Exacum affine*, *Heliotrope regale* hybrids, coleus, *Cuphea platycentra* (cigar plant), schizanthus, *Torenia fournieri*, and ricinus (castor oil plant) to be grown as pot plants for greenhouse or indoor decoration.

Take cuttings of zonal pelargoniums ('geraniums') to give plants that flower next winter. Let cuttings be 2 - 2½ in. long, of sturdy shoots, cut below a leaf or node; allow these to dry off overnight and insert in a sandy porous compost, and give no water until growing.

Sow seeds of *Asparagus plumosus nanus* and *A. sprengeri* in J.I. or U.C. seed compost, with bottom heat of not less than 70°F. (21°C.), preferably in a propagating unit.

Prune *Plumbago capensis*, the Cape leadwort, if this has not already been done, shortening last year's shoots to within about an inch of their base; and water freely.

Pot tubers of *Gloriosa rothschildiana*, and *G. superba*, the climbing lilies, 2 in. deep in 6 - 8 in. pots, and water sparingly at first, increasing with growth, giving ample sun and warmth.

Pot bulbs of *Crinum moorei*, *C. powelli*, *Hippeastrum* varieties for late spring and summer blooming; one bulb to a 6 - 8 in. pot, and water increasingly as growth is made; minimum night temperature of 55°F. (12° - 13°C.).

Divide and repot plants of *Primula obconica*, etc., using J.I.P. 3, or U.C. potting compost; provided plants are robust, vigorous and in good health.

Start repotting or refurbishing house plants towards the end of the month and during April. Tackle first those about to make new growth. In the case of evergreen foliage plants, such as ficus, aralia, cissus, philodendrons, etc., it is often sufficient to remove an inch or two of the top-soil and replace with fresh compost—repotting only when roots are crowding the pots. When indoor azaleas finish flowering, remove spent flowers, but keep growing in cool conditions until they can be placed outdoors for the summer. Do not prune new shoots.

Sow cucumber, and marrow seeds singly in peat-wood fibre pots, with bottom heat of at least 70°F. (21°C.), for planting out of doors in late May or early June.

Syringe on warm days earlier-sown cucumber plants which are intended for inside cropping under glass.

Sow seeds of aubergine or egg-plant, with bottom heat of 60° - 65°F. (15·5° - 19°C.), and air temperature not less than 60°F. (15·5°C.). But give the plants a dryish atmosphere to avoid damping off.

Feed strawberries brought in for forcing with a good liquid manure two to three times weekly; support trusses of fruit on small sticks.

Be ready to control aphides (greenfly) with a derris insecticide, and watch for red spider mite infestation.

April

April, April,
Laugh thy girlish laughter;
Then, the moment after,
Weep thy girlish tears!
. SIR WILLIAM WATSON

APRIL may well be described as a month of transition, when winter is laid by the heels and spring enthroned, for with strengthening sun and heightening temperatures the regeneration and growth of the plant kingdom cannot be denied. Yet sudden changes, drenching showers and knifing night frosts often occur to keep the gardener on his toes.

With growing conditions steadily improving, differences in latitude in the temperate regions become less important, and the month is a busy one of sowing and planting in readiness for the burgeoning of plant development in stem, leaf and flower. In the north, on high ground and in the colder localities, operations out of doors can follow more closely their timing in the south, with a postponement of no more than a week or ten days.

Birth in the plant kingdom is hazardous, and the young are

vulnerable as in the animal world. There are three main threats to plant welfare this month—weeds, spring frosts and emerging plant parasites.

Quite naturally, the native and unwanted plants which we term weeds tend to be quickest off the mark in growing. They menace the more exotic and highly bred garden plants by their vigorous competition for light, moisture and nutrients from the soil.

Prevent competition among outdoor-sown crops and plants by applying a pre-emergent weed-killer soon after sowing. This functions by destroying germinating weed seedlings as they attempt to break through to the surface but loses its toxicity before the slower-germinating plant seedlings appear. Timing is critical, and the maker's instructions should be implicitly followed.

Alternatively, use a flame-gun prior to sowing, to partially sterilise and destroy weed seedlings lying near the surface of seed-beds. A shielded or hooded flame-gun can be used effectively to control weeds among growing plants, but great care is needed as the flame heat is intense.

Remember all weeds must make leaf to grow nad thrive. Deny them leaf growth and they die. Hand-weed and hoe as often as time can be found and when soil conditions are favourable—ideally a drying surface after rain. Use the shallow-sifting Dutch hoe among plants to destroy annual weeds. Keep it razor-sharp to chop up the weeds and work them into the soil to rot. Use the draw hoe to chop out roots of perennial weeds and remove for burning by raking.

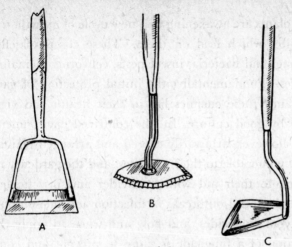

Dutch hoes:
a. Traditional.   b, c. Modern forms.

Smother-mulch weeds in borders, especially the tough ground elder *(aegopodium podagraria)*, first beating down and bruising, sprinkling with sulphate of ammonia, and then covering with an inch or so of compost, moist peat or weathered sawdust.

Be ready to protect early growth of crops and plants and flowers of fruit trees against frost damage in this month and next. The danger comes at night, when heat absorbed by earth and vegetation during the day is radiated back to the atmosphere. The warmed air rises, and cold air flows in to take its place near the ground. This tends to be of freezing temperature on nights when the sky is cloudless and clear after a sunny day, and is most dangerous on low-lying ground to which air can drain from higher up. Precise notes on steps that can be taken are given in the appropriate sections.

91

Just as plants are awakening to a new cycle of growth, so are the parasites which feed on them. These consist chiefly of certain fungi and bacteria, insect pests, eelworms (nematodes) and viruses. Fundamentally, the initial protection of garden plants against these enemies lies in their health and vigour, promoted by good culture. In the contrived environment of a garden, however, arbitrarily chosen and arranged plants are peculiarly vulnerable to their parasites, and the gardener must often come to their aid with fungicides and insecticides to prevent and control outbreaks of infection and infestation.

Know your fungicides, and how and when to apply them. The function of a fungicide is more to prevent and contain infection than to cure it, by means of a chemical ingredient that is toxic to germinating spores. Consequently, fungicides are usually applied to cover all plant surfaces liberally on which spores may alight, either immediately before an outbreak is feared, or when the first signs of infection are seen. A few newer fungicides have eradicant properties, though they are most effective as protectants, preventing disease or its spread. The choice and application of fungicides against specific diseases are given in the monthly notes, but here is a list of fungicides that are useful generally in the garden.

FUNGICIDES BASED ON COPPER: protectant, for application before or immediately on appearance of disease.
Bordeaux mixture: chemical, mixture of copper sulphate and lime in water; used as a spray; effective in controlling potato blight, downy mildews, leaf curl in peaches, scab

and botrytis infections; can be harmful if swallowed.

Burgundy mixture: chemical, mixture of copper sulphate and washing soda in water; used as a spray, chiefly to control canker on fruit trees, while dormant.

Cheshunt compound: chemical, mixture of copper sulphate and ammonium carbonate; used as a solution to prevent or check damping-off diseases in seedlings.

FUNGICIDES BASED ON SULPHUR: protectant, for application before or immediately on appearance of disease.

Lime-sulphur: chemical mixture of sulphur and lime, boiled together; used as a spray, chiefly to control scab disease on tree fruits and powdery mildews.

Sulphur dust: chemical, finely divided, powdered sulphur; used as a dust; effective in controlling powdery mildews, especially on grapes and greenhouse plants.

Wettable sulphur — colloidal sulphur: chemical, finely divided forms of sulphur; used as spray alternatives to lime-sulphur and sulphur dust.

FUNGICIDES BASED ON ORGANIC CHEMICALS: protectant, but with some eradicant properties also:

Captan (N-trichloromethylthio-cyclohex-4-ene-1:2-dicarbo-oxyimide): used as a dust or a spray; particularly effective in controlling fruit scab, and other fruit diseases; botrytis on lettuce, strawberries, chrysanthemums, etc, and black spot on roses. Very low toxicity to humans and animals.

Karathane (dinitro (1-methyl heptyl) crotonate): used as a dust or a spray; particularly effective in controlling powdery mildews on vegetables, flowers and fruits. Very low toxicity to humans and animals.

Thiram or TMTD (tetramethylthiuram disulphide): used as a dust or spray; considered a very safe fungicide for use on foliage to control mildews, rusts, black spot, botrytis, etc. In dust form makes a good seed-dressing to prevent damping-off and foot rot.

FUNGICIDES BASED ON ANTIBIOTICS

Griseofulvin: systemic, being absorbed into the plant and acting through the sap stream; watered on in combination with an organic liquid feed; effective in controlling mildews.

Use insecticides with knowledge and care. Because of their purpose, they are poisonous—some more than others. They are usually designed to kill insects on contact and/or when eaten. Since they do not discriminate between parasitic and beneficial (pollinating or predatory) insects, precision is needed in application and timing. Specific measures against the common insect pests are given in the monthly notes. The most useful insecticides for garden use are:

Aldrin (1:2:3:4:10:10-hexachloro-1:4:4a:5:8:8a-hexahydro-exo-1:4-endo-5:8-dimethanonaphthalene): organic chemical, used chiefly as a dust; effective as a soil insecticide to control wireworms, leather-jackets, chafer grubs, cut-worms, etc; persistent and non-tainting; best used as a seed-dressing, rather than broadcast, to minimise possible toxic effects on beneficial soil life. Hazardous to bird life if misused.

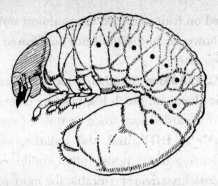

Cockchafer: larval form of the May bug, Melolontha vulgaris.

Calomel (mercuric chloride): chemical: used as a 4% dust in inert carrier; effective against onion and cabbage root fly: has also a fungicidal action against the slime fungus responsible for clubroot in brassicas.

DDT (dichloro-diphenyl-trichloro-ethane): organic chemical, contact and stomach poison; effective in controlling many caterpillars, beetles, weevils, midge flies and thrips, but too slow-acting to be highly effective against aphides (greenfly, blackfly). Used as a dust or spray. May be used on most crops or plants, excepting those of the *Cucurbiteae* family—cucumbers, marrows, melons, etc. Should not be used on plants in flower, particularly fruit crops, when bees and pollinating insects are visiting them, or within 3 to 4 weeks of harvesting food crops.

Derris: natural plant derivative of which the effective constituent is rotenone; controls most pests, aphides, thrips, caterpillars, etc., and red spider mites; used as a dust or spray; has the great merit of being non-poisonous to humans and animals,

95

so may be used on fruit and food crops almost until harvested; toxic to fish, however, and should not be allowed to fall in the water of fish-ponds.

gamma BHC, Lindane (gamma isomer of benzene hexachloride): organic chemical, much less tainting from of BHC, and most suitable for garden use; used as dust or spray; controls pests susceptible to DDT, and also aphides, woolly aphides and soil-frequenting insect pests; often combined with DDT as an all-purpose insecticide; suitable for most plants but not hydrangeas, currants, vines, cucumbers, marrows, other cucurbits or potatoes and root crops. Should not be applied to plants in flower being visited by bees and pollinating insects; not safe for pools where there are fish.

Malathion (S-1:2-di-(ethoxycarbonyl) ethyl-dimethyl-phosphorothiolothionate): organic chemical: used chiefly as a spray; highly effective in controlling aphides, white fly and red spider mites; should not be used when plants are in flower and being visited by bees, etc., or on food crops within 1 to 2 weeks of harvest.

Nicotine: natural derivative of the tobacco plant, used as a spray, dust or 'smoke'; quick-acting control of most sap-sucking and leaf-eating pests, particularly by contact, for summer use at temperatures of 60°F. (15·5°C.): loses toxicity quickly, and may be used on food plants up to within 2 to 3 days of harvest; very poisonous to humans and animals; vapour should not be inhaled.

Pyrethrum: natural plant product, used as dust or spray; controls most plant pests, with quick 'knock-down' effect;

non-poisonous to humans and animals. Often combined with more persistent insecticides for more permanent effect.

Systemics: organic chemicals, designed to be watered on plants and over roots to be absorbed into the sap, and so poison sap-sucking aphides, etc. Menazon is considered safe for use on food crops: needs to be applied in anticipation of infestation and not within 3 - 4 weeks of harvest.

Several of the above insecticides are prepared for use in the form of smoke generators for the fumigation of greenhouses, and as mist-spraying aerosols. They should be used strictly according to the makers' instructions.

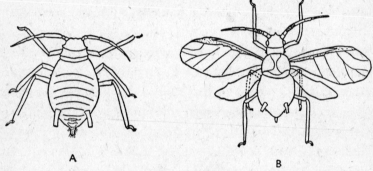

A   B

Aphides or greenfly:
a. The viviparous form.   *b. The winged migratory adult.*

Flowers: Coming into bloom—*Corydalis solida*, *Narcissus triandrus* and vars., large-flowering daffodils and jonquils; *Erythronium dens-canis* and varieties (dog's tooth violets); *Puschkinia scilloides* (striped squill); tulips such as *Tulipa biflora*, *T. chrysantha*, *T. tarda*, *T. fosteriana* and hybrids, *T. greigii*, and *T. kaufmannia*, named varieties; *Fritillaria imperialis* (crown imperials); *Adonis amurensis flore pleno; Arabis albida flore pleno; Bellis perennis* 'Dresden China'; *Doronicum plantagineum; Myosotis alpestris; Primula juliae* and hybrids; *P. vulgaris, P. denticulata; Pulmonaria angustifolia, P. saccharata* (Bethlehem sage); *Sanguinaria canadensis* (blood root).

Continue with weed control, eradicating them in their early stages. Selective weed-killer solutions may be used if they are confined to the weed stems and foliage, by painting on.

Smother-mulch annual weeds (see p. 91).

Continue sowings of hardy annuals (see March notes).

Divide and replant congested clumps of red hot pokers (*Kniphofia* sp.); they appreciate humus-rich soil and bone-meal.

Plant out seedling pansies over-wintered in cold frames.

Sow hardy annuals freely now to fill open spaces in borders, and don't forget the climbers—nasturtiums, *Convolvulus major, Humulus japonicus* (ornamental hop), and *Tropaeolum canariense* (canary creeper)—for the quick covering of trellis, tree stumps, and eyesores.

Make plantings of gladiolus corms at fortnightly intervals to the end of May to give a succession of bloom. Plant corms in well-dug, free-draining soil, 4 in. deep, 6 - 8 in. apart. In heavy soils, put sand beneath and around the corms and fill planting holes up with dry soil. Reject any corms showing fungus mould, or hard centres of rot.

Plant out border and Korean chrysanthemums in latter half of the month, in soil enriched with well-rotted manure or compost and a little bone flour. Water thoroughly.

Plant out border carnations, in good soil, well drained and

enriched with ground limestone if more than slightly acid.

Plant dormant dahlia tubers in well-prepared soil, from the middle of the month onwards, but be prepared to protect young shoots from night frost damage later, by means of cloches or light covering of bracken, straw or sheet polythene.

Prepare beds for half-hardy annual seedlings to be planted out in May; raking, dressing with a general compound fertiliser at 2 oz. per sq. yd.

Plant out autumn-sown antirrhinums and other hardy annuals from their winter quarters, on soil dressed with a little superphosphate (1 oz. per sq. yd.).

Place supports in position for the taller herbaceous perennials. A useful device is 3 - 4 in. mesh coir netting stretched over the plants, through which they can grow.

Paths: Swab stone or concrete flagged paths, driveways and courtyards with a dilute solution of domestic bleach to remove the slimy green growth of algae, on a day when the surfaces are reasonably dry.

Destroy grass growing between the flags of stone pavements by applying a dalapon weed-killer.

Scour out and grout interstices between flags, where no growth is wanted, with cement (2 parts clean washed sand, 1 part cement preferably quick-setting, and just enough water to give a stiffish 'porridge'). Apply in mild weather, cover with damp sacking for 48 hours, until set.

Re-gravel gravel paths after clearing weeds, and applying a residual total weed-killer based on simazin.

Use sodium chlorate as a total weed-killer on paths when the weeds are in leaf. Maximum lethal effect is obtained when the weather has been dry for a few days; such conditions also minimise 'creeping' or dispersion of the salt beyond the area of its application. Do not apply within 12 in. of lawns or borders. Do not let the solution spill or dry on clothing or the coats of animals, as it makes them inflammable. The addition of calcium chloride removes the fire hazard, and Atlacide is a useful proprietary mixture that can be used as a dust for the spot treatment of all weeds in stone paving.

Treat soft stone paving subject to flaking or easy disintegration with a stone-hardening solution. Concrete paths, subject to becoming dusty, need painting with a concrete hardener, as used for garage floors.

Plant up stone flags or paving of terraces and courtyards with carpeting alpines, placed at junctions where room can be made for the plants and a little porous soil compost. Some suggestions—*Acaena microphylla*, *Armeria caespitosa*, *Campanula arvatica*, *C. garganica*, *Dianthus*, dwarf hybrids and species, *Thymus serpyllum* and vars., mossy *Saxifraga* sp., *Sempervivum* sp., *Silene acaulis*.

Hedges: Plant evergreen hedges and screens this month and next. Prepare ground beforehand by bastard trenching. Lighten heavy soils with horticultural gypsum (4 - 6 oz. per sq. yd.), forked in; give body to light soils by forking in clay and thoroughly rotted organic matter. Use no fertilisers except bone-meal, bone flour, or superphosphate.

Weigh maintenance costs and longevity against initial cost of hedging material, and rate of growth. On this basis, yew (but not where cattle or farm stock can reach it), holly or box make the finest permanent hedges.

Use flowering evergreens for informal hedges. *Berberis* x *stenophylla* (to 8 ft.), *B. darwinii* (to 6 ft.), *Cotoneaster lactea* (to 10 ft.), *Escallonia* x hybrids (to 8 ft.), and *Pyracantha rogersiana* (to 9 ft.) are suggestions. *Lavendula spica* (to 2 - 3 ft.), *Erica mediterranea* 'W.T. Racliff' (to 3 ft.) and *Santolina chamaecyparissus* (to 2 ft.) make pleasing though not overlong-lived internal hedges.

Plant *Lonicera nitida fertilis* (syn. *pileata yunnanensis*) for a quick-growing hedge, but remember it needs frequent trimming during the growing season.

Plant coniferous hedges only where the atmosphere remains reasonably clean, not in cities or industrial areas. *Cupressus macrocarpa* is better as a screen than a trimmed hedge, especially for seaside gardens. For quick growth and willingness to stand up to trimming, plant the hybrid *Cupressocyparis* x *leylandii*. Otherwise, *Chamaecyparis lawsoniana*, in a hedging strain makes the best all-round coniferous hedge.

Cut back overgrown laurel hedges this month; they regenerate well from quite severe pruning.

Prune overgrown and neglected hedges of yew, holly and box as soon as new buds show signs of opening. Cutting back can be quite severe into older wood.

Top-mulch newly planted hedges with compost, peat or weathered sawdust, but leave bare within 6 in. of the base.

Spray or syringe all newly planted or pruned evergreen and coniferous hedges with water in dry weather, particularly when easterly drying winds blow.

Shrubs and Trees: Likely to be in flower—*Erica mediterranea superba,* and 'W. T. Rackliff'; *Camellia japonica* and vars.; *Chaenomeles speciosa* and vars., (flowering quinces); *Daphne mezerum* and vars.; *Forsythia* spp. (early part of the month); *Kerria japonica; Magnolia stellata, M.* x *soulangeana* and vars., (towards the end of the month); *Mahonia aquifolium; Osmanthus delavayi; Pieris taiwanensis, P. japonica; Prunus communis* (almond) and vars., *P. persica* (peach) and vars., *P. spinosa purpurea* (sloe), *P. avium* (wild cherry), *P. incisa, P. sargentii, P. subhirtella pendula; Amelanchier canadensis; Rhododendron impeditum, R. pemakoense; Ribes sanguineum* and vars.; *Spiraea arguta* (by mid-April); *S. thunbergii; Vinca major, V. minor.*

Plant evergreen shrubs and trees. Those that arrive with roots in a soil ball and wrapped in sacking only need to have the sacking loosened after being placed in the planting hole. A polythene wrapper must be entirely removed. Plants in 'fyba' pots only need the bottom taken off. Soak planting station after planting if weather is dry, and keep top growth well syringed in cold spells in spring.

Plan magnolias now. Although many are deciduous, they transplant best when growth is just commencing. Avoid injury to their rather fleshy roots.

Plant *Cortaderia argentea* (pampas grass) and its varieties now. Trim and divide established clumps.

102

Prune shrubs which flower late on shoots of the current year's growth, cutting all dead and weak growth away, and reducing other stems to just above strong buds now about to break. Typical kinds are *Caryopteris* x *clandonensis; Artemisia arborescens; Ceratostigma willmottianum; Fuchsia magellanica* and vars.; *Hydrangea paniculata; Hyssopus aristatus; Indigofera gerardiana; Romneya coulteri* and *R.* x *trichocalyx; Sambucus canadensis maxima; Santolina chamaecyparissus, S. viridis; Spartium junceum;* and *Tamarix pentandra* and its varieties.

Remove the spent flowers of last year from the large-flower forms of *Hydrangea macrophylla*, cut out dead wood and weak spindly growth, but do not prune shoots of last year's growth which will carry flowers for this year, unless the tip growth has been winter-killed.

Trim ivy on walls. Remove it entirely where it clambers up trees; kill the roots with sodium chlorate, placed in a small hole made in the severed top of the stem at soil level.

Cut back climbers such as *Aristolochia sipho, Campsis grandiflora, Hydrangea petiolaris, Passiflora coerulea, Vitis coignetiae,* and so-called Virginian creepers of the *Parthenocissus* (syn. *Ampelopsis)* genus.

Roses: Water late-planted roses during spells of dry spring weather until established.

Complete pruning of hybrid tea and bush roses as soon as possible in the month.

Train and tie in new shoot growth on recently planted rambler and climbing roses as it is made.

Syringe soft new growths on all roses with water before the

sun shines on them, after a night of frost. Prevents injury and die-back of promising stems.

Lawn: Sow new lawns this month (see February and March notes). Water with fine sprinkler if no rain falls within ten days after sowing.

Apply complete balanced lawn fertiliser to established lawns, if this has not been done already. (See March notes for fertiliser formula.)

Apply a selective lawn weed-killer, 7 - 10 days after applying the fertiliser and before mowing, *or* 3 - 4 days after last mowing. Weed-killers based on MCPA, 2,4-D or 2,4,5-T will account for most broad-leaved weeds. Where clover is a problem, use a weed-killer containing CMPP (mecroprop). Not all weeds are amenable to selective weed-killers. If speedwells (*Veronica arvensis*, etc.), yarrow *(Achillea millefolium)* and similar prostrate weeds are present, rake to loosen and lift stems before mowing, and use a rotary-scything mower. Too many daisies? Dress with lawn sand as well as selective weed-killer.

Mow lightly, but with increasing frequency as grass growth quickens. A rotary-scything mower may not give the same fashionable finish as a cylinder or reel mower, but it trims coarse grasses more effectively and gives inhibitory control of many weeds.

Compost the cuttings from a lawn treated with a selective weed-killer; but do not use the compost for at least six weeks, when the weed-killer will have decomposed. Do not use the grass cuttings for mulching.

Renovate neglected lawns, after fertilising, by scarifying with a fine-toothed rake, and brushing.

Control moss and broad-leaved weeds like daisies with an application of a mercurised moss lawn sand, if these twin problems exist. Follow this a fortnight later with a selective weed-killer.

Rock Garden: Coming into flower—*Aethionema* x 'Warley Rose'; *Alyssum saxatile* and vars.; *Crocus vernus* and vars.; *Cyclamen repandum; Narcissus bulbocodium, N. juncifolius, N. triandrus* 'Concolour', *N. t.* 'Thalia', *N.* x 'W. P. Milner'; *Erythronium dens-canis* and vars.; *Draba dedeana; Fritillaria meleagris* (snake's-heads); *Hepatica triloba; Leontopodium alpinum* (edelweiss); *Muscari azureum* vars.; *Oxalis adenophylla; Puschkinia libanotica; Scilla bifolia, S. siberica; Morisia monantha; Origanum hybridum; Oxalis enneaphylla; Penstemon* x 'Weald Beacon'; *Polygonum tenuicaule; Potentilla eriocarpa, P. nitida, P.* x *tonguei; P. verna nana; Primula marginata* and vars., *P.* x *pubescens* and hybrids, *P. frondosa, P. rosea; Pulsatilla alpina, P. vernalis, P. vulgaris; Ranunculus alpestris, R. amplexicaulis; Rhododendron chameunum, R. hanceanum nanum, R. pemakoense, R. scintillans; Saxifraga* Kabschia section such as 'Amitie', 'Faldonside', 'Cranbourne', *S.* x *jenkinsae, S. burseriana, S. marginata, S.* x *frederici-augustii, S. griesbachii, S. media; Saxifraga* (mossy section) such as 'Avoca Gem', 'Elf', 'James Bremner', 'Red Admiral', 'Winston Churchill'; *S. oppositifolia* and vars.; *Tulipa clusiana, T. fosteriana* dwarf vars., *T. greigii, T. hageri, T. kaufmanniana, T. stellata chrysantha, T. tarda, T. urumiensis; Waldsteinia ternata.*

Continue planting-up with alpines ex pots, weeding and protecting plants against slugs.

Plant dwarf evergreen shrubs. Choice subjects for any rock garden are: *Berberis stenophylla corallina compacta, Daphne retusa, Erica carnea* and vars., *Helianthemum nummularium* and vars,, and *Polygala chamaebuxus.* For pockets of lime-free, leaf-mould or peat-enriched soil, there are *Andromeda polifolia nana, Cassiope lycopodioides, Leiophyllum buxifolium, Pernettya tasmanica, Phyllodoce breweri,* dwarf rhodendrons (see names listed under 'Coming into Flower' at the beginning of rock garden sections for this month and next); *Vaccinium caespitosum, Calluna vulgaris* and vars. 'Alportii', 'County Wicklow', 'H. E. Beale', 'J. H. Hamilton' and 'Serlei'; *Daboecia cantabrica* and vars., *Erica ciliaris, E. cinerea* and vars. 'C. D. Eason', 'C. G. Best', 'Eden Valley', 'Frances' and 'Rose Queen'; and *E. tetralix.*

Plant dwarf conifers this month and next, watering in thoroughly, and syringing foliage in dry weather and on warm sunny days. True dwarfs are fewer than is generally realised; most useful are *Chamaecyparis lawsoniana nana, C. l. obtusa caespitosa, C. pisifera filifera nana, Juniperus communis compressa, Picea abies gregoryana, Taxus baccata pygmaea, Thuja occidentalis ellwangeriana* 'Rheingold', *T. orientalis minima glauca.*

Sow seeds of perennial alpines available in packets from reputable seedsmen, shallowly in seed pans, covered with a slate or tile, in cold greenhouse of frame. When seeds germinate, remove covering, lift pans nearer to the light but shade from hot direct sun. Water by immersing pans in a bath of water, removing and allowing to drain when the soil is wetted through.

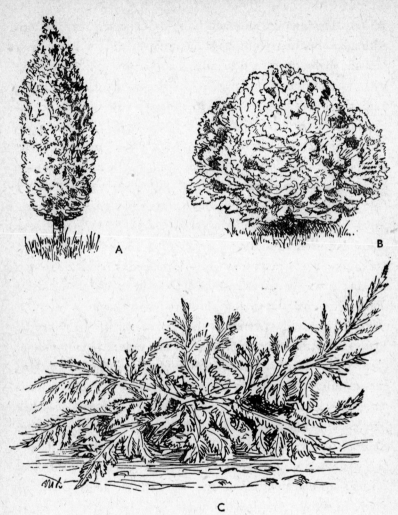

Good dwarf conifers:
a. The Noah's ark conifer, Juniperus compressa communis.
b. The bun-like Chamaecyparis lawsoniana minima glauca.
c. The prostrate-growing Juniperis communis hnrnibrookii.

Water Garden: Prepare new pools for planting. Cover bottom with a layer of heavy fibrous loam or clayey top soil taken from just under the turf of a permanent pasture or old lawn, mixing with it about 4 oz. bone-meal to the barrow load. Press down and firm to a thickness of 5 - 6 in., and top with an inch or two of coarse sand or grit. Use no other fertilisers or strong manures. Add a good sprinkling of well-broken charcoal fro small pools or tub gardens. Add just enough water to make soil thoroughly moist, and it is ready for planting.

Plant up pools before filling. A start can be made in mid-April in mild districts, but May to mid-June is the best planting period (see May notes).

Empty existing pools where base is in need of repair. Remove fish and place temporarily in bath or basin of water in partial shade. Remove plants, and place under wet sacks to keep the roots moist, well covered with litter against spring frosts. Remove soil (for replacement if slimy and reduced to silty mud). Clean pool, wash down with copper sulphate solution ($\frac{1}{2}$ oz. per gallon water) or with a deep pink solution of potassium permanganate, and allow to dry. Seal with waterproof bitumen (see March notes), or by lining with 500-gauge sheet polythene. Replace bottom soil, trim plants of dead and moribund leaves and replant.

Clean up marginal plants and bog garden, cutting away all dead top growth and leaves, and removing debris.

Take steps to control algae growth. Although not harmful to fish or other plants, it is unsightly. Bring scavengers up to strength—ramshorn snails and fresh-water mussels; allow 4 to

6 per sq. yd. of pool. Introduce live Daphnia into pools without fish. Balance planting with sufficient surface-leafing and underwater oxygenating plants (see May notes on planting).

Fruit: Eradicate colonies of the greyish-white, wax-excreting woolly aphides, now easily seen, by brushing with a stiff-bristled brush dipped in a neat solution of a gamma-BHC or malathion insecticide.

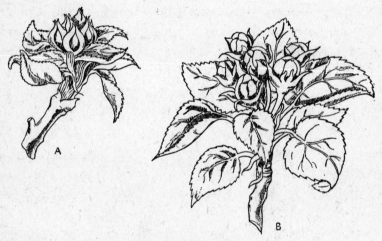

When to spray apples:
a. Green cluster stage of blossom development.
b. Pink bud stage.

Spray apple trees badly infected by scab disease last year with 3 % lime-sulphur or captan fungicide as they come to the green-cluster or green-bud stage of blossom development, in early to mid-April.

Spray apple trees as a routine protection against scab with

lime-sulphur or captan at the pink bud stage of blossom development in late April or early May. Add a DDT insecticide to control apple blossom weevil, winter moth caterpillars and tortrix.

Spray pear trees as a routine measure against scab infection with lime-sulphur or captan at the white bud stage of blossom development, in late April. Add a DDT insecticide to control tortrix and winter moth caterpillars.

Spray gooseberry bushes with a karathane fungicide at pre-blossom stage, when flowers are about to open, to prevent American mildew.

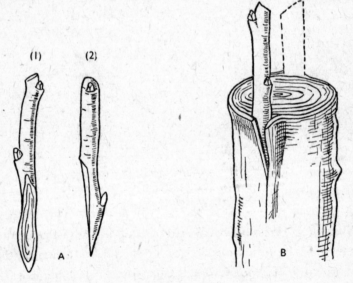

Rind grafting of fruit tree:
a. Prepared scion (i) front view (ii) side view
b. Stock with scion inserted, prior to binding.

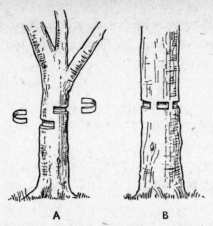

Bark-ringing:
a. Semicircles removed to give severe check to growth.
b. Alternate pieces removed to give a less severe check.

Plant hardy vines ex pots in cold greenhouse and out of doors, in well-trenched soil enriched with bone-meal and limestone grit (if acid).

Graft scions taken earlier in the year on to chosen stocks, preparing the scion and the stock and completing the graft in one operation. Rind-grafting is the simplest way of grafting on to established trees; whip or saddle grafting on to seedling stocks. For success, see that the greenish cambium layers (just beneath the bark) of scion and stock come into firm contact, and bind and seal with grafting wax or tape to exclude air.

Ring the bark of apple or pear trees making too vigorous and non-fruiting growth, between bud-burst and flowering stages. Remove bark in ½ in. wide strips round stem of tree in half-circles on opposite sides, one half-circle inch above the other; or remove alternate short strips in a broken circle round stem.

111

Slit the bark of unfruitful plum or damson or stone fruit trees, cutting through the bark on the north side with a single long cut from the first branch junction to ground level.

Mark strong young strawberry plants for runner production, and remove flower trusses as soon as noted, letting the strength of the plant go into runner formation and give strong maiden plants for propagation.

Spray strawberries to control aphides and red spider mites, where troublesome, with a malathion insecticide in late April.

Vegetables: Make sowings of radish, carrots, broad beans, lettuce and spinach for successional yields.

Sow maincrop peas such as 'Best of All', 'Lord Chancellor', 'Dreadnought', and 'Gladstone', growing 3 - 4 ft. tall.

Stake earlier sown peas when plants are 2 - 3 in. high.

Support broad bean plantings with surround of strong twine on stakes, to prevent being flattened by wind.

Sow under cloches early and forcing varieties of French or kidney beans such as 'Lightning', 'Prince' and 'Early Giant'. Use ground organically manured for a previous crop, enriched with a little superphosphate or bone-flour.

Sow 'Early Purple' sprouting broccoli, late Brussels sprouts ('Cambridge No. 5'), Savoy cabbages ('Giant Green', 'Ormskirk', 'Drumhead'), and autumn cauliflower ('Autumn Giant') in brassica seed-bed.

Sow asparagus seed to raise plants for next year's planting, in lightish soil—'Connover's Colossal' can be recommended.

Sow globe artichoke in a reserve bed where plants can be

112

grown for at least two years. Thin plants to 8 in. apart. Select the best plants only for permanent bed.

Earth up early potatoes when stems are about 8 in. tall, and repeat about three weeks later. Do it with the draw hoe, when the soil is crumbly—unless you are growing the crop under black sheet polythene.

Plant maincrop potatoes by the end of this month. Reduce sprouts to the two most robust on each seed tuber. Cut large seed tubers with two sprouts to each piece, immediately before planting. Plant in or under organic matter; dust sides of drill with a complete fertiliser at 3 oz. per 2 linear yards of drill before covering.

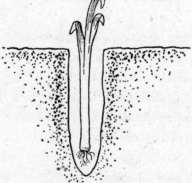

Simple leek planting.

Plant out onions, brassicas, leeks, and other vegetable seeds raised in boxes under glass, after hardening off in a cold frame.

Plant leek seedlings in prepared trench, or in holes made with the dibber at 6 - 9 in. apart, simply dropping the plants in and watering.

Dust seedlings of brassicas in nursery bed with a gamma-BHC (lindane) insecticide if flea beetles are eating the first leaves. Radishes and turnips need protection too.

Prepare celery trenches 12 - 15 in. deep, 15 in. wide for a single row, 18 in. for a double row of plants. Fork over bottom and firm, then put in manure or compost, mixed with any lawn mowings (not treated with selective weed-killer) available, to a depth of 6 in., packed down with a dressing of bone-flour, and leave for June planting.

Sow seeds of herbs on well-drained warm soil, shallowly in drills 4 - 6 in. apart; sweet basil, caraway, coriander, dill, pot marjoram, summer and winter savory, and thyme. Thin plants to 4 in. apart.

Insert cuttings of sage in any reasonably well-drained soil towards the month end; use the ends of shoots, 3 in. long, stripped of lower leaves, and firmed into the soil.

Be ready to protect early sown potatoes from night spring frosts by covering haulms with cloches, tented sacking or polythene, or planks on bricks over the haulms. Spray any blackened or frosted growth with water early in the morning before the sun gets on them.

Sow Swiss chard (leafy beet) in drills 1 in. deep, 18 in. apart, spacing seeds about 8 in. apart, and thinning to one plant at each station later. Grown for its tender, large-ribbed leaves and stems.

Under Glass: Under cloches—sowings of sweet corn, runner beans, and dwarf French beans may be made.

Greenhouse plants you may have in bloom: *Camellia japonica* and vars.; *Cneorum pulverulentum; Abutilon vitifolium; Calceolaria fuchsiifolia;* dwarf rhododendrons and azaleas in pots; hardy hyacinths, narcissus, and tulips started into growth out of doors and brought in to flower; *Ixia* spp.; *Lachenalia* spp.; *Astilbe* spp.; *Cyclamen orbiculatum* and vars. (in large pans); Auriculas; *Dicentra spectabilis; Primula juliae, P. marginata; Salix lanata; Viola odorata* and vars.

In the cool greenhouse (minimum night temperatures 45° to 50°F., 7° - 10°C.): most of the above plants, plus: *Acacia baileyana, A. decora, A. drummondii,* etc.; *Abutilon darwinii; Acrotriche cordata; Agathosma punctata; Boronia megastigma; Bossiaea distachia; Correa speciosa; Epacris* spp.; *Erica caniculata, E. hymenalis* and vars.; *Goodia latifolia; Grevillea thelemanniana, G. lavandulacea; Oxylobium obtusifolium; Pimelia ferruginea; Polygala myrtifolia grandiflora; Prostanthera sieberi; Protea speciosa; Streptosolen jamesonii; Sollya heterophylla; Cyclamen persicum* in variety; *Clivia miniata, C.* x *cyrtanthiflora; Darlingtonia californica; Ranunculus lyallii; Sarracenia drummondii; Ferraria ferrariola; Streptanthera elegans; Sparaxis grandiflora* and vars.; *Tigridia atrata; Zantedeschia aethiopica.*

As days become warmer, ventilate longer, aiming to keep temperatures by day between 60° - 70°F. (15·5° - 21°C.). Water moderately with increasing amount on sunny days; syringe growing plants on warm days before noon. (Refresh ventilating and watering techniques by reading March notes.)

Prick off seedlings of earlier sowings as soon as large enough to handle. The younger the seedling, the quicker it gets over the shock of transplanting. Use a small two-pronged fork for lifting seedlings. Most annuals and half-hardy annuals destined for bedding or planting out are pricked out at $1\frac{1}{4}$ - $1\frac{3}{4}$ in. apart, according to vigour, in boxes 3 in. deep. Specimen plants are pricked off into thumb ($2\frac{1}{2}$ in.) pots or small peat-wood fibre pots singly. Hold seedlings by seed or first pair of leaves, set straight, gently firm in roots, and water. Keep somewhat shaded until making new growth. Use a stronger soil compost—J.I.P. 1 or 2, or U.C.1.

Harden off half-hardy and hardy annuals being raised under glass by transferring to cold frames, where exposure to some-what lower temperatures, greater daytime ventilation, etc., strengthens growth in readiness for transplanting in flowering or maturing positions out of doors. Exposure to harder conditions should be gradual, chiefly by increasing ventilation; but cover frames when night frosts are heralded.

Pot up seedlings of *Primula malacoides*, *P. obconica*, *P. sinensis*, and *P. stellata* and grow on under cool conditions—night temperature 50°F. (10°C.).

Sow zinnias, and seeds of *Lobelia tenuior*, bottom heat 65° to 70°F. (18° - 21°C.).

Sow seeds of greenhouse cineraria thinly for winter flowering, with bottom heat of 65° - 70°F. (18° - 21°C.), and prick off singly into pots when first true leaves form.

Make further sowings of outdoor cucumber, marrows, melons and gourds; single seeds in peat-wood fibre pots, with bottom heat of up to 75°F. (24°C.).

Sow sweet corn for the vegetable garden, and ornamental

maize (*Zea japonica* hybrids) for the ornamental garden, singly in small peat-wood fibre pots about the middle of the month; bottom heat of 65°F. (18°C.) is best.

Start remainder of dahlia tubers into growth by placing in boxes and covering with a mixture of equal parts by volume moist peat and sand; they will then be ready to plant out in late May.

Pot up tubers of *Achimenes coccinea* and hybrids, 1 in. deep, 2 in. apart, in 6 - 8 in. pots, using U.C. soilless compost, greenhouse temperature at 60°F. (15·5°C.).

Bring in potted-up roots of *Dicentra spectabilis* to flower in cool greenhouse. Roots are best potted in late autumn and placed in cold frame until wanted.

Plant bulbs of *Ornithogalum thyrsoides* (chincherinchees), 2 in. deep, six to an 8 in. pot, U.C. compost, in cool greenhouse, for long-lasting summer bloom.

Sow seeds of tomatoes for outdoor-growing in seed boxes or pans, spacing seeds 1 in. apart, J.I. or U.C. seed compost, bottom heat of 65° - 70°F. (18° - 21°C.), about $\frac{1}{4}$ in. deep; prick off singly into small peat-wood fibre pots when seed leaves are big enough to hold in finger and thumb, using J.I. or U.C. potting compost.

Thin forming fruitlets on indoor apricots, nectarines and peaches. Syringe plants and walls on sunny days to keep down red spider mites. If they are evident, spray with a malathion insecticide.

Water ornamental pot plants with a systemic insecticide to protect against sap-sucking aphides and other similar insects,

Train in the lateral shoots of vines, and stop growth at two leaves beyond the first flower truss on each lateral. Extension shoots on young vines can be left unchecked. Keep roots watered.

Continue to feed strawberries in pots weekly with a dilute liquid feed. Thin fruits to the best half-dozen per truss early, and give supports.

Make up border for ring culture of tomatoes, taking out 5 in. of soil, lining trench with sheet polythene and replacing soil with weathered boiler ashes, fine gravel or shingle, or very coarse sand, and water thoroughly. Set out bottomless 9 in. fibre or plastic or clay rings, about three-quarters full with J.I.P. 3 or U.C. 3, ready to receive plants.

Plant up tomato bed in a cool greenhouse from mid-April; in a cold house, not until the end of the month or early May. Choose sturdy plants, about to flower in first truss, preferably grown in soil blocks or peat-wood fibre pots that entail no root disturbance on planting out.

Be prepared to protect greenhouse plants from sudden night frosts. Close house early in the afternoon when the day has been sunny and a clear sky seems likely at night. Interpose some suitable material—newspaper, sheet polythene or aluminium foil—between glass roof and frost-sensitive plants, particularly in the cold greenhouse.

May

But the merriest month in all the year
Is the merry month of May.
'ROBIN HOOD AND THE THREE SQUIRES'

WITH the greater part of the seed-sowing completed and the new stock planted, unfolding leaves, lengthening stems and opening flowers on every side proclaim the new growing season well begun. Nevertheless, as Shakespeare has it, 'rough winds do shake the darling buds of May', and the protection of tender young growth from boisterous winds and sudden dips in the temperature is often necessary.

With day temperatures climbing beyond 60° Fahrenheit (above 15·5 °C.), differences in the timing of garden operations between southern and northen parts of the country become negligible. Local conditions, however, may compel some delay in the planting out of frost-tender plants such as half-hardy annuals and perennials for bedding, and aspect, susceptibility to night frosts, exposure and elevation may all play a part in this. Broadly, spring planting can be done earlier in the west than in the east. But whenever chilling wind blows from the north or east in dry weather, planting should be postponed until softer weather prevails.

Bear in mind that wind, apart from the mechanical damage and distortion to plant growth that it can do, tends to rob leaves of their moisture and so stunts their growth. The drier the wind—and easterly cold winds are usually dry—the more severe their effect. Apart from staking vulnerable plants, arrange windbreaking shelter for them. This does not need to be solid. Open-work trellis, netting, etc., anything that breaks the force of the wind, is usually sufficient.

Just as plants are awakening to a new cycle of growth, so are their parasites and competitors—fungi, bacteria, viruses, insects, birds, animals and weeds. Have the appropriate chemical controls on hand in a safe place. Many insecticides and some fungicides would be harmful to animal pets and children in their concentrated state. Poisonous products should be kept under lock and key.

Weigh advantages and disadvantages of dusts and sprays in regard to your own personal requirements before deciding which to use. Most fungicides and insecticides are prepared for use in both forms. Dusts require no expensive apparatus, and are more easily applied in small gardens. They make you independent of a water supply; also it is easy to see where a dust has been applied and where it has missed. Calm weather is, however, needed for economical application, and the operation will need to be repeated more frequently, as dusts are more at the mercy of rain and weather, and are thus less persistent.

Sprays require an efficient spraying appliance, which is relatively expensive, if it is to be efficient and give a good cover. Spraying is more practical and more economical, especially on a large scale. The spray cover persists longer that the dust, and with good apparatus it is usually a less laborious process.

Keep all dusting and spraying appliances scrupulously clean, cleaning or washing out immediately after use. Spraying appliances are best washed out with a solution of washing soda and water, and then clear water, since some spray solutions such as copper and sulphur are corrosive to metal.

Keep a separate appliance, if possible, for the application of growth-regulating substances (so-called 'hormones'), as these substances are exceptionally potent in residual amounts, difficult to clean from sprayers, etc. A separate watering-can with distributor head is best set aside for the application of selective weed-killers. Paint it red.

Wear protective clothing when applying dusts and spray solutions, not only in the interests of your clothes but also of your health. Although care has been taken in this book to recommend only those materials least poisonous to humans, long exposure to a dust or spray mist may cause minor upset. It is sensible to wear an overall, an old mackintosh or coat, a hat and rubber boots when using sprays or dusts. A simple face mask, especially when working under glass, is a simple precaution for those sensitive to respiratory upset or asthma.

Note that certain substances, notably organophosphorus insecticides such as parathion, TEPP (tetrapyrophosphate) and Systam (schradan), are subject to the Agriculture (Poisonous

Substances) Regulations as being highly poisonous, and should only be used in emergency in the garden, and under recommended precautions printed on the labels of the products.

Flowers: Coming into bloom—many bulbous plants, flowering in April, continue into the month (see April notes): bluebells (*Scilla non-scripta, Scilla hispanica* in variety); *Erythronium revolutum; Camassia esculenta, Hyacinthus amethystinus; Leucojum aestivum; Ixiolirion ledebourii; Muscari plumosum* (feather hyacinth); *Ornithogalum umbellatum; Tulipa batalinii; T. linfolia; T. ostrowskiana;* hybrid large-flowering hyacinths; *Narcissus poeticus recurvus* (old pheasant's eye) and late-flowering daffodils; hybrid triumph, cottage, lily-flowering, Darwin, breeder, parrot, Bybloem, bizarre, Rembrandt, and *viridifolia* tulips; *Iris hoogiana; Allium aflatunense, A. karataviense.* In the border: *Ajuga genevensis; Alyssum saxatile; Anchusa angustissima; Aquilega canadensis*; Arnebia echioides*; Asperula odorata*; Asphodelus cerasiferus;* aubrieta in variety; *Bergenia stracheyi; Centaurea montana* and vars.*; *Cheiranthus cheiri* (wallflower)*; *Convallaria majalis* (lily-of-the-valley); *Corydalis lutea*; Cypripedium calceolus*; Dianthus plumarius*; Dicentra spectabilis; Dodecatheon meadia*; Doronicum plantagineum; Euphorbia wulfenii; Geum borisii* and vars.*; *Lathyrus vernus; Meconopsis superba; Mertensia virginica; Nepeta faassenii; Papaver nudicaule, P. orientale; Polemonium coeruleum; Primula sikkimensis*, P. alpicola*;* pyrethrum in variety*; *Tiarella cordifolia*, T. wherryi*; Trollius europaeus superbus*; Viscaria splendens flore pleno.*

* Continues flowering beyond the month.

There is still time to make sowings of hardy annuals out of doors (see March notes), especially if earlier sowings have not come up to expectations, but get the seeds in as soon as possible.

Detach spent flower heads from daffodils and early-flowering bulbs—unless seed is wanted—but do not cut down the leaves until they begin to yellow.

Lift early-flowering tulips, intact with roots and soil, which have been used in beds where space is now wanted; replant in a trench, re-covered with soil, where they can grow on until the leaves wither. The same plan can be followed with narcissi and other bulbs now past flowering, but naturalised bulbs are best left until leaves wither before lifting to divide.

Replant bulbs which have flowered indoors, taking them out of their containers with roots intact in the rooting medium. Place in a sheltered reserve bed to finish growing. Put bulbs out of doors later. Do not attempt to grow for indoors again, until bulbs have built up for 3 - 4 years.

Plant out half-hardy annuals, hardened off in the cold frame, when frost danger is past. Give night protection with cloches or sheet polythene tented over a wood framework if a late May frost is forecast.

Thin annual seedlings sown in April where they are to flower.

Continue to move half-hardy and hardy annuals sown under glass to cold frames to harden off. At first, close the frames at night, then expose more completely by day, and leave frames slightly open at night. Transplant to flowering positions late in the month.

Give bulbs that have finished flowering a dressing of a nitrogenous fertiliser (Chilean potash nitrate at 1 oz. per sq. yd. is excellent), to encourage good leaf development, and to build up good flowering bulbs for next year. Do the same to offset bulbs (young bulbs that grow at the side of parent bulbs) planted in reserve ground, to build up.

Try to stake border perennials in advance of their need. Place twiggy branches of pea-sticks among annuals for support. If you are growing sweet peas on the cordon system, have your canes in position, and be ready to train and remove side growths regularly from now on.

Divide polyanthus, primroses and cultivated oxlips and cowslips when flowering finishes, lifting and splitting the plants into pieces; each piece should consist of a small rosette of leaves with attached rhizomatous rootstock and roots. Replant in humus-rich soil, in partial shade. A light sprinkling of nitro-chalk is helpful after the divided plants begin to grow again.

Cut out shoots of wallflowers carrying fading flowers, and side growths carrying buds will then flower. But do not be tempted to leave plants in for another year, although they are often perennial. Pull plants up with the roots before they seed, and bruise the tough stems before composting. Burn anything with swollen roots or clubbing, and check for clubroot disease — if evident, mark the area to be kept free of cruciferous plants for two to three years. (See notes under *Vegetables* this month.)

Continue weeding assiduously as time and opportunity affords. Hoe to keep down annual weed seedlings. Smother-mulch ground elder. Paint shoots of horse-tails with a solution of a 2,4-D or 2,4,5-T weed-killer. Gather growing tips of bindweed together, stuff in a jam-jar, half-filling with selective weed-killer solution. But if you are up against trifoliolate, shamrock-like leaved *Oxalis corniculata* or one of its relations, forming bulbils at the base of the leaf stalks, dig or fork the plants out, roots and all, for burning. No weed-killer eliminates it, and hoeing only scatters the bulbils to spread it.

Make sowings of biennials towards the end of the month on reserve bed to provide plants for next year—canterbury bells, sweet williams, wallflowers, *Cheiranthus allionii, Chelone barbata, Cynoglossum amabile,* honesty—on any well-drained soil, given a phosphatic dressing of superphosphate or bone-flour prior to sowing.

Clean up window-boxes ready for summer flowers. Paint inside with a bitumen paint for preservation, never creosote. Fill with soil when dry. Cover drainage holes with perforated zinc squares or fine nylon mesh, then an inch or so of broken crocks or brick or stone, a thin layer of leaves or fibrous peat, and top up with a good soil compost—J.I.P.3., or U.C. Firm, soak with water, and allow to drain. Then plant with annuals and bedding plants, or use begonias for partially shaded windows. For the kitchen window, plant a box of herbs—chives, sage, thyme, mint, parsley, marjoram, etc., will grow, and be at hand for cooking purposes.

Prepare and plant hanging baskets. First line with moss, then with perforated sheet polythene (this ensures better moisture retention), and then soil (J.I.P. or U.C. compost). Plant up with plants out of pots as you fill with soil. Some plant suggestions—ivy-leaved 'geraniums'; *Campanula isophylla*; trailing

Lobelia x 'Sapphire'; Livingstone daisies *(Mesembryanthemum crinifolium); Begonia pendula;* and dwarf annuals.

Finish planting of gladiolus corms by the end of the month, Soil may be watered with a pre-emergent weed-killer after planting to minimise weeding later.

Paths: Should be looking immaculate now. Destroy weeds appearing between interstices of crazy-paving or stone flagging by painting the foliage with an appropriate herbicide—an ordinary selective lawnweed-killer for most broad-leaved weeds, a dalapon herbicide for grasses, and one containing mecroprop (CMPP) for clover.

Make provision for excessive wear on a grass path by inserting stone flags at stepping-stone distances. Place the stones slightly lower than the grass surface to allow the mower to be used in keeping the grass short; or the grass can be dwarfed by spraying with a maleic hydrazide growth inhibitor.

Hedges: Plant evergreen and coniferous hedges and screens as soon as favourable weather arrives. A mild moist period following a spell of dry, chilling wind is ideal.

Planting late? The danger to very late planted evergreens is sun heat and soil dryness in the ensuing summer. But planted with the soil-ball in which the plants arrived, well packed around with a mixture of equal parts by volume moist peat and soil, and kept well watered, they will thrive.

Use the smaller growing conifers for trouble-free and beautiful screens. *Chamaecyparis lawsoniana erecta viridis,* for instance, will grow to 20 - 25 ft. only, but is always shapely, rich green in colour, and excellent for hard weather; var. *lanei* makes a lovely golden foliaged dense screen, ultimately to 30 - 40 ft.; var. *fraseri* a grey-green, spire-like screen of similar height. They need no trimming throughout growth.

Move misplaced evergreen hedges early in the month. Hedges of privet, laurel, yew, box, lonicera, cypress and thuya can be successfully moved to new positions if care is taken. Take out a trench of soil at each side of the hedge, just wide of the branches, 15 - 18 in. deep. Under-cut the roots of the hedge with a sharp spade, then lift in sections, keeping the roots encased in soil (slip strong sacking or sheet polythene under), and move to new position. Finally, pack round with a moist peat-soil mixture, and water well. Old hedges—more than 12 years—are best prepared a year in advance, by cutting the roots back to the dimensions of the soil-ball in which they are to be lifted.

Tip-prune new growth on hedges of lonicera towards the end of the month to induce new branching.

Establish hedges in windy places by sheltering them with a windbreak of chestnut paling, temporary fencing of ex-WD coir netting, wire-netting or pea-sticks. Anything that breaks the wind up into smaller eddies, without actually stopping it, will spare the hedge much buffeting and dehydration.

Shrubs and Trees: Likely to be in flower — *Berberis candidula*, *B*. x *stenophylla* and vars., *B. thunbergii* and vars., *B. verruculosa;* *Viburnum carlesii*, *V*. x *juddii*, *V. tomentosum* 'Lanarth variety',

V. opulus and vars., in late May; *Caragana arborescens; Ceanothus* x 'Delight', *C. dentatus, C. rigidus; Choisya ternata; Corokia cotoneaster; Cotoneaster horizontalis, C. simonsii, C. dammeri; Cytisus albus, C. ardoinii, C. decumbens, C. x praecox, C. x kewensis, C. scoparius* hybrids and varieties; *Daphne* x *burkwoodii, D. retusa; Deutzia pulchra; Kerria japonica; Magnolia* x *soulangeana* and vars.; *Potentilla fruticosa* and vars.; *Rosa cantabrigiensis, R. spinossissima altaica, R. xanthina spontania* ('Canary Bird'); *Rosmarinus officinalis; Spiraea* x *van houttei;* syringa in variety (lilacs); *Thymus nitidus; Ulex europaeus plenus; Weigela* hybrids; *Clematis alpina* and vars., *C. montana* and vars., and large-flowering varieties of the *C. patens* and *C. lanuginosa* group.

On lime-free soils, azaleas in variety; *A. mollis* and *mollis* x *sinensis*, 'Ghent' hybrids, Japanese and evergreen varieties; rhodendrons in variety, including hybrids; and *Enkianthus campanulatus.*

Flowers of Clematis alpina

Trees: *Crataegus monogyna* and var. *stricta, C. oxyacanthiodes maskei* and vars.; *Fraxinus ornus; Sorbus aucuparia; Laburnocytisus* x *adamii; Malus pumila* (flowering crabs); *Prunus serrulata* (flowering cherries in variety); *Pyrus communis* (pear); *Sorbus decora nana; Aesculus hippocastanum* (horse chestnut).

Complete planting of evergreen shrubs, trees and conifers in favourable weather as soon as possible this month. Keep syringed and well watered in dry weather.

Plant bamboos early this month. They welcome moist spots, though successful on most soils except dry chalk. *Arundinaria japonica murielae, A. j. nitida,* and *Phyllostachys flexuosa* and varieties, are most likely to succeed, making good features and being adaptable for screens and hedges. Cut canes fairly hard back after planting to foster new growth; when new canes are growing up, the old can be cut to base.

Prune forsythias as they finish flowering, if necessary. With *F.* x *intermedia* varieties, it is best to cut out only a portion of the flowered and older stems, say one-quarter or one-third, to preserve the symmetry of the plants. Leave most of the young shoots of last year untouched as these will flower next year. On *F. suspensa,* cut back secondary or lateral branches to within a bud of the base, but prune *F. ovata* only lightly.

Prune flowering currants (*Ribes sanguineum* and vars.) by removing a few shoots of the oldest wood each year, cutting out at the base.

Prune the spent flowered shoots of *Spiraea arguta* hard if new growth is needed.

Do not try to prune *Daphne mezereum* or related species; if plants are losing vigour and shapeliness, raise new ones to take their place.

Protect newly planted trees from damage by rabbits or hares in country gardens, placing loose encircling guards of wire-netting round them, 12 - 18 in. high.

Clean out any cavities in established trees caused by canker or branches dying back. Clean to healthy wood, paint with a tree antiseptic (Arbrex), and fill with a bituminous asphalt if large.

Watch out for aphides (green and black fly), especially on euonymus and cherries, and control by early spraying with a malathion or gamma-BHC insecticide.

Prune flowering quinces *(Chaenomeles speciosa)* on walls by cutting back the lateral shoots after flowering.

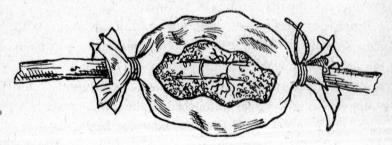

Air-layering of a shrub.

Air-layer young shoots of shrubs difficult to propagate from cuttings, such as magnolia, rhododendron, etc., using the following modern technique: (1) slit the shoot half-way through obliquely from behind a node or bud; (2) wrap the cut area in sphagnum moss, moistened with water; (3) wrap the moss in a polythene sleeve; (4) seal to exclude air, at each end. The cut should be treated with a root-inducing 'hormone' product to stimulate root formation. The layer is severed for soil planting when it is seen that the roots are filling the moss—in about 6 - 12 months' time.

Roses: Water roses and rooting area with a systemic insecticide early this month to prevent infestation by aphides and other sap-sucking insects. Otherwise, spray with a malathion or DDT/pyrethrum insecticide, the moment a developing attack is noticed.

Rose leaf, rolled by the rose sawfly caterpillar.

Prevent rolled up leaves (sawfly infestation) and half-eaten buds (tortrix moth grubs, chafers, etc.) by an early application of a malathion or gamma-BHC or DDT/pyrethrum insecticide; repeat after 3 weeks.

Spray plants with a karathane or sulphur fungicide if the

greyish white spots of Powdery Mildew *(Sphaerotheca pannosa)* appear on young shoots, and repeat in 10 - 14 days. Some varieties are more susceptible than others. Mildew thrives in humid weather.

Watch for sucker growths—shoots breaking from the soil, usually a little wide of the base of the plant, and differing somewhat in colour, leaf and growth from the present top growth. Trace the growth of a suspected sucker to its origin. If it comes from the roots below the bud-union, cut it out at its base with a sharp knife and burn, since it inherits the characteristics of the root-stock and not those of the rose variety.

Lawn: Cut newly sown lawn grasses when about 2 in. high, reducing by one-half. Have mower razor-sharp, as otherwise the grasses may be pulled out; or cut with sharp shears. Roll lightly after cutting. Cut again in a week or so, lowering cut to ¾ in. Cut with increasing frequency as growth demands, but not very close for this season. Hand-weed any grass-smothering weeds. Do not use a selective week-killer until the lawn is at least three months old, and then at dilute strength, about half the normal recommendation. Water by sprinkler if weather turns dry, with occasional (fortnightly) foliar feeding.

Mow established lawns with increasing frequency as growth is made. For ornamental lawns, a ½ - ⅝ in. cut is sufficient, as this gives a well-knit sward that can hold its own with weeds. Frequent, not too close cutting results in the minimum amount of grass being removed in the length of a season, and this conserves the strength of the grasses and fertility of the soil.

Give a supplementary feed about mid-May, such as sulphate of ammonia ($\frac{1}{2}$ oz. per sq. yd.) or on light soils, Chilean potash nitrate at the same rate. In a wet period, apply bulked with sand or sifted peat; in a dry spell, water in.

Give selective weed-killers at least 6 weeks to complete their work. Spot-treat any weeds which have not then succumbed, but leave any further general application until July-August.

Clear clover from lawns where it is not wanted by applying a selective weed-killer based on mecroprop (CMPP), and apply a nitrogenous fertiliser monthly. To increase clover—and this may be desirable in a lawn that suffers readily in drought or in an orchard grassed down—make an application of basic slag (4 - 6 oz. per sq. yd.).

Stunt grass bordering paths and driveways or in places difficult to cut by applying maleic hydrazide growth inhibitor, but do not overdo it. It is hardly suitable for overall stunting of grass growth in lawns, as much repeated use would impair the grasses.

Plant up lawn areas to be developed by means of stoloniferous strains of grasses (*Agrostis stolonifera* v. *stolonifera*) early this month, inserting stolons or runners in prepared soil at about 12 in. apart. Also useful in repairing poor established lawns. Gives a somewhat coarse, green sward, tending to exclude other grasses and weeds, and not requiring so frequent mowing.

Rock Garden: Coming into flower—*Achillea ageratifolia**, *A. clavenae**, *A.* x 'King Edward'; *Aethionema grandiflorum**; *Andromeda polifolia nana; Androsace sarmentosa, A. sempervivoides**;

*Anemone magellanica**, *A. nemorosa; Aquilegia bertolonii**, *A. glandulosa**, *A. scopulorum**; *Arabis albida* 'Rosabelle'*; *Arctostaphylos uva-ursi**; *Arenaria purpurascens**; *Armeria caespitosa**; aubrieta in variety; *Caltha leptosepala**; *Campanula aucheri**; *Cassiope selaginoides; Clematis alpina; Cotoneaster thymifolia**; *Cytisus decumbens, C. demissus**, *C.* x *kewensis**; *Daphne collina**, *D. petraea**; *D. retusa; Dicentra formosa**, *D. oregana**; *Dodecatheon oregana**; *Draba rigida**; *Edraianthus pumilio**; *Epimedium alpinum**; *Eranthis* x *tubergeniana; Erinacea pungens; Erinus alpinus* and vars.*; *Fritillaria meleagris**, *Gentiana acaulis**, *G. verna**; *Geranium sanguineum* v. *lancastriense**; *Geum montanum**; *Haberlea ferdinandi-coburgi**; *Incarvillea grandiflora**; *Iris bucharica**, *I. pumila*, *I. ruthenica**; *Jeffersonia dubia; Lewisia tweedyi**; *Linum alpinum**; *Maianthemum biflorum**; *Meconopsis quintuplinerva**; *Mimulus primuloides; Muscari botryoides; Myosotis rupicola**; *Oxalis adenophylla; Phlox amoena**, *P. douglasii**, *P. sublata**; *Phyllodoce breweri**; *Polygala calcarea**, *P. chamaebuxus**; *Potentilla cuneata**; *Primula auricula, P. forrestii**, *P. juliae, P.* x *pruhoniciana**, *P.* x *pubescens* and vars.*, *P. involucrata, P. japonica* and vars.*, *P. yargongensis; Ramonda myconi**; *Ranunculus amplexicaulis; Rhododendron calostrotum, R. campylogynum, R. cephalanthum* v. *cerbreflorum, R. imperator, R. intricatum, R. racemosum* 'Forrest's form', *R. radicans, R. sargentianum, R.* x 'Carmen', *R.* x 'Cilipense', *R. obtusum* hybrids — 'Hatsu-giri', 'Helena', 'Irohayama'; *Rhodohypoxis baurii* and vars.*; *Rhodothamnus chamaecistus; Saxifraga* x 'Flower of Sulphur', *S.* x 'Red Admiral', *S.* x 'Winston Churchill', *S. umbrosa; Sedum spathulifolium**; *Sisyrinchium filifolium; Thalictrum kiusianum**; *Trifolium uniflorum**; *Trollius yunnanensis**;

Tulipa batalinii, T. celsiana, T. clusiana, T. linifolia; Vaccinium angustifolium, V. caespitosum, V. vitis-idaea minus; Viola cornuta and vars.*, *V. gracilis* and vars.*; *V. saxatilis aetolica*.

Flower of the hybrid Aconite, Eranthis x tubergeniana, with its ruff of green leaves.

Plant empty spaces with late-flowering alpines, ex pots; complete planting of dwarf evergreen shrubs and dwarf conifers (see April notes for choices).

Propagate *Andromeda polifolia* v. *nana* by means of cuttings taken with a heel, inserted in pots of lime-free compost. Alternatively, layer low shoots where the plant grows; nick or slit the stem behind a suitably placed leaf junction, bend this part down and peg in the soil, mound soil over the buried part, and keep moist. Sever the rooted layer next spring.

Propagate *Primula marginata, P.* x *pruhoniciana* and *P. rosea* by dividing the crowns, splitting into pieces equipped with roots

* Continues flowering beyond the month.

135

and potting up in 3 in. peat-wood fibre pots in a cold frame, ready for planting out in autumn. Spring propagation by division can be attempted also with ramonda, saxifrages, sedums and phlox.

Make and plant up a sink or trough garden. Basic essential— good drainage; chisel drainage channels to a main drain-hole, or arrange for the container to have a slight inclination to the drain-hole end; cover base with crocks (broken pieces of clay plant pots) or small stones, then a thin layer of leaves or peat fibre, topped by the soil compost—4 parts by bulk sifted loam, 2 parts leafmould or peat, 2 parts coarse sand or grit, plus 3 oz. bone-meal to the bushel. Pack firm, arrange stones or rock fragments to make a miniature mountain landscape, and plant up with dwarf alpines. A good dozen are: *Campanula arvatica, Dianthus alpinus, Gentiana verna, Androsace lanuginosa, Lithospermum oleifolium, Myosotis rupicola, Phlox douglasii, Primula marginata* vars., *Sempervivum arachnoideum, Aquilegia scopulorum, Saxifraga* 'Kabschias', *Iris pumila*; to which can be added the dwarf conifers *Juniperus communis compressa* and *Picea abies gregoryana,* and a choice of the dwarf shrubs *Daphne cneorum* v. *pygmaea, Genista delphinensis,* or *Pimelea prostrata.*

Lightly dust the soil with a gamma-BHC soil insecticidal dust and rake in to prevent damage to precious plants by cutworms, wireworms, cockchafer grubs, leatherjackets, etc.

Dust base of rocks, and areas where wood-lice hide, with a DDT or gamma-BHC dust, leaving it where the crustaceans are likely to walk and pick it up on their feet.

Watch for aphides, leaf-eating caterpillars, froghoppers and

136

red spider mites infesting plants, and counter promptly with a malathion or derris insecticide.

Control powdery mildew infections with a karathane or sulphur fungicide, after removing seriously infected growth.

Control rusts, characterised by orange or red spotting and blotching of leaves, with a copper-based fungicide.

Water Garden: Plant up new pools this month, with a balanced stock that includes surface-leafing water lilies and plants, submerged underwater oxygenating plants, and free-living surface plants.

A hybrid water-lily, Nymphaea x 'Escarboule'.

Choose water lilies according to depth and size of the pool, as well as for hardiness and flower colour. Depth is particularly important in affecting the subsequent performance of the plants. Some first choices are : for 12 - 18 in. of water, *Nymphaea* x 'Albatross', *N. odorata alba*, *N.* x 'Froebeli', *N. odorata sulphurea;* for 18 - 24 in. of water, *N.* x 'Hermine', *N.* x 'James Brydon', *N.* x 'Escarboucle', *N. marliacea chromatella;* for 2 - 3 ft. of water, *N.* x *gladstoniana*, *N.* x *colossea*, *N.* x 'Attraction', *N.* x 'Col. A. J. Welch'.

Remove dead leaves from plants before planting. Plant the roots (1) direct in the bottom soil, for best results without disturbance; or (2) in wicker baskets or boxes, filled with very well packed soil and placed in position on the base of the pool, when plants usually need dividing and replanting every third or fourth year; or (3) place roots between two inverted large sods, tie together and drop in the pool; or (4) in very deep pools, plant in containers placed on raised brickwork pedestals to the level at which the water lily will grow best.

Plant up with any additional surface-leafing plant—*Aponogeton distachyum*, the water hawthorn, is a favourite for water up to 2 ft. deep. *Nymphoides peltatum* is another.

Plant submerged oxygenating plants simply by pressing the roots into the bottom soil; alternatively, cuttings can be inserted about an inch deep. Do not be afraid of planting too many oxygenators; a dozen per square foot of base area is not too many, and ensures clear water. Useful species, which can be planted in variety, are *Callitriche autumnalis*, *C. verna*, *Elodea crispa*, *E. canadensis*, *Hottonia palustris*, *Potamogeton densus*, *P. crispus*, *Ranunculus aquatilis*, *Villarsia nymphaeoides*.

After planting up the bottom of a pool, run in only sufficient water to cover water lily crowns. To avoid soil disturbance, place a shallow bowl on a sheet of polythene on the bottom, and let the water run into the bowl to overflow gently. Then add a few inches more water at 2- to 3-day intervals until pool is full. Avoids cold shock to newly transplanted stock. Add a few floating aquatic plants—*Azolla caroliniana, Hydrocharis morsus-ranae, Stratiotes aloides*—but avoid the duckweeds, *Lemna gibba* and *L. minor.*

Introduce fish 2 - 4 weeks after planting, to give the pool time to settle. (See June notes.)

Plant marginal aquatics. Choice plants that like shallow water are: *Butomus umbellatus* (flowering rush), *Acorus calamus variegatus, Cyperus longus, Mimulus ringens, Scripus zebrinus, Iris laevigata* and vars., *Sagittaria japonica, Pontederia cordata, P. lanceolata, Typha minima, Caltha palustris* and vars.

Plant the bog garden sparingly. All the marginal aquatics given above do quite well in wet soil. To them can be added *Aruncus sylvestris; Arundinaria murielae;* astilbe in variety; *Cypripedium reginae; Epilobium angustifolium; Hemerocallis* hybrids; *Hosta decorata, H. sieboldiana, H. fortunei; Iris kaempferi* and vars., *I. sibirica; Lobelia cardinalis; Lysichitum camtschatcense, L. americana; Lysimachia clethroides; Mimulus guttatus* and vars.; *Monarda didyma* and vars.; *Polygonum affine; Primula beesiana, P. bulleyana, P. florindae, P. japonica, P. pulverulenta, P. sikkimensis; Sidalcea candida;* and ferns such as *Osmunda regalis, Adiantum pedatum* and *Athyrium felix-foemina foliosum.*

Divide and replant aquatics from the established pool being renovated, on the same lines as for planting new pools. Trim the older thick rhizomatous roots of water lilies, replanting the rootstock and crowns of the plants. Many submerged aquatics propagate readily from cuttings, others by division; but look over plants after 2 - 3 weeks and remove those that have not made any new growth.

Shade open spaces of water with boards floating on them until plants make new leaf and can create natural shade.

Fruit: Carry out routine spraying to prevent fungus infections and pest infestations this month.

Spray apples with lime-sulphur or captan fungicide to protect against scab infection at 80% petal-fall stage of blossom development. Use captan for this on the sulphur-sensitive varieties, notably 'Cox's Orange Pippin', 'Beauty of Bath', 'Lane's Prince Albert', 'Newton Wonder', 'Stirling Castle', 'Laxton's Advance', 'D'Arcy Spice'. Add a gamma-BHC or malathion insecticide to control apple sawfly, late aphides and red spider.

Spray pear trees this month with a captan or thiram fungicide when 80% of the petals have fallen from blossom clusters. It is not usually necessary to add an insecticide, unless the pear sucker insect has been active, feeding on developing fruit buds; when a malathion insecticide can be used.

Spray gooseberries directly the fruit has set with a karathane fungicide to prevent infection with American gooseberry mildew, about mid-May. Add a liquid derris insecticide to control the gooseberry sawfly caterpillars. This pest can defoliate a gooseberry bush almost overnight.

Spray the bottom halves of raspberry canes with a gamma-

BHC insecticide to control cane midge, in the first week of the month; repeat a fortnight later, if necessary. Spray raspberries just before blossoms open with a sulphur or a thiram fungicide if cane spot infection is feared or present.

Spray or dust strawberries with a karathane fungicide during the first half of the month to prevent powdery mildew and grey mould or botrytis disease. The right stage of development has been reached when the first flowers have opened. Add a derris insecticide if aphides are present.

Prune out and burn shoots of cherry or plum which bear collapsing and withered leaves and flowers, infected by bacterial canker. Make a note to spray with a copper fungicide after leaf-fall in the autumn to check reinfection.

Plum blossom at the cot-splitting stage.

Spray plums, damsons and cherries with a derris insecticide to control the plum sawfly at the cot split stage of fruit development—i.e. when the fruitlets split through the brown tissue of the flower.

Thin the forming fruits on wall trees at intervals during the month. Keep such trees well supplied with moisture and an occasional feed of liquid manure in dry weather. Syringe to deter red spider mite infestation.

Disbud trained wall trees of morello cherries progressively through the month, rubbing off the buds from which growth is unwanted.

Weed strawberry beds, put down metaldehyde slug bait pellets, and then 'straw' the plants with clean straw or, better still, with straw mats or sheet polythene, so fruit can develop cleanly.

Keep grass mown in a grassed-over orchard, letting the cuttings return to the ground. A rotary scything mower does the job well. Give an occasional sprinkling of sulphate of ammonia or calcium cyanamide to help the grass mowings to rot. Keep the area immediately around tree trunks as clear as possible of grass.

Vegetables: Sow dwarf French beans, maincrop varieties such as 'Canadian Wonder', 'Granada', 'Golden Waxpod', etc., sowing seeds $1\frac{1}{2}$ in. deep, 9 - 12 in. apart, in rows 18 in. apart. Dust with a seed dressing to avoid faulty germination.

Make main sowings of runner beans 2 in. deep, spacing seeds about 9 in. apart, in double rows. Plant a pair of seeds at each station to allow for low germination. If two seedlings appear, remove the weaker. 'Crusader', 'Streamline', 'Prizewinner' and 'Achievement' are good tall varieties, climbing to 7 - 8 ft.; 'Kelvedon Marvel' and 'Princeps' are shorter, 4 - 5 ft., and crop earlier. For those who do not wish to erect supports for climbing, 'Hammond's Dwarf Scarlet' is suitable and grows no more than 16 in. high.

Make sowings of 'Asparagus Pea', 'Sugar Pea', 'Blue Coco' which is a semi-runner bean, and 'Pea-bean du Pape' if you are fond of the epicurean vegetables.

Plant out sweet corn raised under glass about mid-May; cover with a cloche if night frosts are heralded. Plant in blocks of threes or fours, 9 - 12 in. apart, to facilitate cross-pollination.

Sow sweet corn out of doors 1 in. deep, in double rows about 9 in. apart, choosing an early-maturing variety, such as 'John Innes Hybrid' or 'Kelvedon Glory'. Outdoor tomatoes go well with this crop, and can be interplanted.

Sow the maincrop of beetroot this month, spacing seeds 2 - 3 in. apart, 1 in. deep, in rows 12 in. apart. Actually, the seeds are capsules containing several seeds, and seedlings must be thinned later. Choose long-rooted beets for deep, lightish soils only; for other soils, globe or round varieties are better. See that soil contains lime, but no unrotted manure.

Make a sowing of turnips for late summer use, but only on moisture-retentive soils, sowing $\frac{3}{4}$ in. deep, in drills 9 in. apart. A sowing of swede turnip can be made towards the end of the month for winter supply.

In brassica seed bed, sow seeds of 'Late Purple' sprouting broccoli, winter cabbage ('Christmas Drumhead', 'Winnigstadt') and cauliflower ('St. George', 'Superlative Protecting') for spring next year.

Plant out early Brussels sprouts, autumn cabbage and cauliflower to mature in autumn. Firm in very well, treading with

143

boots, on ground well manured in winter and given a balanced compound fertiliser in spring. Lime must be present. Set plants with first true leaves resting on the soil, and water in. If there is any reason to suspect clubroot infection, dust each planting hole with a teaspoonful of 4% calomel dust before planting.

Finish planting maincrop potatoes as soon as possible this month. Every day of delay will cut the yield now.

Earth up second earlies when haulms are 6 in. high.

Begin cutting asparagus as budding shoots show through, cutting shoots about 6 - 8 in. in length, from well established beds. Do not cut from newly made beds for the first year or until plants are at least three years old.

Thin earlier sown carrots, spacing seedlings 3 - 4 in. apart; firm soil to remaining plants, and dust with whizzed naphthalene or soot to repel the carrot fly, or with lindane insecticidal dust, from mid-May.

Thin onions sown out of doors, and refirm and water soil containing retained plants. Dust with soot or lindane insecticide to control the onion fly pest.

Plant celery towards the end of the month, dressing the prepared trench with a little superphosphate a few days before planting. Firm and water in.

Plant out vegetable marrow, pumpkin and courgette plants raised in peat-wood fibre pots under glass, when the danger of night frosts is past. Traditionally, these are planted on prepared 'hills' of fermented organic matter and soil, but they do quite well on soil that has been well enriched with organic matter and a complete fertiliser, and given adequate moisture. Cover with a handlight or cloche for the first few days.

Make successional sowings of peas, radish and lettuce.

Keep the hoe busy to control annual weeds. Mulch growing crops such as peas, beans, etc., with organic litter.

Plants Under Glass: Remove cloches from crops sown under them earlier in the year, towards the end of this month.

Harden off annuals and bedding plants progressively. If frame space is at a premium, place seedlings under open-ended cloches in a sheltered part of the garden.

Differences between growing conditions in the cold and the cool greenhouse lessen considerably this month, though the availability of heat at night is a frost safeguard.

Greenhouse plants you may have in bloom: many of the plants given under April will extend their flowering into May. Plants coming into flower this month that are worthy of note include:

Acrophyllum venosum*; Adesmia boronioides; Anopterus glandulosoa; Bauera rubioides*; Boronia megastigma; Bossiaea distachia; Callistemon speciosa; Candollea tetrandra*; Chorizema cordata, C. dicksonii*, C. varium*; Dillwynia floribunda*; Epacris longiflora*, E. pulchella; Leucopogon richei; Myrtus ugni; Pelargonium cordatum, P. quercifolium; Petrophila acicularis; Pimelea arenaria, P. spectabilis; Platylobium obtusangulum; Sparrmania africana; Astilbe japonica; Clivia nobilis; Gladiolus cuspidata; Sparaxis tricolor.

* Continues flowering beyond the month.

Ventilate greenhouse freely with rising temperatures, but close down early after sunny days. Water plants more often as growth increases; it will be stimulated by light intensity. Syringe wall plants, and foliage of all plants on warm, clear days in the forenoon, and damp-down by watering paths and staging to give a humid atmosphere on days when growth is bound to be vigorous. Have plant foliage and greenhouse dry by nightfall.

Continue to harden off annuals, vegetable seedlings and tomato plants intended for outdoors.

Pot on rooted cuttings of zonal pelargoniums ('geraniums') intended for winter flowering.

Prune flowered *Acacia* spp., by cutting back the flowered shoots. Repot if necessary; otherwise renew the top inch or so of soil.

Remove spent flower heads from bulbous and cormous plants that have finished flowering, and plunge the bulbs and corms with their soil-balls in the soil out of doors, giving a liquid feed to encourage leaf growth and some build-up of the plants for the future.

Sow seeds of cineraria for winter flowering: *C. stellata* to give large bushy plants, *C. nana multiflora* for compact pot plants. Shade them from hot sun and keep moist.

Sow seeds of herbaceous calceolaria in cold greenhouse, simply pressing the seed into a fine soil compost, and covering box or pan with glass until germinating.

Place plants of perpetual-flowering carnations, raised from cuttings, to summer in the cold frame.

Move chrysanthemums, now in their pots, out of doors in the latter half of the month, after giving the first stop to growth by pinching out the growing point when the plants were 6 - 9 in. high. Place plants in a wind-sheltered spot, on ashes or boards; stake and water daily.

Take short 2 - 3 in. long cuttings of the Cape heaths (*Erica caniculata*, *E.* x Cavenish, etc.) and insert in pots of lime-free compost to root with slight bottom heat.

Continue disbudding of apricots, nectarines and peaches under glass; this consists of pinching out the tip growth of embryo shoots from wood buds from which extension is not required. Select the replacement shoot that is to grow and become the fruit-bearing shoot next year from near the base of the current bearing shoot; pinch the tip out when about 19 in. long, and stop any secondary growth at the first leaf.

Syringe above fruit trees on warm and sunny days.

Thin grape bunches as soon as the embryo fruitlets form, reducing the numbers drastically. Work with long, thin-shanked scissors and do not be afraid of removing too many. Stop secondary sub-lateral growth at the second leaf.

Plant out cucumber plants in greenhouse border, or in prepared beds made up on the staging, 4 - 6 in. deep, consisting of thoroughly rotted organic matter and good loam, and train up wires to the roof. Indoor cucumbers require higher temperatures and more humidity than tomatoes, and if the two crops must be grown in the same greenhouse, choose the variety of cucumber known as 'Conqueror' as the one most likely to succeed under tomato-growing conditions.

Plant tomato plants in cold greenhouse early in the month. They can be grown in borders, in beds on staging, in pots, or in bottomless pots on sterile moist aggregate (ring culture), or in the latest fashion in straw bales. Plant sturdy, short-jointed, dark green, even-coloured plants with first truss of flowers in being. Keep the soil-ball just moist for the first three weeks, until plants are established. In ring culture keep the aggregate of clinker and ashes, or gravel, thoroughly moist to attract roots downward. In straw bale culture, cut a hole to receive the root soil ball; water straw with a dilute solution of liquid manure or fertiliser.

Make a sowing of the biennial *Celsia cretica* and the half-hardy perennial *Celsia arcturus*, for subsequent growing on as pot plants for greenhouse ornament.

Have ready: karathane to control any outbreak of powdery mildew on greenhouse plants; captan or thiram fungicide to deal with damping-off, grey-mould (botrytis), leaf-mould on tomatoes, and rusts; malathion or derris to cope with aphides, white fly, scale insects and mealy bugs; DDT or gamma-BHC dust to control wood-lice, earwigs and ants; and, of course, metaldehyde bait pellets for stray slugs and snails.

Pot up and keep a few plants of African marigold in the greenhouse with tomatoes—they will act as a deterrent to white fly infestation.

June

O, my luve's like a red red rose
That's newly sprung in June.
ROBERT BURNS

THIS month sees plant growth well into its stride, and there is no vital difference in the timing of most garden operations in any part of the country, since temperatures and light intensity are above the critical level for plant growth generally.

It is still necessary to keep weeds at bay, and routine hoeing should never be shirked.

The greatest need of crops and plants in active growth is a constant supply of moisture. This need must be met by the soil, and the soil's available reserves in dry weather depend partly upon its texture—dense clayey soils retain their moisture longer than sands—but even more upon its humus-forming organic content, which holds moisture at rooting levels like a sponge.

In dry weather soils lose moisture directly by evaporation and drainage, and indirectly by plant transpiration. No soil

149

ever completely dries out, but as its water content falls, it may reach a point when its power of retention becomes greater than the plant's ability to extract it, and the plant has to make its own economies by wilting. This can happen at any time in the next three months, though the threat is greater in the drier southern and eastern counties. Plants are affected by diminishing water supplies before wilting point is reached, however. Growth tends to be stunted and to harden prematurely. Some basic rules for watering out of doors are as follows.

Water in advance of plant needs—i.e. before they start to wilt. Just how soon you should water in a period of drought depends on how readily soil moisture is lost. Light, sandy and free-draining soils suffer first from water shortage. High temperatures, strong winds and a porous soil texture make for rapid loss of moisture by evaporation. The more plants per square yard, the more moisture is taken up and transpired, though a good plant coverage leads to efficient plant use of moisture and tends to mitigate losses by evaporation. Obviously, the more shallow-rooting the plant, the more quickly it is likely to need watering. All these factors have to be considered. A practical guide is the state of the soil, ascertained by examining to a depth of 6 - 8 in. with a trowel. When soil shows signs of drying out to this depth, water.

Whether you use watering can or hose, soak the soil thoroughly. Check penetration with a trowel. Watering to wet the surface does more harm than good, tempting plant roots to seek the water where subsequent drying out injures them; 3 - 4 gallons per sq. yd. are not too much.

Water through the air. When possible, water should fall like rain, becoming oxygenated in its fall through the air, and falling on plants and soil with gentle impact. The more mist-like the spray, the better for growth and economical water use. Use trickle irrigation of the soil where the soil has dried out considerably, but combine with spray or sprinkler watering where possible.

Water and leave alone. Unless you have a permanent irrigation system, it is better to water thoroughly and then leave alone for several days, than to water a little at a time often.

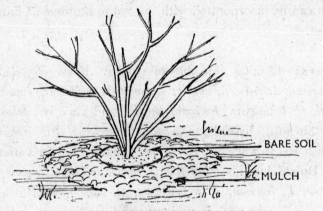

BARE SOIL

MULCH

Mulching a shrub.

Mulch to conserve soil moisture. A mulch is a top cover of organic litter placed over the rooting area of growing plants. It checks evaporation losses, keeps the soil temperature down, helps to suppress weeds, improves bio-chemical activity in the soil, and feeds the plants.

Apply the mulch when the soil is damp, after rain or after

watering. Leave a few inches clear near the base of plants, for the soil must breathe and rain penetrate. Use moist materials —rotted manure, moist peat, weathered sawdust, chopped straw or chaff, lawn mowings (if not treated with selective weed-killers), half-rotted leaves, spent hops, etc.—to a depth of an inch or so. Replenish if and when material dries out and becomes thin. Sprinkle the soil with a little nitrogenous fertiliser (sulphate of ammonia, nitro-chalk, dried blood) before applying a mulch; it fosters micro-organic activity and improves the feeding value of the mulch. Ultimately, the mulch can be incorporated with the soil to improve its humus content.

Flowers: Coming into bloom—bulbs: *Allium albopilosum, A. azureum, A. moly, A. anceps; Alstroemeria aurantiaca; Camassia cusickii, C. leichtlinii; Eremurus* bungei and vars., *E. robustus, E.* x 'Shelford' hybrids; *Gladiolus byzantinus; Iris xiphioides* (English iris in variety), *I. xiphium* (Spanish iris in variety), *I.* x 'Dutch' hybrids; *Lapeyrousia cruenta; Lilium croceum, L. dauricum, L. hansonii, L.* x *martagon, L. monadelphum;* ixia in variety; *Gladiolus nanus* in variety; and *Ornithogalum arabicum.* In the border—*Anchusa azurea* vars.; *Aquilegia canadensis; Armeria plantaginea* 'Bees' Ruby'*; *Bulbinella hookeri*; *Buph-thalmum salicifolium*, B. speciosum*; Campanula persicifolia* and vars.*; *Cichorium intybus*; Dianthus* (border pinks)*; *Dictamnus albus* (burning bush); *Digitalis purpurea* and hybrids; *Draco-cephalum grandiflorum; Filipendula rubra venusta*; Galega officinalis* and vars.; *Gaura lindheimeri; Geranium grandiflorum; G. pratense* and vars.; *Glaucium flavum; Hemerocallis flava; Hesperis matronalis purpurea; Incarvillea grandiflora**; *Inula glandulosa**; *Iris sibirica*, flag or German irises; *Jasione perennis** (sheep's-bit scabious); *Kentranthus ruber* (valerian)*; *Lupinus arboreus* and vars., lupins, Russell strain; *Lychnis arkwrightii**; *L. coronaria* (rose campion)*; *Meconopsis betonicifolia*, *M. integrifolia; Moltkia intermedia**; *Monarda didyma* (Oswego Tea)*; *Oenothera missouriensis**, *O. odorata sulphurea**; paeony, in variety; *Penstemon ovatus; Polygonum affine**; *Potentilla atrosanguinea; Primula beesiana**, *P. pulverulenta**, *P. bulleyana**, *P. florindae**; *Prunella vulgaris* and vars.; *Sanguisorba officinalis; Tunica saxifraga**.

Finish planting of gladiolus corms as soon as possible.

Plant out dahlias grown from cuttings or seeds in soil well provided with organic matter. Place stakes in position for tall-growing varieties.

Plant out bedding begonias, enriching ground with a light dressing of a compound fertiliser beforehand.

Thin annuals sown previously out of doors. Pinch out tops of annuals such as clarkia and antirrhinum to develop bushy plants.

Plant out in the first week or so of the month half-hardy and hardy annuals to complete bedding schemes and fill empty places in the border.

Sow seeds of hollyhock in a cold greenhouse of frame to provide plants for next year.

Plant out biennial seedlings (wallflowers, sweet williams, canterbury bells, etc.) in nursery beds, spacing 3 - 4 in. apart.

* Continues flowering beyond the month.

Lift bulbs when the foliage begins to yellow and wither; dry off, preferably under cover and not in full sun out of doors, then sort according to size and store under cool dry conditions until planting time comes round again. There is no reason, however, why bulbs should not be replanted at once if naturalised in grass. Narcissi, crocus, tulips and most bulbs benefit from being lifted, divided and sorted every three or four years.

Divide crowded clumps of pyrethrums when they stop flowering, replant at once, and give thorough watering.

Stake and disbud border carnations for large blooms, removing the axillary buds as soon as they can be easily rubbed off with finger and thumb.

A pink 'piping', ready for propagation.

Take 'pipings' of dianthus pinks towards the end of the month consisting of the end growths of non-flowering vigorous shoots with three or four pairs of leaves, detached by a gentle pull at a node. Insert in a porous compost in boxes, and place in a cold frame, if many are wanted. Or they will root readily if inserted in the soil under a handlight.

Give plants coming into flower the benefit of a weekly 'foliar' feed, especially gross feeders such as delphiniums, hollyhocks and other herbaceous plants. In dry weather, a 'foliar' feed is preferable where it is not possible to water heavily.

Paths: Painting stray weeds with an appropriate weed-killer solution, or spot-spraying, is the simplest way of keeping paths weed-free. Sodium chlorate (4 oz. per quart water) can be used if the solution is confined to the weed foliage and not allowed to wet the soil or touch garden plants.

Hedges: Spray privet hedges with a growth inhibitor (maleic hydrazide) if you wish to avoid the labour of frequent clipping.

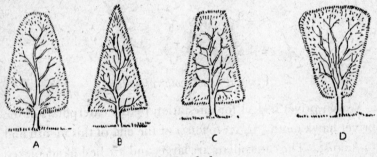

A   B   C   D

Shaping hedges:
a, b, c. Rightly trimmed.   *d. Wrongly trimmed.*

Trim informal spring-flowering hedges such as *Berberis* x *stenophylla*, forsythia, etc., when they go out of bloom, cutting the flowered shoots back to within 3 - 6 in. of their base.

Make a first trimming of fast-growing hedges such as thorn,

lonicera, myrobalan plum and privet; clip leaders that make extending top growth lightly, and side shoots severely. Trim always to keep sides parallel, or tapering from a wide base to a narrowing top; never let the top grow wider than the base, as this would lead to the lower growth being shaded and consequently becoming sparse and dying back. For a close-packed hedge, trim in the first week, and again in the last week of the month.

Spray yew with a white petroleum oil and nicotine insecticide or with a malathion insecticide if infested by scale insects (numerous small shell-like bumps on the stems).

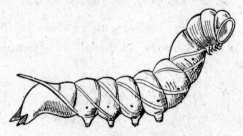

A typical hawk moth caterpillar.

Watch privet hedges for infestation by the caterpillars of the privet hawk moth *(Sphinx ligustri)* at the end of this month and to August. The caterpillars are large, and are best hand-picked and destroyed.

Spray hedges when the foliage is being eaten with a DDT, gamma-BHC or malathion insecticide, as caterpillars or leaf-eating weevils are likely to be responsible.

Mulch newly planted hedges after rain, and if quick growth is desirable, spray monthly with a foliar feeding solution.

Shrubs and Trees: Shrubs likely to be in flower—*Rhododendron luteum* (syn. *Azalea pontica*); *R. maddenii*, R. crassum, R. discolor, R. ferrugineum, R. griersonianum;* '*Cytisus battandieri, Cistus corbariensis, C. cyprius*, C.* x 'Elma'**, C.* x 'Silver Pink'*; *Cornus kousa; Cotoneaster rotundifolia, C. salicifolia rugosa; Daboecia cantabrica*; Deutzia scabra candidissima; Erica cinerea* and vars.*, *E. terminalis*, E. tetralix* and vars.*; *Escallonia* x 'C. F. Ball', *E.* x 'Donard' hybrids; *Fabiana violacea prostrata; Genista virgata*; Helianthemum nummularium* and vars.*; *Helichrysum lanatum; Hypericum androsaemum*; Hyssopus aristatus*; Kalmia latifolia*; Kolkwitzia amabilis; Magnolia sieboldii; Paeonia ludlowi; Pernettya mucronata* and vars.; *Philadelphus* in variety; *Potentilla fruticosa* and vars.*; *Pyracantha atalantioides, P. rogersiana, P. watereri; Rhus cotinoides*, R. cotinus* and vars.; *Robinia hispida,* rose species; *Salvia grahamii, S. officinalis* and vars.; *Senecio greyii*; Spartium junceum*; Symphoricarpos* x *chenaultii*; Viburnum opulus* and vars. Trees in flower: *Aesculus carnea briotii*; Cotoneaster frigida; Crataegus* x *carrierei, C. prunifolia; Laburnum* x *vossii; L. alpinum; Robinia pseudacacia* and vars.; *Sorbus aucuparia.*

Prune, when necessary, the early spring flowering shrubs as they stop flovering. This is only strictly necessary when it is desired to shape the plant, or replenish young wood by cutting out a proportion of the old. There is no need to prune a healthy shrub that is flowering well, and is in a suitable position.

Remove spent flowers only from plants such as lilacs (*Syringa* spp.) and rhododendrons and azaleas.

* Continues flowering beyond the month.

A flowering shoot of Spartium junceum, the Spanish broom.

Prune flowering cherries, and all ornamental trees of the *Prunus* genus (flowering almonds, peaches and plums). This is the time to cut out overhanging or unwanted branches. It is best to do this work when the trees are in full leaf, to minimise bleeding, and preferably this month or next to avoid infection by the silver leaf fungus disease. Paint all cut surfaces well with a tree antiseptic (Arbrex).

Mulch and spray newly plants shrubs and trees when the weather turns dry. Add a little liquid manure or foliar feed to the water to make it even more effective.

See that the soil-bal enclosing the roots of newly planted conifers and evergreens is kept moist.

Spray ornamental cherries and related peaches and plums with a gamma-BHC/DDT or derris insecticide when aphides (greenfly) are seen to be present on the undersides of leaves.

Remove suckers from shrubs and trees grafted or budded on rootstocks of common species, such as lilacs, flowering quinces

(*Chaenomeles* sp.), flowering cherries and stone fruits, etc. Trace the sucker to its base and cut flush with the root from which it springs. Do not chop the root off itself, as that will encourage further suckering. Do not dig deeply around these plants that produce suckers. An alternative method—paint the sucker with sodium chlorate solution (4 oz. per quart water), and it will die back.

Give a top-dressing of an organically based balanced fertiliser to any shrub that is backward, making little or no new shoot growth, and to shrubs that have been hard-pruned. A mixture of 2 parts by weight hoof and horn meal, 2 parts bone flour, and 1 part sulphate of potash, used at 2 oz. per sq. yd., is about right. Cover with a mulch atfer the fertiliser has been raked and rained in.

Roses: The first flush of roses from hybrid teas, floribundas, climbers, and several of the species, makes this month a glory. Alas, pests and diseases rear their heads too.

Keep the growth vigorous by watering in dry weather, and a weekly foliar feed.

Keep powdery mildew under control with karathane, thiram or sulphur fungicide. Watch for outbreaks when cool, dewy nights follow warm days. Make a note of very susceptible varieties.

Watch for black spot fungus infection this month, especially when the weather turns cool and wet. The fungus, *Actinonema rosae*, may over-winter on fallen leaves, and last year's shoots, but rarely does so in the soil. The spores can also be air-borne.

Early signs—faintly purple small blotches on leaf surfaces, gradually deepening to black, spreading to involve all the leaf and producing innumerable, tiny black shining dots over the surface. Spray promptly with a captan, thiram or copper fungicide and repeat at about fourteen-day intervals. Detach seriously infected leaves and burn.

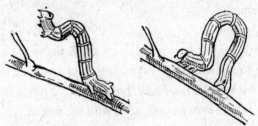

Typical 'looper' caterpillars of geometer moths.

Leaves being eaten? Look for caterpillars, particularly the loopers or geometers, this month and next. Spraying or dusting a 'stomach' poison insecticide would give control. DDT with pyrethrum, malathion, or derris.

Leaves being rolled? Usually the handiwork of caterpillars of tortrix moths or sawflies. Treat as for looper caterpillars, after removing leaves which are very much infested for burning.

Blooms in bud partly eaten? Most probably the work of the garden chafer, *Phyllopertha horticola* or rose chafer, *Cetonia aurata*. Use a DDT/pyrethrum preparation on the plants, and an aldrin or gamma-BHC dust on the soil to frustrate egg-laying female chafers, laying eggs for a future generation.

Leaves skeletonised? The rose slugworm, *Endelomyia aethiops*, has been at work. Use the DDT/pyrethrum preparation.

160

Aphides? Greenflies, clustering up stems, leaves and buds, are best controlled by a quick-acting contact insecticide, dusted or sprayed directly at them suchaspyrethrum, nicotine, derris, or malathion.

The handiwork of leaf-cutter bees, Megachile sp.

Semicircular pieces taken out of leaves? Leaf-cutter bees are responsible; they use the cut portions to make their nests. There is no certain control, but unless numerous the damage is not serious.

Mottled, dryish-looking, yellow leaves, falling prematurely? Often the signs of infestation by red spider mites, *Tetranychus telarius*, particularly active under hot, dry conditions. DDT/ pyrethrum, malathion or derris can be used for control, applying to undersides as well as surfaces of leaves.

Combine summer pruning with cutting. Cut rose stems of blooms to a suitably placed bud, pointing in the direction new growth is wanted. Remember that in removing leaves you reduce the plant's food-manufacturing capacity, so avoid overdoing this. Cut away spent flower heads, however, rather than let them waste energy in hip and seed formation. Cut blooms for indoors in the early morning or late evening, plunging them into a backet of water up to their 'necks' for a few hours.

Give a light dressing of a complete rose fertiliser after the first flush of flowers, and rake gently in.

Lawn: Mow as frequently as possible. Adjust the height of the cut to take less foliage in dry periods, and leave the grass-box off, at least where ornamental lawns are concerned.

Repeat the supplementary feed about mid-June (see May notes), before or just after rain, or when it can be immediately watered in.

Do not use lawn sand or selective weed-killers in drought or dry weather. Lawn sand will scorch, if not kill the grasses; selective weed-killers may inhibit grass growth.

Water copiously when you water. Really soak one area of the lawn at a time. It can then go for a longish period without water. If water supply is limited or restricted, apply a dilute solution of a liquid feed or fertiliser in the evening.

New lawns, struggling to establish themselves, should be shaded from the hottest sun with lath fencing, hurdles or evergreen boughs.

Compost your lawn mowings with a quick-acting herbal activator for quick results. Use an open-ended box-like enclosure for the mowings, water with the activator, and leave 6 - 8 weeks. No need to press down; it turns to a friable mould, very useful for mulching.

Rock Garden: Coming into flower—several alpines will still be in flower from May (see May notes), plus *Achillea tomentosa**; *Aethionema schistosum; Allium sikkimense**; *Androsace lanuginosa**; *Antennaria dioica; Aquilegia discolor; Arenaria montana**; *Asperula suberosa**; *Calamintha grandiflora**; *Calceolaria darwinii, C. polyrrhiza**; *Campanula bellidifolia, C. cochlearifolia**; *C. garganica** and vars., *C. pulla**, *C.* x *rotarvatica**; *Centaurea simplicaulis; Codonopsis clematidea, C. ovata**; *Cytoledon oppositifolia* (syn. *Chiastophyllum oppositifolium*)*; *Crepis incana**; *Daboecia canatbrica* (Irish heath)*; *Daphne arbuscula; Dianthus alpinus**, *D.* x *arvernensis**, *D.* x *alwoodii alpinus* and vars.*, *D. deltoides**, *D.* x *hybridus**, *D. sylvestris**; *Dryas octopetala; Erica cinerea* and vars.*, *E. tetralix* and vars.*, *E. vagans* and vars.*; *Erodium chamaedryoides roseum**, *E. chrysanthum**; *Gaultheria nummularioides; Genista dalmatica**, *G. villarsii**; *Gentiana kochiana**; *Geranium argenteum**, *G. cinereum; Globularia bellidifolia**, *G. cordifolia**; *Gypsophila repens**; *Halimiocistus* x *sahucii**; *Helianthum alpestre**, *H. nummularium* and vars.*; *Hippocrepis comosa* 'E. R. Janes'*; *Hypericum rhodopeum**; *Iris gracilepes, I. innominata, I. lacustris, I. tenax; Leontopodium alpinum* (edelweiss); *Linaria alpina**, *L. origanifolia**; *Linum* x 'Gemmell's hybrid'*; *L. flavum**; *Lithospermum diffusum**; *Mentha requienii**; *Mimulus cupreus**; *Moltkia* x *intermedia**, *M. petraea; Nierembergia repens**; *Omphalodes cappadocica**, *O. lucilliae**; *Onosma albo-roseum**, *O. echioides**; *Papaver alpinum**; *Penstemon barrettae**, *P. menziesii**, *P.* x 'Six Hills'; *Pimelea prostrata; Potentilla aurea plena**; *Primula alpicola, P. bulleyana; Rhododendron fastigiatum; R. nitens; Rosa chinensis* v. *minima** (dwarf roses); *Roscoea cautleoides**, *R. humeana**;

Saponaria ocymoides*; Saxifraga aizoon and vars.*, *S.* x *burnatii, S. cotyledon, S.* x 'Esher', *S. longifolia*, S.* x 'Tumbling Waters', *S. scardica*, S. aizoides atrorubens*, S.* x *primulaize*; Scabiosa graminifolia*; Sedum lydium, Silene acaulis*; Sisyrinchium bermudiana*; Soldanella alpina, S. montana; Spiraea japonica bumalda*; Thymus serpyllum* and vars.*; *Trollius pumilus, T. ranunculinus*; Veronica armena, V. bidwillii, V. buchananii*, V. cinerea*, V. fruticans*, V. spicata nana**.

Propagate *Primula denticulata* after flowering is over, dividing crowns and replanting immediately, every third or fourth year. Treat *P. frondosa, P. involucrata* and *P. yargongensis* similarly, every second year. See each piece has a crown of rosetted leaves, rhizome and roots, and replant in rich moist soil, in partial shade. Alternatively, pot in 3 in. peat-wood-fibre pots, using U.C. compost, and growon in cold frame for planting out in autumn.

Take cuttings of *Hypericum reptans* with a heel and insert in dansy loam in cold frame or under cloches.

Take cuttings of dwarf rhododendrons, insert in lime-free compost of moist peat and coarse sand, and keep shaded and close in frame until rooting. Treatment with a root-inducing 'hormone' helps.

Take cuttings of saxifrages of the Engleria group, detaching single rosettes of the silvery encrusted leaves with attached basal stem, and inserting them in sandy loam, with partial shade until they root.

---

* Continues flowering beyond the month.

Take heeled cuttings of *Verbascum spinosum,* insert in a porous sandy-peat, in cold frame or under cloche.

Lift dwarf bulbs that are getting overcrowded when leaves die down—crocus, scilla, narcissus, etc. Sort and replant the best corms or bulbs forthwith; replant others separately in a nursery bed to grow on.

Plant out dwarf annuals where space is available to give a summer show—*Ageratum* 'Fairy Pink' and 'Blue Mink'; *Alyssum* 'Royal Carpet' and 'Pink Heather'; Candytuft 'Fairy Mixture'; *Delphinium chinensis; Lobelia* 'Cambridge Blue'; French Marigold 'Marionette' and 'Dainty Marietta'; dwarf nasturtiums; *Tagetes signata,* etc.

Deal promptly with incipient weeds—paint dandelions, horse-tails, bindweed, etc., with a 2,4,5-T weed-killer solution.

Water Garden: Finish planting up new pools as soon as practical this month, as plants are eager to grow. Do not worry if newly planted water-lilies do not bloom in their first year; they are all right if they make good new leaves.

Introduce fish when the pool has settled down, the water is clear, and oxygenating plants are seen to be putting out new foliage: roughly 2 - 4 weeks after planting. Avoid over-stocking, as fish will grow and breed under favourable conditions. A rule of thumb is to allow 24 sq. in. of surface area for each inch of body length (excluding the tail) of fish. In practice, this is far too generous. Start with 3 - 4 in. fish, and allow 4 - 6 for a small pool, 8 - 12 for medium to large pools. Introduce fish to the pool by floating or suspending the container in which they are bought in the pool for an hour or two until temperatures are similar; then push the container down and let the fish swim out. Buy plain goldfish for outdoor pools, or shubunkins as the best fancy fish. Golden orfe are also good. (See that ramshorn snails and a few freshwater mussels are also introduced for scavenging purposes.)

Remove growths of blanketweed by hand, by netting, or by inserting a forked stick and twisting it. Blanketweed or silkweed is a form of algae growth. Chemical control is not very effective at the concentrations permissible where there are fish and plants, but balanced stocking with plants and fish should bring improvement.

Clear greening water by making up a solution of potassium permanganate (1 oz. per gallon water) and water through a fine-rose watering can over green areas. Shade open spaces until plants are large enough to do it. In a pool without fish, introduce live Daphnia in quantity. The greening, due to algae multiplying, is not hazardous to fish or plants—only unsightly to our eyes. Changing the water does not help.

Forestall cats and herons from fishing in your pool by fixing a small-mesh nylon netting just about $\frac{1}{2}$ in. below the surface of the water.

Avoid the use of insecticides to control pests on aquatic plants, as most of them—including derris—are toxic to fish. Fish will keep many pests—caddis flies, mosquitoes, etc.—under control. Wash aphides off water-lilies and plants with a hose, and fish will deal with them.

Learn to identify the enemies of fish, so that you can deal

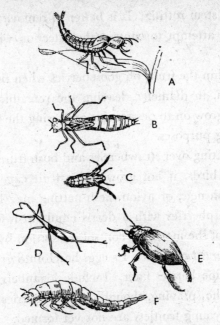

Dangerous inhabitants of the garden pool:
a. Larva of a great diving beetle.
b. Nymph or naiad of a dragonfly, Cordulagaster sp.
c. Back-swimmer, Notonecta glauca.
d. Water scorpion, Renatra linearis.
e. Adult great diving beetle.
f. Larva of the silver diving beetle.

with them promptly. The worst are the great diving beetles
(*Dytiscus* sp.) and their larvae, dragonfly naiads, leeches, water
boatmen (*Notonecta* sp.), water stick insect *(Ranatra linearis)*,
and water scorpion *(Nepa cinerea)*.

Detach leaves being attacked by fungus disease, and burn.
Water-lilies are the most vulnerable, showing leaf-spots, and

sometimes stem rotting. It is better to remove attacked leaves early than attempt to contain the infection with a fungicide.

Fruit: Thin the fruits on gooseberries when the berries reach about ½ in. in diameter, leaving the remaining berries well spaced to grow on to dessert size and using the thinned berries for cooking purposes.

Place netting over strawberries and bush fruits to protect the fruit from birds, if not grown in a fruit cage. Small-mesh, repaired fish nets, or nylon mesh netting may be used.

Spray raspberries with a derris emulsion insecticide in the latter half of the month to control infestation by the raspberry beetle (*Byturus tomentosus*). Its eggs hatch into grubs which will infest the ripe berries later. Include loganberries and black-berries in the spraying, though the blackberries can wait until July if the young fruitlets are not yet formed.

Spray neglected apple trees, subject to serious scab infection, with a captan fungicide about the second week of the month.

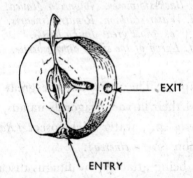

An apple infested by the codling moth maggot.

Put bands of tree-grease round apples (and pears) subject to codling moth *(Cydia pomonella)* infestation; spray trees, particularly the developing fruitlets, with a derris insecticide in mid to late June. This is the insect responsible for the maggoty apple at harvest.

Watch for fire blight afflicting pears if you garden in the Midlands or the South. This is a highly infectious bacterial disease which must be notified to the Ministry of Agriculture under the Fire Blight Disease Order 1958. Infection starts with the blossoms wilting; the spurs and branches are then attacked and become girdled with cankers; leaves turn dark brown or black and hang on the tree so that shoots look as if scorched by fire. 'Laxton's Superb' pear is particularly susceptible. There is no cure, and trees are best destroyed as soon as the infection is confirmed.

Thin pears about mid-June, leaving two to three fruits per cluster on trees well furnished with foliage. The foliage is the key to number of fruits it is wise to leave, since it is in the leaves that the food is manufactured to swell the fruit. Young trees should be spared the burden of heavy cropping, but established trees with much foliage can carry quite big crops.

Thin apples after the 'June drop'—when many apples shed their excess fruit naturally. Go over the early maturing cooking apples first, thinning the clusters to two or three apples, removing the short-stalked 'king' apple that forms in the centre of the cluster. Some apples, such as 'Grenadier', 'Monarch', 'Newton Wonder' and 'Rev. W. Wilks' are the better for being thinned to singles, spaced evenly on the branches. Thin dessert apples, including 'Cox's Orange Pippin', towards the end of the month, leaving pairs or singles. What you lose in numbers, you gain in added size of the remaining apples.

Mow the grass under trees and allow it to return to the soil. A sprinkling of nitro-chalk or sulphate of ammonia or Chilean potash nitrate (for dessert apples particularly) will speed its rotting and benefit the trees.

Vegetables: Make successional sowings of French beans, carrots, and saladings such as lettuce and radish.

Sow early (i.e. quickly maturing) peas for a late crop— 'Feltham Advance', 'Kelvedon Wonder', 'Early Superb', etc.

Sow parsley on good rich soil, after rain, to give fresh leaves for the winter.

Make sowings of colewort and endive for winter greens.

Give onions a fortnightly feed with liquid manure or a balanced liquid fertiliser.

Continue to plant out celery and leeks early in the month.

Plant out seedlings of sprouting broccoli, late cropping Brussels sprouts, savoys, and autumn and early spring cauliflowers; protect against the cabbage root fly and its grubs with a dusting of 4% calomel dust in the planting hole, and on the surface. The same dust also helps to prevent clubroot infection.

Plant out tomatoes on sunny, sheltered borders, but away from potatoes, their near relations. Stake, and after three weeks give first fortnightly feed with a tomato fertiliser.

Stop cutting asparagus at the end of the third week of the month. Remove weeds and give a top-dressing of a balanced fertiliser, such as 3 parts by weight steamed bone-flour, 2 parts superphosphate, 1 part sulphate of ammonia, 2 parts sulphate of potash, at 8 oz. per sq. yd., and rake in.

Finish earthing up of potatoes. Eradicate any plants showing stunted growth, yellowing of leaves in a mosaic pattern, and much leaf-curling, as they are probably infected by virus disease. The tubers can be harvested for food, but do not use them for seed.

Pinch out tops of broad bean plants, particularly if infestation with aphides (black fly or dolphin) is beginning. A watering with a solution of potash nitrate ($\frac{1}{4}$ oz. per gallon water) strengthens the plants and makes them more distasteful to the pests—a trick worth trying with all vegetables liable to aphid attacks.

Keep saladings well watered during dry weather; soak marrow and cucumber 'hills' in the evening.

Plants under Glass: Use the next three months, when heating is no longer necessary, as an opportunity to overhaul heating apparatus, and make any needed alteration.

Greenhouse plants you may have in bloom: those marked with an asterisk* in May notes will still be blooming, to which may be added some of the following:

Adenandra fragrans, A. amoena; Calceolaria sp.*; *Chrysocoma coma-aurea; Coronilla glauca; Crowea saligna*; Cytisus canariensis*; Darwinia frimbiata; Embothrium coccineum*; Gompholobium polymorphum*; Grevillea robusta; Hovea celsii; Nerium oleander*;* pelargonium in variety*; *Philesia buxifolia; Prostanthera* *lasianthos; Psoralea aculeata*, P. pinnata*; Rhododendron edge-worthii, R. javanicum*, R. maddenii* and hybrids; *Sarmienta repens; Solanum atropurpureum*, S. capsicastrum*, S. pseudocapsicum*; Agapanthus orientalis*; Commelina coelestis; Drosera binnata*; D. capensis*; Linum flavum*; Mirabilis jalapa* ('Marvel of Peru') and vars.*; *Stachys coccinea*,* Bulbous plants—*Albuca nelsoni; Babiana stricta* and vars.; *Crocosmia aurea*; Lilium brownii, L. concolor, L. hansonii, L. henryi, L.* x *maculatum, L. pumilum, L. regale, L. rubellum, L. sulphureum; Ornithogalum thyrsoides* (chin-cherinchees); *Tigridia pavonia*; Watsonia densiflora.* Climbers —*Cobaea scandens; Maurandya barclayana; Mitraria coccinea; Pharbitis learii; Phygelius capensis; Solanum jasminoides; Streptosolen jamesonii.*

Keep temperatures within the range of 60° - 75°F. (15·5° to 24°C.) as far as possible; give free ventilation, frequent damping-down or watering of paths and stages, syringe plants, and increase water supplies as growth comes to full vigour.

Shade during the heat of the day. In this climate variable shade is preferable by means of blinds, lath frames, opaque polythene sheeting, etc. If semi-permanent shade is wanted, use a proprietary product or a simple paste of flour and water painted on the glass, which can be easily removed later.

Stake chrysanthemums and pot plants now growing freely.

Dry off early-flowering bulbs when leaves begin to wither at the tips, and store.

Place spring-flowering shrubs such as azaleas, daphnes, etc.,

* Continues flowering beyond the month.

out of doors, in sheltered quarters, keeping them well watered in dry weather.

Give liquid feeding to perpetual flowering carnations now coming into bud.

Stop decorative chrysanthemums a second time, about mid to late June, if the variety calls for this. As a rule, exhibition plants only require stopping once, but plants being grown to give several medium-sized blooms need stopping twice.

Sow seeds of streptocarpus for plants to come into flower under heated greenhouse conditions next spring.

Sow seeds of *Gerbera jamesonii* hybrids as greenhouse perennials to grow under cool conditions.

Sow seeds of alpine plants as they ripen. Many germinate freely when fresh. Sow thinly and shallowly in a porous compost (J. I. Seed compost answers excellently—omit the lime for the lime-intolerant plants), in pans, cover with a slate or asbestos tile and place in cold greenhouse of frame.

Syringe frequently cucumbers being grown under glass, and shade from hot sun.

Keep fruit tree borders well watered.

Finish thinning out the fruitlets on grapes, and continue to stop sub-lateral shoots at their second leaf.

Spray tomato flower trusses, when open, in the morning to encourage a good 'set' of fruit. If you use a fruit-setting 'hormone' spray, only use it once on each flower truss, otherwise fruits are grossly distorted.

Take cuttings of greenhouse shrubs, such as *Acacia* sp., *Fabiana* sp., *Abutilon* sp., *Erica* sp., *Epacris* sp., *Fuschia* sp., etc., as suitable side shoots develop to the half-ripe state. Where possible, take with a heel.

A leaf cutting of Camelia japonica, prepared for propagation.

Take cuttings of *Camellia japonica*, consisting of a leaf with bud and a sliver of the branch wood, and insert in sandy-peat compost in propagating unit, keeping fairly close. May be slow to root. The ideal with evergreen cuttings is to root them in a mist propagation unit.

Feed tomatoes being grown in rings or pots. Under ring culture feed the roots in the ring only, watering the base aggregate. Feed according to growth and weather conditions, withholding when dull cloudy conditions and diminished light intensity check growth. Once every 7 - 10 days is usually sufficient. Use a balanced 'feed', rich in potash; either proprietary or a mixture of 1 part by weight sulphate of ammonia, 2 parts dried blood, 3 parts superphosphate, 1 part steamed bone flour, 2 parts sulphate of potash and 1 part sulphate of magnesium: used at a rate of a level teaspoonful per plant watered in.

Remove shoots from leaf axils cleanly, as soon as they are seen when training tomatoes up supports. Similarly, cut or make clean breaks when removing leaves. Paint cut surfaces with a little sulphur fungicide. Remove all cut pieces from the house, to avoid grey mould infection.

July

The English winter — ending in July.
LORD BYRON

WITH suitable growing conditions now prevailing, a
gardener's main concern will be with routine work that
keeps plants vigorous and healthy—mulching, feeding, watering
and weeding. Broadly, plants have two main phases in their
growth period; first, they are active in building up their
structures and assembling materials to foster their second
phase, which is chiefly one of ripening, hardening their tissues
and exploiting what they have garnered during the first phase
for the production of flowers, fruits and seeds. During the first
phase, they benefit from all the help we can give them to make
good growth; in the second they chiefly need sustenance, and
over-stimulation with feeding may delay maturity.

Feed plants with discretion. Given proper winter preparation,
organic manuring, correction of acidity, and basic fertilisation,
most plants grow very well without supplementary feeding.

176

It is chiefly food crops and certain specialised ornamental plants such as chrysanthemums and plants grown in soil of limited resources, as in the case of pot plants, that need feeding. The choice of a supplementary feed lies between (1) dry quickly-soluble fertilisers, which are applied and watered in; (2) highly soluble and concentrated chemicals, usually designed for solution in water and to be applied as a liquid feed; (3) liquid 'fertilisers', highly concentrated solutions requiring dilution with water for application; and (4) foliar feeds, of readily soluble chemicals for application in dilute solution to the foliage and stems of plants. In practice, (2) and (3) can often be used as foliar feeds also. Since plants respond most quickly to liquid feeding, (2) and (3) are becoming the more popular supplementary feeds. Whatever feed is used, it should be balanced to suit the plant. As over-feeding can be harmful, follow instructions given with proprietary materials implicitly, and do not be tempted to feed too often or too much.

Master the simple art of compost-making. Compost, in this sense, means the rotted-down organic and plant waste of garden and home for the provision of humus-forming matter, which is the foundation of fertility in the soil. It makes you independent of farmyard or animal manure.

Use all eligible organic materials for the compost—plant remains, leaves, lawn mowings, soft prunings, kitchen waste, shredded newspaper, straw, hay, haulms and stalks of harvested crops and flowers, etc.; but exclude tough perennial weed roots, flowering or seeding weeds, diseased garden plants, and wood (though sawdust can be added in moderation).

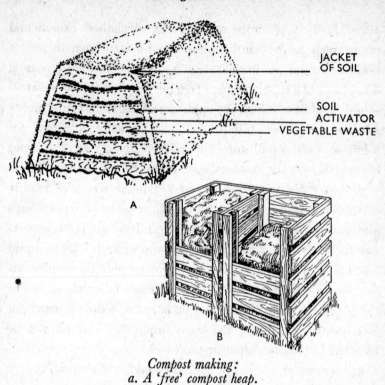

JACKET
OF SOIL

SOIL
ACTIVATOR
VEGETABLE WASTE

A

B

Compost making:
a. A 'free' compost heap.
b. A compost bin.

Stack materials, as available, in reasonably compact heaps.
Free heaps need to be at least 4 -5 ft. wide, and as high and as
long, to decompose satisfactorily. In most gardens it is best to
confine the organic waste in a simple container, such as a
wooden bin made with open slatted wooden sides, or a stout
wire-netting enclosure, or, for greater permanence, a bin or
bunker of open-work brickwork, which can be from about
2½ ft. wide, 2½ - 4 ft. long and 3 - 4 ft. high.

The heap is best built on the soil—not on an impervious surface that stops micro-organisms and worms entering the heap from the soil. Stack material as it accumulates in layers 4 - 6 in. thick, nicely moist, with the rougher, coarse material mixed with the finer. Add an activator or accelerator of decomposition between each layer, and a sprinkling of soil. An activator can be a nitrogenous fertiliser (calcium cyanamide, nitro-chalk, dried blood, sulphate of ammonia) or a thin inch or two of animal manure (cow, stable, poultry or pig) in a reasonably fresh state, or a proprietary product. Repeat layers until heap is complete. Cover incomplete heaps, during building, with sheet polythene. Allow to rot and heat until the heap begins the fall in the centre; then it is advantageous—though not vital—to turn the heap top to bottom, sides to middle, and re-stack thoroughly mixed. It takes 8 - 16 weeks to complete the rotting, when a sponge-like, brownish back mass is ready for distribution and incorporation with the soil, as a manure or a mulch. It is best to have two compost bins: one containing compost materials being assembled; the other, compost on its way to complete decomposition.

Flowers: Coming into bloom—bulbs and corms: *Agapathus africanus*, A. orientalis* and vars.*; *Allium beesianum*, A. narcissiflorum*; Alstroemeria* 'Ligtu hybrids'; *Galtonia candicans*; Gladiolus tristis, G. dracocephalus; Lilium brownii, L. candidum, L. davidii, L. pardalinum, L. regale, L. superbum; Orchis latifolia; Tritonia hyalina*.* In the border—*Achillea filipendula*; Aloe aristata; Anemonopsis macrophylla; Aquilegia longissima*; Ascle-*

pias tuberosa*; *Campanula lactiflora* 'Loddon Anna'*, *C. pyramidalis* and vars.*; *Centaurea macrocephala**; *Cephalaria tartarica**; *Chrysanthemum maximum* and vars., (Shasta daisy); *Cimifuga americana**, *C. dahurica**, *C. foetida intermedia; Clematis recta**; *Codonopsis ovata; Coreopsis grandiflora* and vars.*; *Crambe cordifolia**; *Cyananthus lobatus**; *Cynoglossum nervosum; Delphinium* hybrids; *Dianthus* (border carnations); *Dierama pulcherrimum**; *Dracocephalum forrestii; Erigeron macranthus**; *Eryngium planum; Filipendula purpurea**; *Helenium* 'July Sun'*; *Heliopsis scabra* and vars.*; *Hemerocallis* hybrids*; *H. thunbergii**; *Heuchera sanguinea* and vars.*; *Hosta fortunei, H. lancifolia; Inula ensifolia**; *I. helenium**; *Kniphofia uvaria**; *Lathyrus latifolius**; *Lavandula spica**; *Liatris spicata; Ligularia hessei**; *Limonium latifolium; Linaria purpurea**; *Lobelia milleri**; *Lychnis flos-jovis**; *Lysimachia clethroides**, *L. punctata**; *Lythrum salicaria* and vars.* (purple loosestrife); *Macleaya cordata**; *Morina longifolia; Nepeta* x 'Souvenir d'Andre Chaudron'; *Phlox paniculata* and vars.*; *Phygelius capensis coccineus** (Cape figwort); *Physostegia virginiana**; *Platycodon grandiflorus**; *Potentilla* x 'Wm. Rollison'*; *Rodgersia pinnata; Romneya coulteri**; *Rudbeckia speciosa**; *Santolina chamaecyparis; Saponaria officinalis* and vars.*; *Senecio macrophyllus**; *Sidalcea* hybrids*; *Stachys lanata; Tanacetum vulgare**; *Thalictrum dipterocarpum* and vars.*; *Verbena rigida**; *Veronica longifolia subsessilis**; *Zauschneria californica**.

Remove faded flowers of annuals and border plants promptly in order to encourage new buds and flowers to form.

* Continues flowering beyond the month.

Lift tulip bulbs now the foliage is fading, dry off in airy place but out of hot sun, and sort for storing until October-November when bulbs can be replanted. Give careful attention to tulips with much reddened leaves (tulip 'fire' or botrytis disease); burn foliage, only retain sound clean bulbs, and dust with thiram before storing. Mark places where the bulbs have grown, and do not plant tulips there next year.

Stake border phlox, Michaelmas daisies and other tall-growing border plants which need support.

Divide and replant bearded irises after flowering, if the weather is dampish and the soil in a good moist condition to promote rooting. Otherwise, wait until autumn.

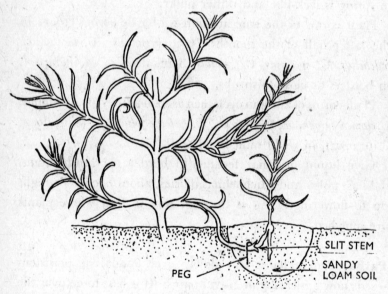

A layered border carnation.

181

Dust base and soil around the base of dahlias with an aldrin or gamma-BHC insecticidal dust, to prevent earwig infestation; *or* place plant-pots, stuffed with hay, inverted on the tops of stakes as traps, and inspect and empty of earwigs periodically.

Continue to take 'pipings' of pinks for propagation.

Layer border carnations as suitable shoot growth is made, using young non-flowered shoots, slitting half-way through a node, and pegging this part in the soil to root.

Plant bulbs of the so-called autumn crocus, *Colchicum autumnale* and vars., and *C. speciosum*, 6 in. deep and 3 in. apart, in any soils that are well-drained; in corners of the border, under shrubs or in grass; remembering that the foliage which comes in spring is leek-like and rather bulky.

Plant corms of the true autumn-winter flowering crocus in the latter half of the month: *Crocus byzantinus*, *C. medius*, *C. pulchellus*, *C. speciosus*, *C. zonatus*, 3 in. deep, 3 - 4 in. apart, in borders or close to shrubs.

Plant corms of autumn cyclamen as soon as they are available: *Cyclamen europaeum*, *C. graecum*, *C. hederae folium*, 1 - 2 in. deep, 3 in. apart, in well-drained leafy soil.

Give liquid or foliar feeding to border chrysanthemums, dahlias, phlox and Michaelmas daisies, about once a fortnight up to flowering. This is the best way to feed where plants are mulched.

Paths: Run a flame-gun slowly over annual or persistent weeds now appearing in gravel paths. It is best to go over the weeds at slow walking pace once, to cause them to wilt, and then go over again a few hours later to burn them off. Alternatively, spot-treat with a total weed-killer, such as one based on simazine.

Hedges: Trim the fast-growing hedges again, as soon as new growth begins to stick out spike-like. The price of quick growth and lost first cost is in the extra amount of time that must be spent on maintenance.

Clip quick growing thorn, gorse, lonicera and privet hedges again this month.

Propagate lonicera from cutting of firm half-ripened shoots, 12 in. long, inserted for half their length in well-drained soil, this month and next. They root readily.

Trim established formal hedges of beech, hornbeam, cypress (*Chamaecyparis* sp., and *Cupressus* sp.,), thuya, holly, box, yew and *Euonymus japonicus* with shears.

Trim hedges of laurel, Portugal laurel, *Aucuba japonica* and *Elaeagnus pungens* with secateurs, cutting straggling shoots back fairly hard. Clipping leads to cut leaves which brown and spoil the looks of a hedge.

Trim informal hedges of flowering shrubs such as *Buddleia alternifolia*, *Ceanothus dentatus*, *Chamaemoles speciosa*, *Philadelphus* sp., and *Rosa moyesii* by cutting back the flowered shoots to within 4 - 6 in. of their base.

Water lagging recently planted hedges with a dilute liquid feed every ten days.

Plant cuttings of lavender, santolina and artemesia to make a hedge of these plants, taking new shoots which have not flowered, with a heel of older wood, and inserting for a third of their length in the soil; pack around with sand if the soil is heavy.

Syringe and water newly planted hedges, especially evergreens and conifers, in dry weather. Do not worry if holly shows a disposition to shed its leaves—this is an indication of active rooting as a rule.

Shrubs and Trees: Shrubs likely to be in flower—*Abelia* x *grandiflora**; *Berberis aggregata* 'Buccaneer', *B. wilsonae, B. rubrostilla crawleyensis; Buddleia davidii* and vars.*, *B. alternifolia; Clerodendron trichotomum montanum**; *Cotoneaster dielsiana, C. franchetii, C. frigida, C. lactea; Erica* x 'Dawn'*, *E. vagans* 'Lyonesse', *E. v.* 'Mrs. D. F. Maxwell'*; *Eucryphia glutinosa**, *E.* x *intermedia**; *Fuchsia magellanica riccartonii** and vars.; *Genista aetnensis; Veronica anomala**, *V.* x 'Hielan Lassie'*, *V.* x Marjorie'*; *Hydrangea acuminata* 'Blue Bird'*, *H. macrophylla* and vars.*, *H. paniculata* and vars.*; *Hypericum patulum* and vars.*; *Indigofera gerardiana**; *Lavendula spica* and vars.*; *Romneya* x *trichocalyx**; *Santolina chamaecyparissus nana**; *Senecio laxifolius; Spiraea japonica* 'Anthony Waterer'*; *Stephanandra tanakae; Clematis* of the Lanuginosa, Jackmanii, Texensis and Viticella groups*; *Hydrangea petiolaris; Lonicera periclymenum serotina**; *Passiflora coerulea**; *Polygonum baldschuanicum**. Trees: *Catalpa bignoniodes,** *Liriodendron tulipifera.*

Prune May and June flowering shrubs that need it, as they

---

* Continues flowering beyond the month.

finish flowering: cut brooms back by reducing the flowered shoots by about two-thirds their length; cut out to base the flowered shoots of deutzias, easily distinguished by the greyer colour; remove spent flowered shoots of escallonia; but leave alone shrubs grown for their berrying later.

Layer shrubs difficult to propagate from cuttings, such as rhododendrons and other evergreens, by bending well-placed low branches to the soil, slitting or nicking behind a node at the lowest point of the bend, pegging down and mounding over with soil. Leave a year before severing.

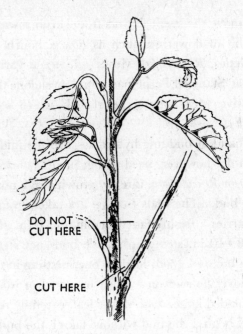

Pruning a cherry branch that needs to be curtailed.

185

Look over trees, and cut out all dead and diseased wood, especially on cherries and *Prunus* species, and burn the wood. Dead wood left lying about often becomes a source of infective parasitic fungus. It is a good time also to prune out unwanted, badly placed or overgrown branches on deciduous shrubs and trees, but remove to base, trim bark and cut smooth, and paint with a tree antiseptic (Arbrex). Prune maples, walnuts, and similar trees that tend to bleed if pruned at other times. Pruning now also minimises the chances of infection by fungus spores, particularly the silver leaf fungus, *Stereum purpureum*.

Roses: Remove the spent flowers from shrub roses that have a repeat habit of flowering, such as *Rosa* x bourboniana; *R. chinensis* varieties, *R.* 'hybrid Musks', *R. rugosa* varieties, and *R. spinosossima* 'Stanwell Perpetual'; but leave alone thoses roses with distinctive hips coming later such as *R. moyesii* and *R. pomifera duplex*.

Try your hand at budding hybrid roses in the middle of the month. You do, however, need young plants (stocks) of brier *(Rosa canina)* or *R. multiflora*, already growing in a nursery bed, on which to bud. The buds (scions) are taken from a robust shoot that carries a freshly faded bloom, cut from about half-way on an 8 - 10 in. stem; up to five buds per stem can be taken if each bud is a good, healthy one, nestling in the axil of a leaf. Remove the bud on a sliver or shield of wood with a sharp, thin-bladed knife. Cut off the leaf, carefully remove the whitish wood behind the bud without taking the bud out, and the bud is ready. Keep it moist in a damp cloth, while preparing the stock. Make a T-cut in the bark of the stock at about ground level, raise and peel back the right angles of bark (the readiness with which the bark is freed is an indication of the right time for budding). Slip the bud into the opening thus made, matching the greenish slimy layer with that of the stock, and then tape the bark and bud together with budding tape or moist raffia. A successful budding is soon shown in subsequent growth.

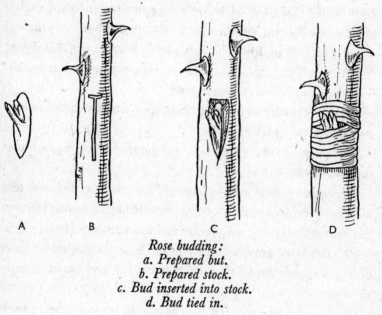

A   B   C   D

Rose budding:
a. Prepared but.
b. Prepared stock.
c. Bud inserted into stock.
d. Bud tied in.

Bud standard roses on trained stocks of *Rosa rugosa*, kept to a single stem by rubbing out all lateral buds, except at the top where lateral shoots, more or less opposite, are allowed to grow. Buds are then inserted in these laterals as close to the

187

main stem as possible. When the buds have taken, and are growing out, the laterals are cut short.

Propagate favourite roses from cuttings towards the end of the month—use firm, well-ripened shoots of this year's growth, about 9 in. long, cut just below a bud; remove leaves from lower two-thirds and insert and firm the cuttings in the soil, under cloches or handlights.

Propagate rambler and climbing roses by layering from mid-July until September. Choose young flexible shoots, bending towards the ground, slit the stem half-way through from behind a node, 15 - 18 in. from the end, and insert and peg this down, covering well with moist porous soil, and severing for transplanting when rooted early next spring.

Repeat spraying to control black spot when weather is cool and damp (see June notes).

Dust or spray with a 'stomach' poison insecticide when leaves continue to be eaten.

Serpentine tunnellings in leaves? The work of the rose leaf miner (*Stigmella anomalella*), best controlled by removing infested leaflest and applying a systemic menazon insecticide.

Reddish wiry growths on stems? These are the mossy galls of a gall-wasp *(Rhodites rosae)*, best cut off and burnt as soon as seen.

Give a complete rose fertiliser as a light top-dressing to bush roses, and to ramblers and climbers, to encourage strong new growth.

Remove spent blooms on bush roses whether hybrid teas, floribundas, polyanthas or grandifloras.

Lawns: In drought, take a higher cut with the mower, leave the grass-box off, and water copiously. If water restrictions are in force, spray with a foliar feed in dilute solution, since the grasses will then take in some nutrients through their leaves, and make less demand on soil.

Prepare sites now for new lawns to be sown in late summer. Old grassland or worn out lawns can be treated with a grass weed-killer based on dalapon or a new total herbicide based on Paraquat. Allow 6 weeks to elapse before taking the ground in hand and cultivating. Add a selective 2,4-D/mecroprop weed-killer to the grass herbicide if many broad-leaved weeds are present.

Rock Garden: Several alpines will still be in flower from June (see June notes), plus: *Achillea clavenae*; Asperula hirta*, A. nitida*; Astilbe simplicifolia*; Calluna vulgaris* 'County Wicklow'*; *Campanula arvatica* and vars.*, *C. carpatica* and vars.*; *Clematis tangutica*; Crassula sarcocaulis*; Erigeron leiomerus*; Frankenia thymifolia*; Geranium wallichianum*; Hypericum nummularium*, H. olympicum*, H. polyphyllum*; Jasminum parkeri*; Origanum hybridum*; Potentilla nitida*; Sedum cauticola*; Selliera radicans*; Sempervivum* x *calcaratum, S. ciliosum, S. pumilum, S. tectorum; Silene schafta*; Spiraea bullata*; Teucrium polium*; Thymus caespititius*, T.* x *citriodorus aureus*; Trachelium rumelianum*; Veronica cattarractae*, V. lyalii*.*

Propagate spring and early-summer flowering alpines from

---

* Continues flowering beyond the month.

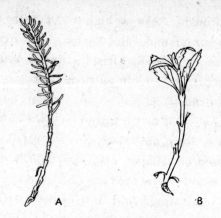

'Heeled' cuttings prepared for propagation:
a. Cutting of Erica sp.
b. Cutting of Aubrieta sp.

cuttings this month and next. Cuttings should consist of shortish shoots of this year's growth, detached with a small heel of the older stem to which they are attached. Insert in a moist but porous soil compost (a mixture of 1 part by bulk loam, 1 part sphagnum moss peat and 2 parts coarse sand suits most alpines), in a small box, seed pan or pot. A useful device is

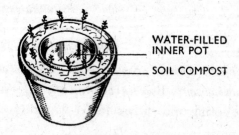

WATER-FILLED
INNER POT

SOIL COMPOST

A simple device for propagating soft-stemmed alpine cuttings.

190

a large pot with a smaller empty pot (with its drainage hole corked) inside it, and the space between the pots filled with soil compost, into which cuttings are inserted. The empty pot is then filled with water to seep into and keep the rooting medium moist. Easy plants propagated by cuttings are: *Aethionema* spp.; *Alyssum* sp.; *Androsace* sp.; *Aubrieta* sp.; *Cotyledon* sp.; *Cyananthus* sp.; *Gypsophila* sp.; *Helianthemum* sp.; *Phlox douglasii, P. subulata; Pimelea prostrata; Saxifraga,* Euaizoonia section; *Spiraea* sp.; *Teucrium* sp.; *Viola* sp. In the same way, raise new plants from the heeled cuttings of dwarf shrubs such as *Calluna vulgaris,* *Erica* sp., *Ceratostigma plumbiginoides, Cotoneaster* sp., *Jasminum parkeri, Vaccineum* sp., and dwarf conifers of cypress, juniper and yew.

Propagate rhizomatous-rooted alpines by lifting and dividing the rhizomes, planting each piece with attached roots. *Anemone blanda, A. nemorosa, Dodecatheon* sp., *Doronicum cordata, Geum montanum, Iris bucharica, I. chamaeiris, I. ruthenica, I. tenax,* lend themselves to this treatment this month.

Continue to sow seeds of alpines as they ripen. The Pasque flowers, *Pulsatilla vulgaris* and vars., for instance, germinate readily now.

Plant *Sternbergia lutea,* the so-called autumn-flowering daffodil, 6 in. deep in rich soil.

Layer shoots of *Clematis alpina* and *C. tangutica* for increase. It is sufficient to crack the stems between nodes by twisting gently, and bury this part in the soil.

Beware of slugs in humid weather, and renew metaldehyde slug bait around young plants.

Water Garden: Keep water clear of decaying foliage of plants. Top up with clean water to meet evaporation losses.

Wash infestations of aphides and other insects seen on the leaves of water-lilies and aquatics, by hosing or by submerging the leaves, and let the fish deal with the pests.

Detach pieces of the stems of underwater oxygenating plants, and insert in the bottom soil to increase the number of plants in a new pool.

Feed fish regularly, at the same times each day, preferably early morning and again in the afternoon. The best foods are: earthworms, woodlice, caterpillars, scraped raw lean meat, shredded fish, scrambled egg and oatmeal, and chopped shell-fish. Only give as much as the fish will take readily at a time.

Too many snails: the signs are leaves of plants being much eaten. Float a cabbage leaf on the pool surface, and remove periodically to take the snails off.

Watch the temperature of a small shallow pool in hot weather. Check it rising much above 70°F. (21°C.) by shading.

Fruit: Pick strawberries daily. Remove any fruits showing grey mould, distortion of hard core, for burning. Train runners to root either in a trough of soil enriched with peat and a little bone-meal; or, for superior plants, into plant pots sunk in the soil near the plants and filled with a good soil compost.

Clear strawberry beds of more than three years old that are obviously past their best.

Prepare new ground for planting with strawberries by bastard-trenching, clearing perennial weed roots; enriching

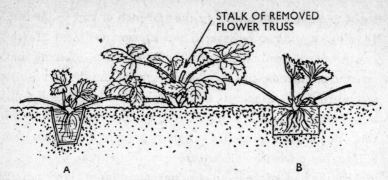

STALK OF REMOVED
FLOWER TRUSS

A   B

Propagating strawberries by runners:
a. Into pots.
b. Into a trough of enriched soil.

as liberally as possible with rotting manure, leaf-mould, compost or spent hops, plus bone-meal at 4 oz. per sq. yd.

Complete thinning of late dessert apples early in the month, and thin heavily cropping plums drastically.

Bud fruit trees this month and next. You can bud peaches, plums, cherries and nectarines as well as apples and pears. Prepare your buds with a shield of bark (as for roses, q.v.) from robust shoots of this year's growth, and insert them into T-cuts on young shoots in the same way as when budding roses. In this way you can propagate your own fruit trees, using seedling root stocks, or you can bud existing trees to carry more desirable varieties.

Train wall trees as new growth is made.

Stop the shoots of outdoor figs early in the month, just removing the tip growth, without removing swelling fruits.

Tip-layer new shoots of loganberries and cultivated blackberries if extra plants are wanted. Bend the tip of a growing shoot to the ground and bury the end inch or two in the soil. It will root and can be severed and transplanted next March.

Cut out all dead wood from plums, damsons, cherries and ornamental members of the *Prunus* genus before the end of the second week of this month, and burn. The Silver Leaf Regulations of the Ministry of Agriculture compel you by law to do this. You are not compelled to remove growth carrying silvered foliage, but obviously infected trees need attention. Feed well, and slit the bark of the main stem next spring (see March notes) to encourage recovery.

Begin summer pruning of apples and pears towards the end of the month. It should be spread over a few weeks. In its simplest form it consists of shortening the new growth on lateral shoots to within three leaves of its base, not counting the basal rosette of leaves. This should be done as the growth matures and becomes hardened and stiffish. Any sub-laterals or side shoots on the laterals are pruned back to just above one leaf. The leader or extension shoots of the main stem and/or branches is left untouched.

Spray or dust blackberries with a derris insecticide to prevent spoliage of fruit by the blossom beetle, early in the month.

Spray strawberries after the harvest is over with a malathion insecticide to control aphides and mite infestation, and the danger of virus infection.

Vegetables: Take up shallots and garlic when tops of plants begin to yellow, preferably in a dry spell. Dry off thoroughly, store dry and cool.

194

Lift early potatoes, as needed, or when the haulms begin to yellow. Rake ground smooth, giving a light dressing of super-phosphate ($\frac{1}{2}$ - 1 oz. per sq. yd.), and sow with turnips ('Golden Ball'), or quick-maturing carrots ('Perfect Gem') or round beet, to give tender roots for autumn.

Make a sowing of spring cabbage in brassica nursery bed — 'Wheeler's Imperial' is a very suitable variety.

Sow where it is to grow, thinly in rows 9 - 12 in. apart, 'Hungry Gap' kale, in districts where green vegetables are scarce in late winter and spring.

Plant out seedlings of 'Late Purple' sprouting broccoli, mid-season and late savoy cabbages, and cauliflower for late spring, from the nursery bed.

Still time to make a sowing of a quick-maturing lettuce, prickly spinach, and the shorter varieties of runner beans.

Spray potatoes and tomatoes to prevent and control the fungus disease, Blight *(Phytophora infestans)*, with a copper (Bordeaux Mixture) or captan fungicide, aiming to wet all leaf and stem surfaces. Disease is apt to appear and spread in cool, wet weather. First signs are brownish patches on the leaves and stems; these patches turn black and spread rapidly. Spray early in the month in the south-west, by mid-July in the Midlands and the North; and repeat every 2 - 3 weeks in unfavourable weather conditions to protect new growth.

Earth up maincrop potatoes for last time, prior to spraying against blight.

Give priority to celery, celeriac and saladings when watering in drought.

Syringe flowers of tomatoes, runner beans and French beans in dry weather to ensure that flowers will 'set'.

Use a derris or a pyrethrum insecticide to control insect pests on food plants near to maturity.

Give liquid feed to globe artichokes, celery, leeks and newly established leafy greens.

Sow a green manure crop on vacant ground that needs organic improvement. A mixture of mustard and clover will suit chalky or limy soils; one of oats and vetches for heavy clay soils; one of barley and white lupins on sands. Allow to grow 6 - 8 in. high or until flower buds start forming, then trample down, top-dress with nitrochalk or calcium cyanamide or sulphate of ammonia (on chalk soils) at 2 oz. per sq. yd.; leave 2 - 3 days, and then turn into the soil.

Watch the asparagus bed for the appearance of small red, yellow and black beetles, which eat the young shoots and foliage. Apply a derris or nicotine insecticide, when present.

Plants Under Glass: Clean and repaint frames which are empty. Repair cloches and wash glass with a dilute solution of domestic bleach to remove greening algae growth.

Greenhouse plants you may have in bloom: several plants will still be in flower from June (see June notes), plus *Adenanthos obovata; Bouvardia triphylla* and vars.*; *Eugenia buxifolia*; Platylobium formosum*; Salvia fulgens; Tweedia caerulea; Astilbe rubra; Begonia sutherlandii*; Francoa ramosa, F. sonchifolia*; Nerine flexuosa*;* and climbers—*Plumbago capensis*; Tropaeolum tricolorum.*

* Continues flowering beyond the month.

Sow *Humea elegans* (incense plants), preferably in small peat-wood fibre pots so that there is no transplanting disturbance of roots. Grow on in cold greenhouse or frame and pot on as needed, finally to 8 - 9 in. pots; bring into cool greenhouse for wintering to flower next July.

Sow the sweetly scented *Nicotiana suaveolens* and *N. sanderae* hybrids, half-hardy annuals, to provide late autumn fragrance in the greenhouse.

Take leaf cuttings of *Begonia Rex* and other strongly veined leaved plants. Slit the veins or ribs at junctions on the back of the leaf, and peg the leaf down on moist compost, to form buds and eventually young plants at the points of incision.

Pot on cyclamen being raised from seed to final 5 - 6 in. pots and keep cool in partial shade.

Pot on calceolarias sown earlier in the year, using J.I.P. 2 compost.

Take late cuttings of mid-season and late varieties of chrysanthemums for Christmas flowering, or buy them from a grower who has the stock plants. Root in peat-wood fibre pots, in U.C. compost, and pot on into larger pots when growing well and roots are penetrating the peat-wood fibre pot walls. Grow without check or stopping in the greenhouse. Good varieties— 'Balcombe Perfection', 'Fred Shoesmith' and its sports, 'The Favourite'.

Take cuttings of *Hydrangea macrophylla* varieties—short, stubby non-flowered shoots to root in greenhouse.

Keep fruit borders well supplied with water, and syringe in hot sunny days.

197

Stop tomatoes at about the seventh truss, if crop has to be cleared in September to make way for chrysanthemums. Continue to suppress axillary shoots, feed regularly up to the end of August, then withhold. Watch for leaf-mould, and combat promptly with captan or a copper fungicide.

Screen ventilators with muslin or fine-mesh nylon to keep out unwanted insects, especially where there is ripening fruit.

Keep day and night temperatures as equable as possible, between 60° - 75°F. (15·5° - 24°C.), by proper use of ventilation, damping-down and syringing, and so reduce stress on plants.

August

To recommence in August.
LORD BYRON

HARSH as we may think Lord Byron's appraisal of our climate with winter ending in July to begin again in August, it must be admitted that August can be a tempestuous month, with thunderstorms and chilling rains to suddenly cool warm sunny spells. A month in which the gardener has to be alert to changes, and yet in its more agreeble passages a month that contributes tremendously to the approaching climax of the active growth phases of plant life.

As plants come to their maturity in flowering, fruiting or seeding, the need for feeding diminishes. Within reason, weed competition can be observed with a closing eye, though it is still necessary to deal promptly with the weed in flower before it seeds, particularly weeds like willow-herb, ragwort, dandelions and others that menace our own and our neighbour's gardens when left alone.

Climatically, latitude begins to exert its effect. Nórthern gardeners must begin to plan their operations for the future knowing that autumn and winter come to them earlier than to their brethren in the South, and this means that operations such as sowing must be carried out 1 - 3 weeks in advance of average timing.

Flowers: Several plants will still be flowering from last month (see July notes). Others coming into bloom—bulbs and corms: *Amaryllis belladonna* (Belladonna lily); *Colchicum agrippinum; Crinum longifolium, C. moorei, C. powellii; Dierama pulcherrimum**; *Leucojum autumnale**; *Lilium giganteum, L. henryi, L. tigrinum; Tigridia pavonia**; *Tritonia pottsii*. In the border: *Acanthus mollis latifolius**; *Aconitum napellus* 'Sparks' var.; *Anaphalis triplinervis**; *Anemone hupehensis japonica* and vars.*; *Aster amellus* vars.*, *A. novae-angliae* and vars.*, *A. novi-belgii* and vars.*; *Boltonia asteroides**; *Centaurea dealbata**; *Coreopsis verticillata**; *Cyananthus sherriffii; Cynara scolymus glauca**; *Echinops ritro; Helenium autumnale* and vars.*; *Helianthus decapetalus* and vars.*, *H. mollis**; *Limonium eximium**; *Phlox paniculata**; *Salvia uliginosa**; *Sedum spectabile**, *S. telephium**; *Solidago ballardii**; *Zauschneria californica canescens*; hybrid dahlias and gladioli in profusion.

Order bulbs for autumn planting, and prepare planting stations when there is an opportunity.

Remove spent flower-heads from dahlias promptly, and cut out the flowered stems of border plants.

* Continues flowering beyond the month.

Continue giving a weekly or fortnightly feed to late flowering border plants such as asters (Michaelmas daisies).

Disbud early chrysanthemums if large blooms are wanted, simply pinching or rubbing off the smaller buds that threaten to compete with the one chosen to flower.

Cut away flowering stems of gladioli before they start forming seed pods, as seed formation will mean poorer corms for next year.

Lift and divide eremurus (foxtail lilies) where they have been in for four years or more. Lift carefully, so as not to break the brittle thong-like roots. Replant in deep, good soil, with tuber and crown 6 in. deep. Plant new varieties at this time.

Start planting bulbs such as muscari (grape hyacinths), *Erythronium dens-canis* and vars. (dog's tooth violets), *Anemone fulgens* and *Ornithogalum pyramidale*, this month; 3 - 4 in. deep, in groups to the front of borders.

Plant the early spring-flowering cyclamen—*C. orbiculatum* and its vars. *coum*, *atkinsii* and *ibericum*—about 2 in. deep, in the shrubbery or corners of borders where they can remain undisturbed. Later planting often means poorer performance in the first year or two.

Treat weed-infested ground, vacant of garden plants, with selective weed-killers—dalapon for couch grass, a 2,4,5-T or 2,4-D/mecroprop product for broad-leaved weeds. Then after 6 - 8 weeks it can be brought into cultivation. Alternatively, use the Scarlett Process for very weedy ground being freshly brought into cultivation: (1) rough harrow and flatten weed cover; (2) apply 2 oz. calcium cyanamide per sq. yd to the weed cover; (3) leave a few days, then sow a green manure crop of tares (vetches), and work in with rough raking; (4) when tares and weeds are growing again and have reached 6 - 8 in. high, flatten very thoroughly by beating down and rolling to form a mat; (5) dress with calcium cyanamide at 2 oz. per sq. yd. again and leave 3 - 4 days; (6) when green cover is beginning to rot, turn it under the top-soil, by spade or plough.

Paths: A start can be made on remaking paths that have sunk or become irregular on the surface. Paths subject to waterlogging can be taken up, and a foundation of aggregate (broken, stone or brick, crushed clinker, etc.) put down to a depth of 3 - 4 in. This can be topped with sand, and the stone flagging or crazy paving relaid.

Repair and re-surface asphalt paths with modern bituminous asphalt which allows drainage.

Hedges: Trim established hedges which, for economy reasons, are only given one clipping annually. Box, holly, beech and yew will stand up to this treatment, though it tends to create coarse hedging, and is more appropriate to loose screening.

Clear hedge bottoms of grass and weeds, likely to give shelter to pests seeking winter quarters.

Shrubs and Trees: Shrubs likely to be in flower—several shrubs will still be flowering from July (see July notes), plus: *Abelia chinensis** (sheltered gardens); *Aesculus parviflora; Calluna vulgaris** and vars.**; *Ceanothus* x 'Autumnal Blue'**, *C.* x

burkwoodii*, *C.* x 'Gloire de Versailles', *C.* x 'Topaz'; *Ceratostigma willmottianum**; *Clethra alnifolia paniculata; Colletia cruciata;
Fuchsia* x 'Chillerton Beauty'*, *F.* x 'Madame Cornelissen'*,
F. x 'Mrs. Popple'*, *F.* x 'Tom Thumb'*; *Hibiscus syriacus*
and vars.*; *Leycesteria formosa; Magnolia grandiflora**; *Olearia
haastii; Perowskia atriplicifolia**; *Tamarix pentandra* and vars.;
Ulex nanus*; *Veronica* x 'Autumn Glory'*. Climbers—*Clematis*
of the patens group, flowering on new wood; *C. tangutica*
'Gravetye variety'; *Jasminum officinale**; *Solanum crispum.*

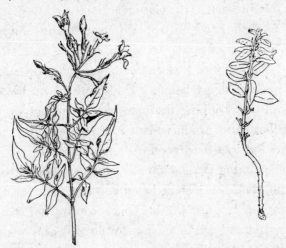

*Summer-flowering jasmine, Jasminum officinale (left).
A 'heeled' shrub cutting, Cotoneaster sp. (right)*

Propagate shrubs this month by means of cuttings consisting
of semi-ripe shoots of the current year's growth, detached with
a 'heel' from its parent branch. The 'heel' is simply the base

* Continues flowering beyond the month.

or joint between the shoot and the branch, and being made up of a concentration of growth cells tends to make new roots readily. Shrubs readily increased in this way include: box *(Buxus sempervirens)*, ceratostigma, corokia, corylopsis, coton-easter, chanaemoles, *Daphne mezereum;* *Erica carnea* and vars., escallonia, exochorda, fabiana, fatsia, forsythia, fothergilla, fuchsia, hibiscus, holly, lavendula, olearia, phyllodoce, pieris, pyracantha, salix (willow), santolina, syringa, tamarix and viburnum; but the method is worth trying with any shrub offering suitable material. Cuttings should be 3 - 6 in. long, stripped of their lower leaves, and inserted into sandy loam if out of doors, or a sand-peat compost in a frame, and well firmed. Covering with a cloche or handlight and shading for the first week or so are helpful. Odd cuttings can be covered with a jam-jar. Dipping the base of the cuttings in a root-inducing 'hormone' product tends to hasten and increase root action, but cuttings need good care afterwards.

Prepare planting stations for the autumn planting of ever-greens and conifers; loosen the subsoil and if clayey work in some gypsum; balance the top-soil according to its needs—organic matter and grit to a heavy soil; moist peat or compost to a sandy or light soil. No fresh manure or stimulatory ferti-lisers should be used. On poor soils, a dressing of 2 parts by weight hoof and horn meal, 2 parts bone-meal, and 1 part sulphate of potash, at 3 - 4 oz. per sq. yd., would be helpful, however. Planting can be done from the end of the month, and the earlier in the autumn the better.

Prune lavender bushes after flowering, cutting back only

flowered shoots and not the young unflowered shoots forming to carry bloom next year.

Unwanted old tree in an awkward place? Drill ½ in. holes about 1½ in. deep, 6 in. apart, at a downward slant, around the base of the tree; fill with a neat solution of a brushwood killer, based on 2,4,5-T; and seal with tape. As the solution circulates in the sap through the tree, both top growth and roots are killed. By winter it is often possible to rock the tree and its main roots out of the ground. Top growth should be removed as soon as the foliage dies.

Roses: Feed rather less frequently from now on, and choose a feed with a high phosphatic content and less nitrogen, so that, while the bushes will still flower well, they will also ripen their new wood and be hardy for the winter.

Repeat appropriate fungicidal treatment if either black spot or mildew persist—captan for the former, karathane or thiram for the latter.

New leaves being skeletonised? Likely to be the work of caterpillars of the yellow-tail or buff-tip moth; spray or dust with a malathion or derris insecticide.

Were many blooms eaten on one side in the summer? Did you notice many round, fattish and clumsy beetles about, especially at dusk in May or June? Then it is fairly certain that you have chafer beetles in your garden, and chafer larvae (white grubs) in the soil of the rose bed. Dress with an aldrin soil insecticide and rake this in.

Prune wichuraiana ramblers when they finish flowering,

cutting away the flowered shoots to their base, and training in the new growth. This means roses such as 'Crimson Shower', 'Dorothy Perkins', 'Excelsa', 'Lady Godiva', 'Mary Hicks', 'Minnehaha', and 'Sanders White'.

Prune large-flowering wichuraiana ramblers ('Albertine', 'Easlea's Golden Rambler', 'Emily Gray', 'Golden Glow', 'Leontine Gervais', 'Thelma',) and wichuraiana climbers such as 'The New Dawn', 'Dr. W. Van Fleet', 'Chaplin's Pink' and 'Paul's Scarlet' less drastically, chiefly removing only a few of the old stems.

Lawns: Cultivate, firm and rake level the area being prepared for sowing. Give careful attention to drainage. Lighten a heavy subsoil with gypsum and grit. On a low-lying site, it is well worth putting a 3 - 5 in. layer of crushed clinker and ash under the top 3 in. of soil. Pre-fertilise at least a week before sowing with a mixture of 4 parts by weight superphosphate, 1 part steamed bone flour, 2 parts sulphate of ammonia, and 1 part sulphate of potash, at 2 oz. per sq. yd., raked in.

Sow a new lawn, given favourable weather, in the latter part of this month, especially in the North. Choose a seed mixture suited to the lawn's purpose, and its soil. Cover lightly with sifted sand. Germination is usually rapid, and an August sowing enables the grass to get well established.

Lightly fork, fertilise, rake and sow bare areas in the established lawn. If the whole lawn is thin, scarify it thoroughly and sow with seed at $\frac{1}{2}$ oz. per sq. yd., bulked with sand; and top-dress the lawn with sifted loam and lawn peat to $\frac{1}{8}$ in depth.

Watch for signs of fungus disease when the weather is dull, mild and humid. Brownish-yellow, roundish patches of collapsed grass from penny-size to a foot or more across may be symptoms of fusarium patch disease *(Fusarium nivale)*. Place a jam-jar over the affected grasses, and if a pinkish white mycelium or fungus growth develops, it confirms the diagnosis. Apply a mercury or a malachite green/bordeaux mixture turf fungicide to the whole lawn, and repeat after 3 - 4 weeks. Bleached grasses, covered with a reddish, thread-like fungus in the form of pink needles on the tips of the grass blades, means corticum disease *(Corticium fuciforme)*. Treat with a mercury turf fungicide or a malachite green/bordeaux mixture.

Go over areas affected by fairy ring fungi thoroughly with a hollow-tine fork. Water with a turf fungicide to wet the soil; and a few days later, water with a solution of potassium permanganate ($\frac{1}{2}$ oz. per gallon water to 2 sq. yd.). If this fails, strip the turf and burn, then fork over and break up the soil thoroughly, and sterilise, before re-turfing or re-seeding.

Rock Garden: Coming into flower—everal alpines will still be in flower from July (see July notes), plus: *Calluna vulgaris alba plena**, *C. v.* 'H.E. Beale'*, *C. v.* 'J. H. Hamilton'*, *C. v.* 'Mrs. Ronald Gray'*; *Clematis tangutica* 'Gravetye variety'*; *Cyananthus lobatus**, *C. microphyllus**; *Cyclamen cilicium**, *C. europaeum**; *Gentiana farreri*, *G.* x *macauleyi**, *G. lagodechiana**, *G. septemfida**, *G. sino-ornata**; *Hypericum reptans**; *Oenothera acaulis**; *Sedum ewersii*; *Verbascum spinosum*; *Zauschneria californica**.

* Contioues flowering beyond the month.

Propagate by simple division of the plants the evergreen alpine herbs such as *Acaena* sp.; *Acantholimon glumaceum; Achillea* sp.; *Antennaria dioica; Aster alpinus, A. flaccidus, A. subcaeruleus; Globularia* sp.; *Meconopsis quintuplinervia; Ranunculus alpestris, R. amplexicaulis; Saxifraga oppositifolia* and vars.*, *S.* x *primulaize; Trillium grandiflorum.* Division implies the gentle separation into separate parts, each consisting of a top crown and leaves and roots. Replant at once, and water in.

Propagate by stem cuttings taken with a 'heel' the following: *Arabis* sp.; *Arnebia echioides; Campanula garganica* and vars., *C. pulla, C.* x *pulloides*, and *C. rotarvatica; Cassiope lycopodioides; Draba* sp.; *Molkia petraea; Penstemon scouleri, P.* x 'Six Hills', (see July notes for methods).

Plant corms of *Cyclamen orbiculatum* and its vars., and *C. repandum* (in warm sheltered localities).

Plant bulbs of winter aconites, *Eranthis cilicia, E.* x *tubergeniana,* dog's tooth violets, *Erythronium dens-canis, E. revolutum, E. tuolumnense, Crocus* sp., *Muscari botryoides* and the dwarf daffodils, *Narcissus bulbocodium, N. cyclamineus,* etc., *Puschkinia scilloides,* and *Scilla bifolia.* Give them all well-drained spots where they can remain up to three years undisturbed.

Water Garden: Clear duckweed (*Lemna* sp.) from the surface by netting it, driving it to one corner with a flat water jet from the hose and scooping it out, or by attaching a piece of sacking or rough cloth to the back of a wooden rake and drawing over the pond surface to collect the weed, which can then be scraped off. Duckweed does not harm pond-life, but it is unsightly and should be removed now, before hibernating buds sink to the bottom of the pool for the winter.

Remove scum, often caused by the presence of manures or organic matter in the bottom soil. Spread a layer of shingle or stone chippings over the soil at the base of the pool.

Persevere in removing silkweed or blanketweed, without changing the water. When aquatic plants and under-water oxygenators have grown sufficiently, they will take up the nutrients on which the algae growth lives.

Fruit: Take up strawberry mulch material, such as straw mats or sheet polythene, used to facilitate picking of fruit in a clean condition. If loose straw was used, this can be set alight and allowed to burn away. Remove old discoloured leaves around the base of plants, together with unwanted runners in the established strawberry bed, and finally prick over the soil between the rows of plants in readiness for winter.

Water late-fruiting strawberries of the alpine or perpetual type if the weather is hot and dry.

Plant up the new strawberry bed as soon as well-rooted runners become available. Water plants in well, on prepared ground (see July notes).

Cut down the fruited canes of raspberries to ground level and burn. There is no point in putting this job off until the winter, especially if the canes harbour grubs of the raspberry beetle or raspberry moth, or have shown signs of any infection. Tie in the most robust of the new canes to grow on. Clean up the soil of weeds. Couch and coarse grass can be safely killed by applying a dalapon grass-killer. Earmark robust new canes growing away from the stools of row plants for severance and propagation, but pull other growths up.

Prune black currants, cutting out older fruited shoots to base; leave the strongest of the new shoots to grow on. Prune to keep the bushes open to sun and air in the centre.

Cut out the fruited canes of loganberries to ground level, as soon as fruit has been gathered. Clear base of plants of weeds.

Prune early-fruiting nectarines and peaches as soon as fruit has been gathered, removing the unwanted fruited wood.

Spray early-ripening apples, such as 'Beauty of Bath', 'Laxton's Advance', 'Tydeman's Early Worcester' and 'Worcester Pearmain', with a special pre-harvest 'hormone' product to prevent much loss of fruit in premature windfalls. Wet the fruit stalks by spraying about three weeks in advance of picking date. This assures that the fruit will stay on the trees to ripen and mature fully.

Prepare ground or planting stations for new fruit trees by bastard-trenching and conditioning to give a good soil balance. Work in gypsum with heavy subsoils; give basic slag to acid soils; fork in organic matter and a potash fertiliser with light sands.

Choose and order new fruit trees, bearing in mind that all apple varieties and pears (except 'Conference'), all plums (except 'Victoria') and all sweet cherries, fruit best when planted with a cross-pollinating variety that is compatible and which flowers at about the same time. If only one apple tree is to be planted, choose a 'family' tree, consisting of three or more compatible varieties grafted or budded on the same rootstock. For small gardens, choose standard or half-standard trees for specimens only; give preference to bush, pyramid or cordon trees, on dwarfing root-stocks where space is at a premium.

Tie open-ended or perforated cellophane or polythene bags round choice ripening pears to prevent wasp and bird damage. Use fine nylon netting to keep birds away from ripening fruit on dwarf trees.

POLYTHENE BAGS

Protection for ripening pears, against birds and wasps.

Watch the line of flight of wasps attacking fruit as they leave the orchard so that you can trace the insects to their nests. Mark the nests, and at dusk place a spoonful of pyrethrum, DDT or gamma-BHC insecticidal dust just within the entrance. Wasps entering and leaving are soon contaminated with the dust, and the colony dies out.

Vegetables: The harvest begins; have storing places ready. Lift second early potatoes when the tops begin to yellow.

There is no point in leaving the tubers in the soil for marauding slugs and wireworms once plants stop growing. Clear the haulms first; burn if blighted. Lift on a dry day; let tubers dry off for an hour or two in the air and light, and then gather. The traditional method of clamping in thick layers of straw, covered with soil, is apt to prove wasteful and inconvenient. Place potatoes in fibre-board or wooden boxes, and store in cool, frost-proof, light-proof sheds, cellars or rooms. They must be in the dark; light turns them green and a poisonous alkaloid is formed.

Harvest maturing onion. First, sever the roots by lifting plants in the soil with a fork; second, bend over the tops at the neck; third, lift and dry off for roping and storing about three weeks later. Onions can be stored in the light, and do quite well in an attic.

Give another anti-blight spray to maincrop potatoes still growing vigorously, and to outdoor tomatoes.

Stop outdoor tomato plants after the fourth or fifth truss of flowers has formed, and continue with liquid feeding.

Leave surplus foliage from leafy greens — lettuce, beetroot, turnips, carrots, etc. — behind on the compost heap, when gathering vegetables for use.

Earth up celery in stages, taking particular care that soil does not trickle down between the leaves.

Clear the haulms and leaves of peas and beans as soon as the crop is finished. Cut off at soil level; remove top growth for compost; leave the roots to rot and enrich the soil.

Sow winter lettuce ('Attractie', 'All the Year Round', 'Arctic',

'Imperial') on a warm, sheltered border early this month, thinning plants to 9 in. apart later, and growing on under cloches.

Plant out seedlings of 'Late Purple' sprouting broccoli still available; plant out winter cabbage, firming the roots in well.

Make a sowing of onions in drills about 5 in. apart, ½ in. deep, to give produce for next July to October, on a well-drained seed-bed. An autumn-sowing variety is essential, such as 'Autumn Queen' for transplanting and growing on in spring, or 'White Lisbon' to grow on or to pull when green. Hardly a worthwhile crop for gardens exposed to winter frosts.

Watch all brassica crops for infestation by the white cabbage butterflies, which lay their eggs in yellow patches on the undersides of leaves. The eggs hatch in a few days into caterpillars which can soon defoliate plants. Hand-pick, or dust or spray with a derris or pyrethrum insecticide. Look for similar trouble on nasturtiums in the flower garden.

Plants Under Glass: Continue to give free ventilation and ample watering to plants, and temper hot midday sun with shading. Damp down and syringe plants, except when the weather turns close, thundery and humid, since too moist an atmosphere invites mildew and moulds.

Greenhouse plants you may have in bloom—several plants will still be in flower from July (see July notes), plus: *Calceolaria* sp.; *Datura knightii*; *Ceratostigma griffithii*, *C. willmottianum*; *Cassia corymbosa*; *Fuchsia fulgens*, *F. serratifolia*, *F. hybrids**; *Gazania uniflora**; *Iochroma fuchsioides*, *I. lanceolata*; *Leschenaultia* *biloba; Limonium* x *profusum*; Agapanthus orientalis flore pleno; Lagerstroemeria indica*; Lotus jacobaeus*; Nerine fothergilli*; Pelargonium* sp.*, *Stokesia cyanea*; Verbena venosa**. Bulbs: *Brunsvigia josephinae; Crocosmia aurea; Cyrtanthus collinus, C. sanguineus; Gladiolus primulinus* and vars., *G. pupureo-auratus;* stemrooting lilies: *Lilium brownii, L. henryi, L. pumilum, L. sulphureum; Lycoris aurea; Zephyranthes candida*. Climbers: *Hoya carnosa*; Mandevilla suaveolens*; Tibouchina semidecandra**.

The climbing wax flower, Hoya carnosa.

Take cuttings of bedding 'geraniums' (*Pelargonium zonale* vars.) to provide plants for next year; root in an open sandy compost. Let cuttings lie overnight on greenhouse bench to dry cut surfaces; to avoid black-rot, do not overwater.

Re-pot old corms of *Cyclamen persicum* as they begin to bud

---

* Continues flowering beyond the month.

new growth after the summer rest, using J.I.P. 3 or U.C. Potting Compost.

Give final potting to *Cyclamen persicum* raised from seeds last year. Place in light shade, and under cool temperatures.

Pot roman hyacinths for late November and December flowering. Pot prepared hyacinths for Christmas flowering, in bulb fibre ('Ostara', 'Delft's Blue', 'L'Innocence', 'Pink Pearl', 'Jan Bos' and 'Anne Marie' are good varieties). Pot polyanthus narcissi—'Paper White', 'Soleil D'Or'—wanted for Christmas flowering. Place all these bulbs at the base of a north wall, cover with ashes or leaves, and leave for 6 - 7 weeks, then bring into the cool greenhouse for forcing. Pot *Iris tingitana* for unusual early bloom; treat as the above bulbs.

Pot bulbs of *Lachenalia bulbifera* (syn. *L. pendula*), six to a 6 in. pot, to bloom about Christmas, and *L. aloides* and vars. to bloom in the early spring.

Pot on plants being raised from seeds for winter flowering— cineraria, calceolaria, *Begonia rex* (for foliage), *Primula obconica*, *P. malacoides*, etc.

Pot up *Zantedeschia aethiopica* (syn. *Richardia africana*), the arum lily or calla, singly in 5 or 6 in. pots, or two or three to an 8 - 10 in. pot, and bring into the cool greenhouse, but do not force with high temperatures.

Take cuttings of choice coleus to over-winter in cool greenhouse.

Rest gloxinias going out of flower, withholding water and drying the tubers off. Then store where the temperature will not fall below 50°F. (10°C.).

Feed chrysanthemums coming into bud, about every 7 - 10 days, until flowers open, using a balanced chrysanthemum feed or a simple solution of $\frac{1}{2}$ oz. nitrate of potash to 1 gallon water. You can delay flowering by switching on light at night for two hours, from about the end of the third week of the month until late September. A 40-watt lamp hung above the plants will give sufficient illumination for about 15 - 16 sq. ft. Flowering is delayed by three to four weeks. To hasten flowering, you must lengthen the time the plants spend in total darkness: a less easy matter, though it can be done with black sheet polythene screening quite well.

Tomatoes in Trouble? Blackish-brown sunken area opposite to the stalk end indicates blossom end rot—no cure; caused by water shortage at an earlier critical stage of development; prevent on later trusses by seeing to it that plants do not dry out. Fruits remaining small, without swelling, is symptomatic of dry set—caused by lack of moisture and still air when flowers are open, with resultant lack of fertilisation; prevent by syringing flowers with water, and/or tapping the flower stalk gently to dislodge pollen; cure by spraying faulty fruits with a fruit-setting 'hormone' spray within a fortnight of flowering. Leaves curling upwards, although foliage is healthy and green, usually means that the plant is too well fed with nitrogen; this often happens after planting, and is not damaging; cure by reducing the nitrogenous feeding. Ripening fruits green in patches, other than around the stalk end may be caused by insufficient potash in the feeding; by the effect of direct sun on the fruit; or by erratic culture. Can be prevented to some extent by growing a variety not susceptible to this trouble. Fruit splitting? A physiological trouble, chiefly caused by fluctuations in the water supply of the plant, though often in conjunction with wide temperature changes—a period of dull, slow-growing weather broken by high temperature and sun, for example; high humidity can cause it, or excessive watering following a dry period.

Suspect any plant showing signs of a mosaic mottling, or alternate blotching of yellow and green on tomato leaves, of virus infection. If there is no improvement and the plants fail to make normal growth, eliminate them—there is no cure.

Other signs of virus infection are: brown spots on the leaves, and brown dead streaks on the stems (streak or stripe virus); abnormal growth, such as twisted, tendril-like leaves, and stunted bushy growth; bronzing of the leaves, with downward curling, and a stop to growth. As there is no cure, it is wise to pull up such affected plants and burn them in the interests of the healthy plants remaining.

Sow seeds of tomato early this month for February-March cropping, but only possible where winter temperatures above 55°F. (13°C.) can be maintained. Sow seeds singly in small peat-wood fibre pots, and pot on without root disturbance.

Paint outside of greenhouse, if necessary, towards the end of the month, when the wood is dry. Traditional colour is white, but it can be any colour desired where the outside is concerned.

Avoid letting grape vines over-fruit. Carrying too many bunches, especially when the vine is young, leads to the physiological disorder known as shanking, when the grapes start to shrivel and turn dark prematurely.

September

The swallows are making them ready to fly,
Wheeling out on a windy sky:
Goodbye, Summer, goodbye, goodbye.

G. J. WHYTE-MELVILLE

OFFICIALY, summer will not run its course until the end of the third week of this month, but horticulturally the month brigns us to a season of change, and many plants are showing signs of having run their course.

Weather-wise, with the shortening of the days, latitude exerts its effect on the timing of garden operations more markedly, and in the North and localities where autumn and winter come early, it is necessary to do things such as sowing and planting and pre-winter operations one to three weeks earlier than in the south.

Every effort should be made to prevent weeds from flowering and seeding, even if there is only time and opportunity to remove top growth with shears or a sickle.

Flowers: Several plants will be flowering from last month (see August notes) — dahlias, begonias, gladioli, and many annuals will persist in flowering until falling temperatures check their vigour, and the first sharp night frost cuts them down. Flowers coming into bloom are fewer, but worth noting are—bulbs and corms: *Colchicum autumnale, C. speciaosum; Crosuc zonatus; Cyclamen cilicicum; Gladiolus alatus; Leucojum roseum; Nerine bowdenii; Schizostylis coccinea; Sternbergia lutea; S. macrantha.* In the border: *Aconitum fischeri; Aster amellus* 'Sonia', *Aster novae angliae* 'Barr's Pink', 'Barr's Violet', *Aster novi-belgii* in variety; *Aster* dwarf hybrids, especially 'Audrey', 'Little Red Boy', 'Snow Sprite'; *Astilbe chinensis pumila*; Chrysanthemum koreanum** in variety; *Helianthus* x 'Monarch', *H. salicifolius*; Kirengeshoma palmata; Sedum telephium* 'Autumn Joy'; *Solidago* x 'Golden Wings'*.

Trim the stems of border plants which have finished flowering. If tough, place at the base of a compost heap; or chop up with a sharp spade before adding to the heap.

Take the opportunity to divide and re-establish overcrowded clumps of kniphofia, hemerocallis, nepeta, and even polyanthus, if they have not been seen to earlier. Broadly, most spring and early summer flowering border plants will stand being transplanted now.

Plant bulbs in earnest this month—narcissi, iris species, and spring-flowering crocus, chionodoxa, etc.; set at a depth of about twice their own length.

Plant crown imperials *(Fritillaria imperialis)* 6 in. deep, in good soil.

* Continues flowering beyond the month.

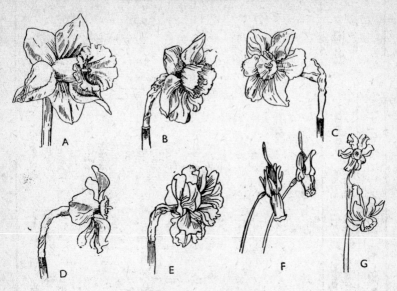

Some types of narcissus:
a. Trumpet daffodil.
b. Large-cupped narcissus, or Narcissus incomparabilis.
c. Small-cupped narcissus, or Narcissus barii.
d. Narcissus poeticus.
e. Double narcissus.
f. Narcissus cyclamineus.
g. Narcissus triandus.

Plant out rooted pink pipings where they are to flower next year. Sever layered border carnations and move a week or two later.

Sow sweet peas in light, well-drained soil, enriched with organic matter, in a sheltered site; plants to be protected during the winter by cloches.

Take cuttings of pansies and violas, consisting of shoots

BULBS AND CORMS FOR AUTUMN PLANTING

Species	Plant	Depth in inches	Inches apsrt	Flowering time	Colour	Height
Alstroemeria aurantiaca	Sep-Oct	4	12	June-Aug	orange-yellow	3 ft
Allium karatavi-ense	Sep-Dec	2 - 3	3 - 4	May	reddish	1 ft
Allium moly	Sep-Dec	2 - 3	3	May	yellow	1 ft
Camassia sp.	Oct-Nov	4	6	June-July	blue, white	3 - 4 ft
Crocus sp.	Sep-Dec	2 - 3	3 - 4	Mar-Apl	various	6 in
Eremurus sp.	Sep-Oct	6	12	June-July	various	5 - 8 ft
Galtonia candicans	Sep-Oct	6	18	July-Aug	white	3 ft
Iris (bulbous)	Sep-Oct	3	6	June-July	various	15 - 18 in
Leucojum sp.	Oct	3	3	Aug-Sep	white	4 - 6 in
Lilium spp.	Oct-Nov	6 - 8	6 - 9	July-Aug	various	3 - 6 ft
Narcissus sp.	Sep-Nov	4 - 6	6 - 9	Mar-Apl	various	6 - 24 in
Nomocharis sp.	Oct-Nov	3 - 4	4	June-July	pinks	15 - 24 in
Ornithogalum sp.	Sep-Nov	3 - 4	2 - 4	June	white	6 - 12 in
Puschkinia libanotica	Sep-Nov	2	4	Mar-Apl	white & blue	4 - 6 in
Scilla sp.	Sep-Nov	2 - 3	3 - 4	May-June	blue	4 - 12 in
Sternbergia sp.	July-Aug	3	4	Sep-Oct	yellow	6 in
Tulipa sp.	Nov-Dec	3	4 - 6	May	various	6 - 24 in

removed to their base, and insert in a porous compost in boxes or seed-pans in cold frame.

Plant out herbaceous perennials, propagated from cuttings earlier in the year, in their flowering stations.

Lift, sort and replant bulbs of the flowering onions such as *Allium caeruleum*, *A. moly*, *A. rosenbachinum*. Gather seeds and store dry and cool for sowing in February.

Paths: Renovate worn patches of grass paths by inserting new turf. Lightly fork over the soil, dress with a little superphosphate, and lay the turf cut thinly to about $1\frac{1}{2}$ in. Then dress with coarse sand.

Hedges: Move established hedges which have to be placed in new positions from the middle of the month onwards, whether deciduous or evergreen, so that the plants can make new roots before the onset of winter.

Begin planting evergreen hedges and coniferous hedges and screens from mid-September to early November, on well-drained soils. On soils subject to waterlogging in winter, it is better to attend to drainage and plant in the spring.

Give a final trimming to the quick-growing hedges—thorn, lonicera, etc.

Take cuttings of privet *(Ligustrum ovalifolium* and its variety *aureum)*, consisting of 6 - 8 in. shoots with a heel of older wood, and insert in a V-slit trench filled with sand. Remember, however, that against the advantages of a quick-growing, dense hedge there are the drawbacks of a soil-robbing plant that needs much clipping and attention as a hedge.

A laurel cutting, prepared for propagation.

Take cuttings of the cherry laurel, *Prunus laurocerasus*, for hedging or bank covering, this month; insert in warm soil, and shade for a week or two, until rooting.

Shrubs and Trees: Shrubs likely to be in flower—several persist from July (see July notes), plus: *Calluna vulgaris* 'C. W. Nix'*, *C. v.* 'Goldsworth Crimson'*; *Caryopteris* x *clandonensis**; *Cortaderia argentea* (pampas grass)*; *Hydrangea villosa; Sambucus canadensis maxima; Yucca filamentosa.* Climbers—*Clematis flammula, C.* x 'Lady Betty Balfour'*, *C.* orientalis*, *C. ascotiensis, Campsis grandiflora, C. radicans; Lonicera japonica halliana**.

Continue propagating shrubs by means of 'heeled' cuttings (see August notes). Many will succeed inserted in the soil out of doors in southern gardens and mild localities, but if in doubt, it is better to use a cold frame.

Move deciduous shrubs and trees that need to be re-located

* Continues flowering beyond the month.

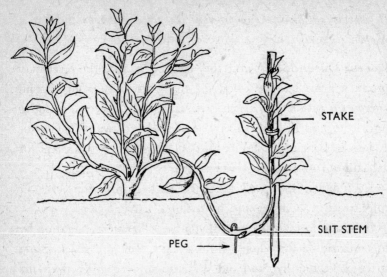

STAKE

SLIT STEM

PEG

An evergreen shrub, with a shoot ground-layered for propagation.

as soon as leaves begin to turn colour; there is no need to wait until they have fallen completely.

Go ahead with planting of evergreen shrubs and conifers. It is well worth while collecting these from the nurseries as early as possible, for ready establishment.

Layer evergreens such as holly, *Arbutus unedo*, rhododendrons, etc., this month, bending suitable low-growing shoots to the ground; prepare at the lowest point by slitting, nicking or ringing the bark, and dress with a root-inducing 'hormone' powder; peg down and mound over with loam, and leave for $1\frac{1}{2}$ - 2 years before severing and planting separately.

Plant shrubs wanted for winter flowers—*Erica carnea* and its varieties; *E. mediterranea* and its hybrids; *Hamamellis mollis*,

225

H. japonica; Chimonanthus praecox; Viburnum fragrans and vars.;
Mahonia japonica, etc.

Roses: Discontinue stimulatory feeding, so that the roses may
produce firm, mature wood for the winter, and not expend
energy on proud growth that is susceptible to frost. Remove
hips from hybrid bush roses, unless seeds are wanted for propagation, bearing in mind that in takes at least 5 years for
a seedling rose to show its merits.

Keep black spot well in check with captan fungicide or
sulphur dust. Gather and burn fallen leaves.

Continue to take cuttings, if you want to try propagation by
this means; on the whole, white, cream, pink and red varieties
strike most readily, and old varieties more readily than the
newer bi-colours and rich yellows (see July notes). It takes
about 2 years before you will see a flower.

Lawns: Sow new lawns as soon as possible this month, certainly
before the end of the second week in the North, and before the
end of the month in mild southern gardens; but in any locality,
the earlier, the better, provided the site is prepared and weed-
free. Dress the seed with a fungicidal dressing (thiram) to
prevent seedling losses from damping-off or foot-rot diseases.
Spray the sown area with a pre-emergent weed-killer, specially
formulated for grass, to avoid trouble from a smothering of
chickweed or other weed annuals.

Re-turf worn patches in tennis courts and on play lawns as
soon as practicable, co that the new turf may knit well and be
in good condition early next year.

Treat areas suspected of fungus infection with the appropriate fungicide (see August notes).

Paint or spot-spray areas of lawn invaded by the flat-growing, brownish-black and grey lichen, *Peltigera canina*, with a copper fungicide or 7½ % tar oil wash. Then take steps to improve soil fertility.

Switch lawns with a long flexible bamboo cane to disperse dew in the mornings (minimises the risk of fungus infection) and to scatter worm casts.

Eradicate earthworms, if necessary, by applying a proprietary worm-killer when the worms are ejecting their casts actively at the surface. Compensate for worm control and their usefulness as soil aerators by periodic slitting, spiking or forking of the turf.

Go over lawns on heavy soil thoroughly with a hollow-tine

SOIL CORES

Aerating the lawn with a hollow-tine fork.

fork, removing cores of soil, which can be placed on the compost heap. The top-dress with coarse sand, and brush in.

Make a last application of selective weed-killer where weeds are noticeable. Daisies are more susceptible now than in the spring to weel-killers based on MCPA or 2,4-D. For clover, hop trefoil, and bird's-foot trefoil, use a mecroprop product, specially formulated for clover control.

Rock Garden: Coming into flower—several alpines persist in bloom from last month (see August notes), but new flowers are more scarce, chiefly: *Astilbe chinensis* v. *pumila**, *A. simplicifolia**; *Crocus zonatus**, *C. pulchella**; *Leucojum autumnale**; *Liriope graminifolia**; *Mertensia echioides*; *Sedum cauticola, S. spurium* 'Schorbuser Blut'; *Sternbergia lutea.*

Plant hardy alpines ex pots where they are to flower, and where good drainage is assured. With heavy soils, and damp areas, it is often wise to delay until eraly spring. After planting, place a layer of stone chippings or gravel around plants to ensure good surface drainage and dryness about the crowns.

Propagate the following by simple division early in the month: *Artemesia lanata; Aubrieta* in variety; *Campanula* x *stansfieldii; Centaurea simplicaulis; Epimedium alpinum; Jeffersonia dubia; Nierembergia repens; Ramonda myconi; Rhodohypoxis baurii; Sedum* sp.; *Veronica spicata nana.* Each division should consist of a piece of the plant with roots, planted direct in the rock garden, or on a nursery terrace or border, with good drainage.

Be assiduous in protecting precious alpines from slugs, and

* Continues flowering beyond the month.

228

the tiny snails that often eat their leaves. A spraying of the plant and soil with a metaldehyde emulsion gives excellent results. Carefully collect and destroy clusters of whitish, tapioca-like eggs found in forking the soil and cleaning up rubbish.

Water Garden: Remove old decaying leaves before they sink through the water to the bottom.

Propagate bog and marginal plants by division, such as monkshood (*Acontium* sp.); *Buphthalmum speciosum; Cimicifuga cordifolia; Cypripedium* sp.; *Hemerocallis* sp.; *Hosta* sp.; Elecampane (*Inula* sp.); *Ranunculus aconitifolius; Senecio aquaticus.*

Weed the bog garden, and thin out plants which have made rampant growth, while the water level is low.

Gradually begin to withhold food from the fish as they become more sluggish in their movements with the coming of the colder weather.

Fruit: Plant new strawberry beds from bought plants as soon as possible this month. Nurseries send them out during late August to the end of October, but the sooner they are planted, especially in the North, the better their performance next year. 'Royal Sovereign' is still a premier strawberry, if of a virus-free strain, and 'Talisman' is exceptional. 'Cambridge' varieties are new strains of good repute, and disease-free strains of 'Sir Joseph Paxton' are now available for late-fruiting. Soak the soil after planting.

Plant strawberries of the so-called 'perpetual' type for long-fruiting season, in flushes up to October. Prepare ground well as for other strawberries, though this type is easier to grow and is much more tolerant of lime in the soil. Good varieties are: 'Red Rich', 'Sans Rivale', 'St. Claude' and 'Hampshire Maid'.

Plant the so-called 'climbing' strawberry ('Sonjana') where its robust runners may be trained and fastened up a trellis or netting fence; give it rich soil and a sunny position. Feed regularly to get the best crops.

Grease-band apple and pear trees just below the first branch junction on half-standard and standard trees, near the base of the main branches on bush trees. Use a modern 'grease' based on vegetable oils, and apply direct to the bark in a band of about 3 in wide. It traps many insects, particularly wingless winter moths, capsid bugs and March moths, seeking to lay their eggs in crevices of bark, etc., on the tree.

Harvest early dessert and cooking apples as required, direct from the tree. Do not expect them to keep beyond a week or two without losing some of their flavour. Better to go round the trees and pick the ripest every few days for use within a few days.

Harvest early pears by the calendar, but bear in mind that they should be gathered a day or two before they are fully ripe. Gather varieties such as 'William's Bon Chretien' while green, and bring into a warm room to ripen fully. 'Clapp's Favourite', 'Dr. Jules Guyot', 'Hessle', 'Jargonelle', 'Laxton's Superb' and 'Souvenir de Congres' are all pears to gather and eat before this month is out.

Harvest plums for cooking as soon as they begin to colour. Gather dessert plums fully ripe, detaching from the tree with the stalk.

Harvest cob nuts and filberts towards the end of the month, when the husks turn brown, and the nuts fall readily out of the husks. To keep—layer in sand; an inch of sand in the bottom of a box, then a single layer of nuts, a covering of sand, and repeat until box is full; store in a cool place, but not beyond the New Year, as nuts will tend to shrivel if kept too long.

Harvest cultivated blackberries, Himalaya berries and other hybrid berries as they ripen. When all fruit has been gathered, cut out the old fruited canes to their base, and train the new growing canes on the wires or supports for next year.

Take up and burn exhausted strawberry plants, and bush fruits such as currants, gooseberries and raspberries, with as much root as possible; and do not replant for a season or two with the same kind of fruit. Crop with vegetables for at least a year, replenishing the ground with organic matter, and digging deeply.

Vegetables: Harvest maincrop potatoes when the haulms begin to yellow. Clear haulms first, and burn if there has been any blight infection. Lift tubers on a dry day, allow to dry off for an hour or two, and gather for storing (see August notes). When lifting, take the trouble to gather weeds, and so leave a well-cleaned soil. This is essential where potatoes have been grown as a ground-cleaning crop prior to planting more permanent material.

Earth up celery and leeks grown in trenches for the last time, when the soil is fairly dry and friable.

Lift root crops of mature size towards the end of the month, during a dry spell. Remove tops of carrots, beets and turnips (spring or early summer sown) close to the crown of plants without cutting the crowns. Store, layered in sand or peat in boxes, or bins, in a shed or cellar. Put down a 2 - 3 in. layer of sand or peat, then a layer of carrots, beetroot or turnips packed reasonably closely together, cover completely with sand, then add another layer of roots, and so on, until all the crop is stored. Make mouse-proof with fine-mesh netting or strong-gauge polythene, or bait with a Warfarin bait.

Place cloches over late maturing vegetables, such as lettuce, 'Golden Ball' turnips, etc. Plant out spring cabbage and coleworts, if not already done; firm in well.

Gather herbs for drying. Cut mint shoots at the ground level; cut sage, removing shoots of the current growth almost to base; spread out on clean paper and oven sheets; wilt and dry steadily in very slow oven, (about 100°F., 37·5°C.), turning occasionally; rub when dry, and store in airtight bottles. Parsley leaves can be gathered a few at a time as available; wilt quickly in temperature of 110° - 120°F. (43° - 50°C.), and then dry steadily at 100°F. (37·5°C.). Thyme and pot marjoram can be dried similarly; but the whole plant of sweet marjoram should be pulled up for drying.

Raise mint from cuttings taken in late September, consisting of short 2 - 3 in. shoots from branching stems stripped of their lower leaves and inserted in sandy loam, 4 in. apart in a cold frame.

Plants Under Glass: While good ventilation is important in controlling late fungus diseases, it will be necessary to curtail ventilation earlier in the afternoon, now that night temperatures are falling. Water with care, giving enough to keep plants growing but without creating too much humidity or waterlogging the soil. Damping down will only be needed on the hottest days, and then only in the morning.

Greenhouse plants you may have in bloom: some of the plants will still be in flower from July, see those marked with an asterisk in July notes. To them can be added: *Coronilla glauca variegata*; Coffea arabica; Punica granatum nana*; Salvia involucrata bethellii*; Pinguicula bakeriana**. Bulbs—*Amaryllis belladonna; Crinum moorei*; Lycoris aurea; Nerine sarniensis*; Polianthes tuberosa** (tuberose); *Urginea maritima; Zephyranthes candida**. Climbers—*Cestrum purpureum*; Lapageria rosea*; Streptosolen jamesonii.*

Continue to pot up bulbs weekly of fortnightly, so that they can be brought in for forcing in succession and give an unbroken flowering display in the new year and early spring (see chart, page 222). Place potted bulbs out of doors under north wall, covered with ashes or peat or vermiculite; exmine after 6 weeks and bring in those showing tip growth to cool conditions in frame or greenhouse.

Pot *Lilium longiflorum* singly in 6 in. pots, using J.I.P. 1 compost; keep cool and in the dark until shoots are showing, then bring into cool greenhouse to grow on.

Pot on *Solanum capsicastrum* and *S. pseudocapsicum.*

---

* Continues flowering beyond the month.

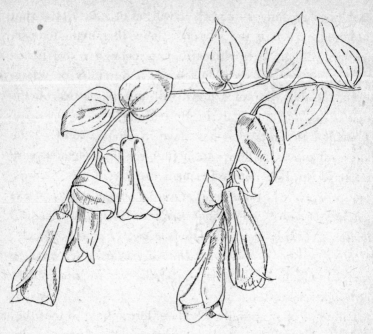

A lovely greenhouse climber, Lapageria rosea.

Pot up freesias, 6 - 8 to a 5 in. pot, 2 in. deep, in J.I.P. 1, and place out of doors under ashes for about 6 weeks; then bring into cold greenhouse or frame. No temperatures above 65°F. (18°C), or 50°F. (10°C.) by night.

Bring in tender shrubs towards the end of the month, such as indoor azaleas, etc., to cold greenhouse.

Keep *Cyclamen persicum* growing under cool conditions not more than 60°F. (15·5°C.); give a liquid feed about every 10 days once the buds show.

Sow a few seeds of annuals to be grown as pot plants and to

234

give springtime flowers: *Clarkia elegans*, godetia, larkspur and schizanthus are popular. A pinch of seed in a small peat-wood fibre pot is sufficient; thin when quite small, and pot on 2 or 3 plants to a 6 in. pot, and grow in cool greenhouse.

Sow sweet peas to give bloom under glass in spring. May be sown in borders, 1 in. deep, seeds spaced 2 - 3 in. apart. Chip the black seeds as for outdoor sowing.

Plant *Anemone* x 'St. Brigid' in cold frame to give early spring bloom, unblemished by the weather.

Clear tomato plants towards the end of the month if chrysanthemums are to be brought in for winter bloom. Healthy haulms may be composted, but any plants suspected of virus infection should be burnt. If possible, clean the house before the chrysanthemums are brought in. Remove all plants, and wash down with a solution of Jeyes fluid, or $2\frac{1}{2}$ % cresylic acid, wearing old clothing. If disease has been present, fumigate with a sulphur candle or two. Air the house thoroughly before reintroducing any plants. If pests have been troublesome, control by means of an insecticidal smoke generator.

Overhaul heating apparatus for the cool greenhouse. Have electrical equipment thoroughly tested. See that oil-heaters are meticulously clean.

If buying new heating apparatus, consider running costs, ease of maintenance and reliability, as well as the initial cost. Solid fuel boilers and water piping a probably the cheapest and most reliable, but need regular attention, usually twice every 24 hours. Oil or gas firing of boilers eases maintenance problems at higher fuel cost. Oil heaters are useful for intermittent or occasional added heat, but expensive for continuous heating, and require periodic attention. Electrical heating is reasonable in the cost of installation, most convenient to manage and undemanding in maintenance (barring power cuts) and, given thermostatic control, makes full use of all current consumed.

October

The skies they were ashen and sober;
The leaves they were crisped and sere —
The leaves they were withering and sere;
It was night in the lonesome October
Of my most immemorial year.
                              EDGAR ALLAN POE

IN SO far as it can be said that the gardening year has an end, it comes this month, when deciduous plants cast their leaves, herbaceous plants die down, and most plants, having matured their fruits and seeds, enter a period of dormancy and rest, with the beat of life within them at its slowest. For the gardener, it is the end of one year and the beginning of a new, when the fruits of harvest are his, and the prospects of the future beckon. In nature, there is, however, no clear-cut division of one year from another. Endings and beginnings merge. Even if October is discouraging with its first sharp frost, it also has promise, often shown in those few soft, warm days it gives us as the Indian Summer.

Broadly, the gardener has three objectives to fulfil this month: (1) to round off the year of active growth in harvesting vegetables and fruits and lifting tender perennials for winter protection; (2) to prepare the ground for future cultivations; and (3) to start new planting.

Flowers: Though several plants will continue to flower from September (see September notes), few new ones come into bloom. We may, however, look for the following bulbs and corms: *Crocus longiflorus, C. medius, C. speciosus; Schizostylis coccinea* 'Mrs. Hegarty'; and in the border: *Aster ericoides* 'Blue Star', *A. e.* 'Chastity', *A. e.* 'Ringdove'; *Salvia ambigens; S. uliginosa; Cortaderia argentea* and its varieties.

Take up spent bedding plants and consign them to the compost heap while still green. Refurbish the beds with humus-forming organic matter (manure, compost, spent hops, etc.) and a slow-acting phosphatic fertiliser such as bone-meal or basic slag.

Plant out spring bedding plants in prepared beds such as wallflowers, Brompton stocks, polyanthus, forget-me-nots, pansies and arabis as soon as possible this month, and firm them in well.

Clean up the herbaceous border; remove stems and foliage of plants; collect, clean and store stakes; and plant new herbaceous stock to fill gaps.

Lift border chrysanthemums now finishing flowering, place roots ('stools') together in a deep box or cold frame covered with soil, and store to provide cuttings for next year.

Lift, divide and replant old clumps of paeonies in their fourth to sixth year. Cut out the old centre parts of the roots, and replant the bud crowns, with roots attached, in well-dug soil. Firm and mulch with rotted organic matter.

Lift dahlia roots and tubers when the top growth has been killed and turned black by the first severe frost. Cut main stem to within 2 in. of its base, dry off tubers and remove soil; place in boxes, on a layer of peat and covered with peat, and store in a frost-proof shed, attic or room, where they are kept cool—about 45°F. (7°C.). Alternatively, dry coarse sand or vermiculite can be used. Label the root-stools as they are put away.

Lift gladioli corms as and when convenient towards the end of the month, particularly the large-flowering hybrids, even if foliage remains green. Remove surplus soil, and hang to dry in airy, well-ventilated place. Sorting can be done later; retain the large new corms formed above the old for flowering next year. Dust with thiram fungicidal dust and store in peat, vermiculite or coarse sand, in layers in boxes, in a frost-proof shed or attic or cellar. The tiny cormlets ('spawn') can be stored separately, to be planted for growing on to flowering size in nursery beds, if increase is wanted. In mild gardens, it is reasonably safe to leave corms of *Gladiolus primulinus* and vars. *in situ* for 2 - 3 years, marked and covered with litter for protection during the winter.

Lift begonias when top growth collapses; dry off tuberous roots and store in the same way as gladioli.

Lift corms of the newer large-flowering varieties of montbretia and crocosmia, treat and store as for gladioli.

Plant out biennials raised from seed such as canterbury bells, evening primroses, foxgloves, sweet williams, *Cynoglossum amabile* and Siberian wallflower *(Cheiranthus allionii)* where they are to flower.

Continue planting most bulbs this month, including *Allium* sp.; *Alstroemeria aurantiaca; Camassia* sp.; *Eremus* sp.; *Galtonia candicans; Iris juncea, I. xiphioides, I. xiphium; Leucojum* sp.; *Lilium* sp.; *Nomocharis* sp.; *Narcissi* sp.; and towards the end of the month, tulips.

A successful root cutting of Papaver sp.

Take root cuttings—$\frac{1}{2}$ - 1 in. lengths of thick roots, inserted vertically, the same way up as they grow naturally, for two-thirds their length in pans or boxes of a sandy compost, then covered with coarse sand, and placed in the cold greenhouse or frame, covered with a sheet of glass and treated as for seeds. *Papaver orientale, Gaillardia* sp., *Eryngium* sp., *Romneya* sp., *Erodium* sp., *Phlox decussata* and *P. paniculata* may be increased in this way. When cuttings show top growth and are rooting, they may be potted up separately.

240

Plant lily-of-the-valley (*Convallaria majalis* and vars.) in woodland and shady places. The pink-flowering form, *rosea*, is exceptional for colouring and scent.

Paths: In planning and re-planning paths, keep garden vistas well in mind. Apart from their utilitarian functions as means of access to the garden, paths provide lines of sight along which the eye is inevitably taken. Let paths have a focus, terminating in a well-placed object—seat, statue or ornamental feature— enticing one into further exploration, or inviting one to a worthwhile view.

Hedges: Plant box, holly or yew hedges this month, in ground that has been bastard trenched. Despite high initial cost, these plants still provide the finest screening, boundary and background hedges, suited to all soils except extremely dry or wet. Undeservedly rejected because of their reputed slow growth, the fact is that after the first year growth is quite respectable, and good well-knit hedges of 3 - 4 ft. are attained in about 4 - 5 years. High first cost is offset by low maintenance costs and durability. Yew, however, should not be planted where it might be eaten by cattle, sheep or horses.

Plant box edging for old-world surrounds to beds; *Buxus sempervirens* v. *suffruticosa* is the form used.

Plant *Cupressus macrocarpa* for an inexpensive windbreak or screen in south and west coastal gardens, but pay a little more and plant *Cupressocyparis* x *leylandii* when you intend to limit height and clip the growth annually.

241

Push ahead with the planting of other evergreen hedges on well-drained soils. *Berberis* x *darwinii*, *B*. x *stenophylla* and vars., *Cotoneaster lactea*, *Escallonia* x 'Donard Seedling' and *Pyracantha rogersiana* are good flowering evergreen subjects, but need about a 4 ft. width in which to flourish.

The strawberry tree, Arbutus unedo, which flowers while carrying its red fruits developed from the previous year's flowers.

Shrubs and Trees: Shrubs in flower are fewer, though some will persist from last month (see September notes). Coming into flower are: *Arbutus unedo**; *Fatsia japonica**; *Salix bockii*. This is, however, a season of fruits and berries, and of autumn foliage colour. Particularly rewarding amongst berrying shrubs in autumn are: *Berberis aggregata*, *B. prattii*, *B. wilsonae*; *Cotoneaster dammeri*, *C. lactea*, *C. wardii*, *C. horizontalis*; *Euonymus europaeus*; *Ilex aquifolium* and vars.; *Pernettya mucronata*; *Pyra-*

cantha sp.; *Skimmia* x *foremanii;* *Viburnum davidii;* *Viburnum opulus.* Fruiting or berrying trees: *Cotoneaster salicifolia rugosa; Crataegus* x *carrierei; Malus pumila* vars. 'Dartmouth', 'John Downie', 'Golden Hornet'; *Malus* x *robusta; Sorbus aucuparia* and vars.; *S. hupehensis.* Outstanding for autumn colour in foliage are: Shrubs—*Aronia arbutifolia,* many deciduous azaleas; *Berberis thunbergii* and vars.; *B. wilsonae; Cotoneaster bullata, C. dielsiana; Enkianthus campanulatus; Eucryphia glutinosa; Euonymus europaeus* and vars.; *Hamamelis mollis; Ribes aureum; Viburnum opulus* and *V. lantana.*

Trees: *Acer griseum, A. palmatum* and vars., *A. rubrum; Amelanchier canadensis; Gleditschia triacanthos; Koelreuteria paniculata; Liquidambar styraciflua; Parrotia persica; Prunus* x *hillieri* 'Spire'; *P. sargentii; Quercus rubra; Rhus cotinoides, R. cotinus* and vars., *R. typhina; Sorbus discolor, S. hupehensis, S. matsumurana, S. scalaris.*

Continue to plant evergreen shrubs and conifers as soon as available. It is essential that they should be rooting again before the winter comes, in order to support their leaves.

Lift and transplant any shrubs and trees within the garden that are misplaced. First dig a trench around the roots under the outer rim of the branches, and then undercut and loosen with roots in a soil-ball. Slip strong sacking or sheet polythene under the root ball and remove with a minimum of root disturbance. If the plants are very large and fully mature, however, it is best to prepare the specimen this year for moving next

* Continues flowering beyond the month.

year; first, sever the roots by digging a trench around and undercutting, as before, then fill in the trench with moist peat and soil mixed together, and leave at least 12 months. By then there will be a mass of roots in the peat-soil mixture, and the plant can be moved with a more compact root system.

Sow the seeds of magnolia when freshly ripe—if and when your magnolias set seed—preferably singly in $4\frac{1}{2}$ in. pots, sunk in the soil or in the cold frame, to facilitate transplanting.

Propagate deciduous shrubs difficult to grow from cuttings such as *Chaenomeles speciosa*, *Cydonia oblonga*, *Daphne odora*, *D. retusa*, *Hamamelis mollis*, *H. japonica*, lilacs (*Syringa* sp.), *Corylopsis* sp., and *Clematis* sp., by ground-layering suitably placed low branches in the same way as for evergreen shrubs last month (see September notes).

Stratify the ripe berries of shrubs and trees you wish to increase by growing from seed, such as cotoneaster, crataegus (thorn), ilex (holly), pyracantha (firethorn), rosa (roses), rowan (sorbus), daphne, prunus, etc.; alternate a layer of berries with a layer of sand. Keep in a cool, dry place. Rub out the seeds for sowing in spring. The rest is essential to mature the seeds.

Trim ivy on walls where it has become overgrown.

Roses: Lift and transplant roses within the garden, shortening the thick coarse roots, but leaving the finer fibrous roots intact. Replant bush roses with the bud union just below soil level.

Prepare beds for new roses by bastard trenching. Fork in gypsum and limestone grit to improve heavy clay soils. Do not plant new roses where roses have been grown previously for some years, as the soil is likely to be rose-sick. Trench well, organically manure, and grow annuals, dahlias or begonias for a year or two before reverting to roses.

Plant new roses of all kinds as and when they come available (see November notes).

Lawns: Cut a newly sown lawn when the grass is 2 - 3 in. high, on a dry day, using a well-sharpened mower or shears to reduce the grass height by about half. Roll lightly. Repeat cutting in 3 - 4 weeks' time.

Spike, slit or fork the established lawn prior to top-dressing. This is more valuable than rolling and should be carried out when the surface is dry.

Apply autumnal top-dressings to improve soil texture and structure. On heavy soils, use a mixture of equal parts by bulk coarse sand and lawn peat; on light soils, use equal parts by bulk of loam and peat. Alternatively, sifted rotted compost can be used instead of peat. Apply to cover the lawn up to $\frac{1}{8}$ in. thick, no more.

Apply coarse sand or grit and crushed charcoal (4 : 1) on soils subject to waterlogging and much moss invasion.

Apply autumnal fertilisers with the top-dressing. On most average ornamental lawns, this can simply consist of fine bone-meal at about 2 oz. per sq. yd. For a hungry lawn on light or sandy soil, a mixture of 1 part by weight hoof and horn meal, 3 parts bone-meal and 1 part sulphate of potash, at 2 - 3 oz. per sq. yd., would answer very well. Proprietary fertilisers low in nitrogen can also be applied at the rates recommended.

Mow the lawn without the grass box until the end of the year. Letting the clippings return to the soil will tend to deter moss invasion and give a greener look to the lawn in winter. Earthworms should be well under control.

Weed non-grass lawns such as chamomile and lawns made from creeping plants like thyme, pennyroyal, etc., by hand. Selective weed-killers can only be used for spot treatment of broad-leaved weeds, being confined to the foliage and crowns of the weeds.

Rock Garden: Coming into flower—plants asterisked* in September will still be flowering, plus: *Crocus longiflorus, C. medius, C. speciosus* and vars.; *Cyclamen neapolitanum; Gentiana sino-ornata; Oxalis lobata; Saxifraga fortunei;* and for autumn colour in foliage and berry, *Gaultheria procumbens, Vaccinium caespitosum* and *Berberis thunbergii atropurpurea nana.*

Two ways of protecting alpines:
a. Glass positioned in a wire frame.
b. Half-moon of clear plastic.

Plant miniature flowering bulbs during this month and next, preferably in groups or drifts, with due consideration of their height and foliage character. See chart on pp. 248-9.

Place small 'roofs' of glass or clear plastic over alpines with woolly or hairy leaves, and those from high altitudes to shelter them from winter rains, and so preserve them from basal rot.

Top-dress established rock plants with fine sifted loam and sand. Add grit for those needing good drainage, granite or sandstone for the lime-intolerant, limestone for the others.

Water Garden: Clear fallen leaves that may have blown into the pool, daily. Any great accumulation of rotting organic matter at the base of the pool will lower the oxygen content of the water and foul the pool to the detriment of fish.

Clean pool surrounds of green algae growth and slime by washing with a domestic bleach solution, but do not let it get into the water.

Stop feeding the fish when they start to stay deep and become less active. At the first cold weather the fish will hibernate, and even if quickened into some activity by a spell of mild weather, do not need feeding as they cannot digest the food, and are better off without it.

Plant bulbs of *Camassia esculenta*, *C. cusickii* and *C. leichtlinii* in the bog garden, 3 in. deep, in groups of a dozen or so, and leave to naturalise.

Plant lily-of-the-valley (*Convallaria majalis* and vars.), Solomon's seal (*Polygonatum multiflorum*), *Cypripedium reginae*, and *Arisaema candidissimum* in the rich, moist soil of the bog garden.

CHOICE MINIATURE FLOWERING BULBS FOR THE ROCK GARDEN

Species	Plant	Depth in in.	Inches apart.	To flower	Height in in.	Colour
Allium moly	Sep-Nov	2 - 3	3	May-June	9	yellow
Allium anceps	Sep-Nov	2 - 3	3	June-July	6	pink
Allium cyaneum	Sep-Nov	2 - 3	3	June-July	6	sky blue
A. narcissiflorum	Sep-Nov	2 - 3	3	July-Aug	9	deep wine
A. ostrowskianum	Sep-Nov	2 - 3	3	June-July	6	rose
Anemone appenina	Sep-Nov	2	3	Apl-Mar	6	blue, pink
Anemone blanda	Sep-Nov	2	3	Apl-Mar	6	blue, white
Brodiaea sp.	Sep-Nov	2 - 3	3 - 4	May-June	4 - 6	various
Bulbocodium vernum	Sep-Nov	2	3	Apl-Mar	2 - 3	pink
Chionodoxa luciliae	Sep-Nov	2	3	Apl	6	blue, white
Crocus biflorus	Sep-Nov	2	2	Feb-Mar	4	various
Crocus chrysanthus	Sep-Nov	2	2	Mar	3	various vars
Crocus susianus	Sep-Nov	2	2	Feb-Mar	2½	golden
Crocus tomasinianus	Sep-Nov	2	2	Mar	3 - 4	lavender
Crocus vernus	Sep-Nov	2	2	Mar-Apl	3½	blue, white
Cyclamen orbiculatum	Aug-Sep	2	4	Jan-Mar	4	carmine

Eranthis cilicica	Sep-Nov	2	3	Feb-Mar	3	yellow
E. x tubergeniana	Sep-Nov	2	3	Mar-Apl	3	yellow
Erythronium dens-canis	Aug-Oct	3	4	Mar-Apl	6	pink
Fritillaria meleagris	Aug-Oct	3	3	Apl-May	12	various
Galanthus elwesii	Aug-Oct	3	3	Feb	4	white
Iris danfordiae	Sep-Nov	2 - 3	2	Feb-Mar	6	yellow
Iris reticulata	Sep-Nov	2 - 3	3	Feb-Mar	6	violet, gold
Leucojum autumnale	July-Aug	3	3	Oct	6	white
Leucojum vernum	Sep-Nov	2 - 3	3	Feb-Mar	4 - 6	white
Muscari botryoides	June-July	3	3	May	6	blue, white
Narcissus asturiensis	Aug-Oct	2 - 3	3	Mar	3	yellow
N. bulbocodium	Aug-Oct	2 - 3	3	Mar-Apl	6	yellow
N. cyclamineus	Aug-Oct	2 - 3	3	Mar-Apl	6 - 9	various
N. triandrus & var.	Aug-Oct	2 - 3	3	Mar-Apl	6	yellow
Puschkinia scilloides	Sep-Nov	2 - 3	3	Apl	4	blue
Scilla bifolia	Sep-Nov	2 - 3	3	Mar-Apl	6	blue
Scilla siberica	Sep-Nov	2 - 3	3	Mar-Apl	4 - 6	various
Tulipa clusiana	Sep-Nov	3	4	Apl-May	8	white, red
Tulipa kaufmanniana	Sep-Nov	3	4	Apl	6	various
Tulipa praestans	Sep-Nov	3	6	Apl	8	red
Tulipa tarda	Sep-Nov	3	4	Apl	3	yellow

249

Plant ferns to give foliage beauty by the water's edge and along a stream. *Adiantum pedatum* (hardy maidenhair), *Athyrium filix-foemina, Onoclea sensibilis, Osmunda regalis* (for lime-free soil), *Polystichum angulare congestum, Scolopendrium vulgare* (hart's tongue fern), *Struthiopteris germanica, Blechum spicant*, and *Polypodium vulgare* and its varieties, are suggestions.

Fruit: Harvest culinary and dessert varieties of apples as they are ready. Generally speaking, the longer an apple keeps the later it is picked. A good test is to lift a fruit up to the horizontal, and if it starts to part from the tree at the stalk junction, it is ready to pick. Avoid bruising of fruit. If possible, lay out on the orchard floor on sheet polythene for several nights before putting into store.

Store apples and pears under cool, well-ventilated and somewhat damp conditions, for long keeping. A shed with a well-insulated roof, a door at each end which may be left open, and framed wire-netting insets, in the coolest (lowest) part of the orchard, answers well. A cellar is better than an attic. An even temperature of about 40° - 45°F. (4.5° - 7°C.) is desirable, and an earth floor. Lay fruit on shelves. Wrapping in oiled paper isolates the specimen that rots prematurely.

Gather late pears that keep, when colouring well and when the fruits part from the tree on being lifted just above the horizontal. Carry straight into store, placing separately on shelves, and if possible, keeping apart from apples. It is best not to use oiled paper wrapping for pears as it tends to ripen them too quickly.

Gather walnuts when nuts begin to fall naturally. Beat other fruits off with a long cane. Remove every scrap of husk from the nuts before storing. If many, put in a tub half filled with water and sand, and churn with a stiff brush until cleaned of husk; then dry well on trays. Store stratified in clean sand in boxes, under cool conditions. Do not attempt to keep too long; walnuts grown under our temperate conditions are not too 'meaty' and soon shrivel.

Check greasebands occasionally to see that they have not been bridged by leaves or debris falling on them.

Harvest fruit of autumn-bearing raspberries when the berries can be gathered dry. Leave fruited canes to be cut back next February-March.

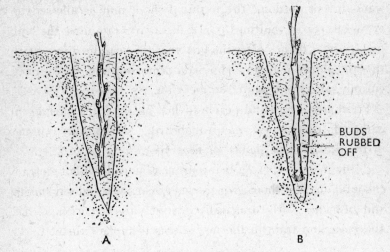

Propagating soft fruits from cuttings:
a. Black currant.
b. Red currant or gooseberry.

251

Propagate black currants by taking cuttings of this year's shoots, 8 - 10 in. long, and leaving all buds intact; insert in narrow trenches with the top two buds only above ground. Place cuttings about 6 in. apart, and ram the soil very firmly into position about them. After one year the rooted cuttings may be planted out in their permanent fruiting positions.

Propagate red and white currants and gooseberries early in the month by taking cuttings of this year's shoots, 9 - 12 in. long. From these remove all the buds except the top three or four, and insert in the soil with these buds above ground. This is to ensure that the plant grows with a single main stem, and growth branches from the buds on it. For plants to grow as standards or cordons, the terminal shoot only is allowed to grow on. Space cuttings 6 - 12 in. apart, ramming the soil firmly about them. After the first year they can be lifted, have the roots trimmed and thinned, removing the upper ones entirely, and be replanted to grow on.

Prune nectarines and peaches when all the fruits have been gathered, cutting out the fruit-bearing shoots and training in the replacement shoots for next year.

Prune morello cherries being trained on walls with a view to encouraging new shoot growth every year. Cut out old shoots and branches fairly drastically; paint cut ends with a tree antiseptic and train in the new shoots to replace them.

Vegetables: Complete the harvesting of potatoes and root crops (see September notes).

Strip sweet corn plants of their cobs when the tassels of silky hair begin to turn brown.

Cut down the yellowing 'fern' on the asparagus bed and weed thoroughly. Then cover with a top mulch of 2 - 3 in. of farmyard manure or good compost and soil for the winter.

Cut globe artichokes to base, and cover crowns with organic litter for the winter.

Gather unripened trusses of fruit from tomato plants and bring into a warm room. It is warmth that ripens, not light. There is no need to decorate window ledges with the fruits. Simply lay in boxes between sheets of newspaper, in rooms with temperatures of about 65°F. (18°C.), and take for use as they ripen. Or hang in warm kitchen, attached to a piece of the haulm.

Plants Under Glass: Give good ventilation to combat diseases such as grey mould which thrives in humidity. Water with care, ensuring plants and all surfaces of staging, paths, etc., are dry by dusk. Close the ventilators ahead of the fall in temperatures at night. Give a little heat to keep night temperatures above 55°F. (13°C.), to maintain good growth in ripening fruits or tomatoes and growing plants. For plants such as begonias, primulas, *Cyclamen persicum* and cool greenhouse subjects, a night temperature of not less that 45°F. (7°C.) is best. Chrysanthemums are happy with temperatures above 40°F. (4·5°C.).

Be meticulous in gathering yellowing leaves, foliage and parts of plants affected by rot or decay. Remove spent plants in pots promptly.

Greenhouse plants you may have in bloom: most of the plants flowering in September will persist in flower (see September notes), plus: *Bocconia frutescens; Bouvardia leiantha*; Calceolaria bicolor*; Fuchsia microphylla*, F. simplicicaulis; Grindelia glutinosa*; Luculia gratissima*; Salvia rutilans*; Begonia* in variety; chrysanthemums.

Plant some of the less hardy bulbs in pots to grow in the cool greenhouse—ixia, brodiaea, sparaxis, streptanthera, triteleia, tritonia, and watsonia. After potting, put in cold frames for 6 - 8 weeks, plunged in peat, and then bring into the cool greenhouse for flowering.

Pot plants of *Dicentra spectabilis* (Dutchman's Breeches) and *D. eximia;* place in cold frame, to bring into the cool greenhouse later for gentle forcing.

Complete potting up of bulbs intended to be forced in the new year and early spring (see September notes and chart).

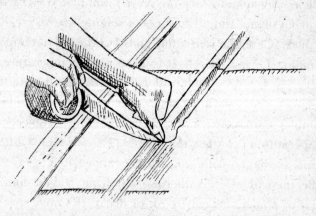

Sealing along greenhouse glazing bars with adhesive tape.

Bring in plants of *Primula obconica*, *P. malacoides*, to the cool greenhouse from cold frames.

Pot up roses, and stand out of doors on ashes until December, when they are pruned and brought in to be forced under cool greenhouse conditions.

Prune peaches and nectarines being grown under glass, removing the spent fruited wood.

Make a sowing of tomatoes to be grown in warm greenhouse for early summer fruiting.

Sow winter lettuce ('Cheshunt Early Giant', 'Cheshunt 5B') about the middle of the month, to be transplanted next month into prepared beds or deep boxes.

Begin to winter-proof the greenhouse when time and opportunity permit. Seal glass along the glazing bars with special sealing tape. Replace broken glass. Line the inside of the greenhouse with sheet polythene or P.V.C., carrying this up to about three-quarters the way on the roof, and fastening with flat-headed pins, tape or proprietary fastenings. Insulates and minimises heat loss. Put draught sealing round doors.

November

No shade, no shine, no butterflies, no bees.
No fruits, no flowers, no leaves, no birds — November!
THOMAS HOOD

Aᴅᴍɪᴛᴛᴇᴅʟʏ, nature and the gardening world reach their
nadir in November, but the garden scene need not be as
empty and drear as Thomas Hood's poem would suggest.
Since the whole world has been opened up to us horticulturally,
we may have flowers and colour, both out of doors and in the
greenhouse and home, although native plant growth may have
gone to sleep. Nevertheless, the month is largely one of
preparation and renovation for the year now looming.

Put soil cultivations in hand as soon as possible before the
winter rains start. Dig deeply or bastard-trench all new ground
being prepared for planting. Digging one spit deep is, however,
sufficient for vacant ground which was trenched within the
past three years or so. Early cultivation before the turn of the
year is most urgent in the case of heavy soils.

Enrich the soil with humus-forming organic matter as

liberally as possible. Humus is the foundation of soil fertility, and all soils need it. It is formed when organic matter decomposes, and improves the soil physically by giving it structure and moisture-retaining capacity; biologically and chemically as a base for bacterial activity and chemical reactions; and, finally, by providing nutrients for plants.

Be familiar with humus resources and their nature. Technically and theoretically, any material of an organic nature that is moribund decomposes and forms humus in the process. In gardening practice, however, the important resources of humus are as follows.

Animal manures, with or without plant material such as straw, used for bedding. Plant nutrient content is useful but variable, often deficient in phosphates. Cow or farmyard manure (a mixture) is traditionally beneficial on the lighter soils; stable or horse manure on heavy soils. Pig manure is wet and slightly caustic when fresh. Sheep manure is richest in plant nutrients and excellent on all counts. Poultry manure (including pigeons') is held to be rich in nitrogen and potash, low in phosphates, but otherwise an adequate alternative to any other manure. If used in their fresh state, animal manures are best applied in autumn or early winter so that they may rot before the growing season begins.

Compost—a mixture of plant and organic waste, pre-rotted before use—is an adequate humus alternative to animal manure, and when properly made is, weight for weight, richer in plant nutrients.

Peat, the partially decomposed remains of bog plants, is a good source of humus for all soils. There are usually two kinds offered—sedge peat and sphagnum moss peat—and both are useful for garden purposes in granulated or prepared horticultural grades. Peat is poor in plant nutrients, and needs the supplement of balanced fertilisers. It should be applied moist, except to heavy wet soils in autumn or winter.

Spent hops, direct from the brewery, are splendid humus-forming material for all soils, though low in plant nutrient content. Hop manure is usually a prepared proprietary product to which fertilisers have been added to make it a complete manure.

Seaweed is well worth gathering for sea-coast gardens, rotting readily and being fairly high in potash content.

Sewage sludge —the wet sticky residue of sewage treatment—may be used for its humus value on light or chalk soils in autumn or early winter. Plant nutrient values are very low. The modern dried sludge is more convenient to handle, and may be used on most soils as a source of humus-forming material, equivalent to that of farmyard manure, though less rich in plant nutrients.

Municipal wastes—the treated compost product of certain local authorities, offered under various names, is cheap and quite good for humus; plant nutrient value is usually quoted, but is comparatively low and unbalanced.

Poultry litter—the refuse of poultry houses, consisting of poultry dung mixed with litter material over a period of some months. Its value depends upon the litter used. If peat, the material can be used freely in autumn and winter, worked into the soil. If sawdust or wood shavings are present, it is wise to moisten the litter and stack for further decomposition before applying to the soil.

'Shoddy'—the wastes of woollen mills—is useful for most soils; it is added in autumn or early winter to give it time to rot. Fairly rich in nitrogen, it is often used for potatoes in the North.

Work in unrotted or partially rotted organic material into vacant soil in the autumn or early winter. Rotted material can be added at almost any time, and should be preferred in late winter and early spring manuring.

Flowers: Most flowers in evidence this month are of plants persisting from October so long as the weather is benign. No new flowers open, unless it is the precocious polyanthus, pansy or wallflower responding somewhat wrongheadedly to a mild weather spell. Bloom may linger among the asters, Korean chrysanthemums and late salvias until there is regular frost.

Plant tulips this month, at least 4 in. deep. Rub off the old 'tunics' or skins, and if there are signs of greenish or greyish mould, dust with a thiram fungicidal dust before planting. On heavy soils plant on a base of coarse sand, and cover bulbs with sand up to their points. Except for formal bedding and colour schemes, plant tulips in groups or drifts.

Begin forking over of herbaceous borders, removing debris and weeds. Prick in a steady and slow-acting fertiliser. Bone-meal is safe and helpful, at 3 - 4 oz. per sq. yd., but a more balanced dressing is one of 2 parts by weight hoof and horn meal, 2 parts bone-meal and 1 part sulphate of potash at 4 oz.

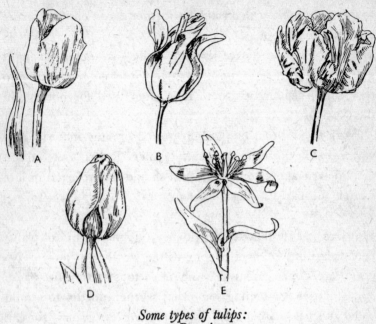

Some types of tulips:
a. Darwin.
b. Lily-flowering.
c. Parrot.
d. Breeder.
e. Water-lily.

per sq. yd. Then top-dress with an inch of sawdust, covering crowns of herbaceous plants. The sawdust will weather through the winter and be drawn gradually into the soil.

Make alterations in border lay-out, perhaps re-drawing the frontal edge. Use the garden hose when planning to make a more serpentine edge to a border.

Make a bonfire of woody waste, unsuitable for composting; add rose prunings, brambles, and any dead wood lying about

260

that might harbour parasitic fungi, like silver leaf or coral spot. Save the ash when cold, and keep it dry: useful as a potassic fertiliser for vegetables and can be applied to the soil at 6 - 8 oz. per sq. yd., in winter or spring. Wood ash is also rich in lime, however, and is more valuable on the acid soils. Do not use for lime-intolerant plants.

Hedges: Do not be tempted to plant evergreen or coniferous hedges once the weather turns cold, unless in very sheltered quarters. The plants lose moisture more quickly than they can regain it when they have to face low temperatures after being transplanted, although they may not show much damage until the spring.

Plant deciduous hedges from now on, when the weather is mild, the soil workable and open. The biggest danger to deciduous plants is not frost, but waterlogged soil conditions, which mean poor aeration and root-rot.

Plant beech *(Fagus sylvatica)* for an economical hedge or wind-break screen, both in unitial outlay and maintenance cost, on light soils, chalk or limestone, or any soil except the waterlogged. Plant hornbeam *(Carpinus betula)* on heavy soils and on low-lying sites, as it is more frost-resistant than beech. Both retain their browned leaves throughout the winter, when clipped.

Plant quick-thorn *(Crataegeus monogyna)* for quick growth and cheap cost on any soil, in double rows, staggered .·.·.·.·.

Plant *Berberis thunbergii atropurpurea*, the purple-leaved barberry, for a coloured foliage hedge up to 4 ft. For a floral effect, plant *Prunus cistena* ('Crimson Dwarf'), flowering in spring. (See Roses for rose hedges.)

Plant deciduous trees for screens. Sycamore *(Acer pseudo-platanus)* is one of the quickest growing, and most useful for exposed sites, but needs room. The Lombardy poplar *(Populus nigra italica)* gives a tall screen; the Manchester poplar *(Populus nigra betulifera)* does well in industrial areas and towns, but no poplar should be planted within 30 - 40 ft. of a building, as its roots soon undermine foundations. For more beautiful and safer screening of gardens, the shorter fastigiate forms of flowering trees such as *Prunus serrulata erecta*, *P. hillieri* 'Spire', *Pyrus communis* 'Beech Hill', *Crataegus monogyna stricta* or *Sorbus decora nana* are suggested.

The winter-flowering jasmine, Jasminum nudiflorum.

Shrubs and Trees: shrubs coming into flower—*Erica carnea* 'King George'*, *E.* x *darleyensis**, *E. vagans grandiflora* (persisting from September); *Garrya elliptica; Viburnum fragrans* and var.

*Continues flowering beyond the month.

candidissimum*; Jasminum nudiflorum*; Prunus subhirtella v. *autum-nalis*;* Colour may also be added to the winter scene by shrubs with coloured bark such as *Cornus alba* v. *atrosanguinea* with red bark, *C. stolonifera* v. *flaviramea* with yellow bark; *Salix vitellina* with golden bark, and its var. *britzensis* with scarlet bark; and *Rubus cockburnianus* with white waxy stems.

Plant deciduous shrubs and trees from now on until the end of March, provided that the weather is sufficiently mild and the soil can be easily worked. Superficial frost need be no deterrent; simply remove the frost crust and place on one side, to be put back when the plant has been installed. Since shrubs and trees are permanent plants, it is essential and worth while to plant them well.

(1) Dig the planting hole somewhat larger than the spread of the roots, one spit deep, and place the soil on one side on a sheet of sacking or polythene film.

(2) Fork over the subsoil. If it is hard, stony or rock-like, break up with a pickaxe. With all soils, mix a little rotted manure or organic matter in the subsoil. If clayey and sticky, add horticultural gypsum (6 - 8 oz. per sq. yd.), mixing well with the soil.

(3) Roughly finish the base of the planting hole convex like an upturned saucer, and tread firm.

(4) Mix top-soil with moist peat, leaf-mould, or rotted organic matter, using one-fourth to one-third its bulk, and perhaps a little bone meal (2 - 3 oz. per shrub or tree), but no strong fertilisers. Place the shrub or tree in the hole, spreading roots out evenly down the slightly raised subsoil. Planting depth

should be to same level as in the nursery—gauge by the soil mark on the stems. It is important to avoid over-deep planting, especially with trees, as this means the tree does not make normal growth later, but remains stunted and weakly.

(5) Insert stake at this point, if one is needed, so that roots remain undamaged.

(6) Cover roots with soil a little at a time, making sure that the roots are in full contact with it, with no air pockets being left. A liberal sprinkling of moist peat at this point helps plants in light soils to root readily. Then fill up with soil, and firm well by treading on it with the heels. If the soil is wet, wait for a few drying days and then firm.

(7) Cover with organic litter or mulch to keep frost out of the recently disturbed soil.

Plant more shallowly on poor soils—where the subsoil is near the surface, where there is rock near the surface and the soil is thin, where the soil is a made-up one such as on a waste tip, where the soil is easily waterlogged and poorly drained. Follow the same planting technique, but mound good topsoil over the roots. In time, the soil can be brought up to the same level by added soil and organic matter.

Plant deciduous wall shrubs and climbers well. Soil near walls tends to become easily dried out in summer. Prepare planting stations as for shrubs; place plants with their base and roots at least 1 ft. away from the wall itself, leaning the stem or stems to the wall. With wall shrubs and climbers that are not self-clinging it is better to arrange supports, such as wires, trellis or square mesh netting, to stand a few inches off the wall, so that air can circulate behind the stems of the plants—minimises trouble with red spider mite infestation, mildew infection and accumulations of dead leaves and debris.

Space new shrubs and trees adequately with regard to their ultimate spread and height, and not to their present size. If the ground looks a little bare, interplant with 'filler' shrubs or perennial flowers that are not particularly long-lived and which can be removed later when the permanent occupants require the room. Useful fillers among shrubs are lavender, santolina, brooms (*Cytisus* sp. raised from seed), sage (*Salvia officinalis* and vars.), *Salix vitellina* and vars., (planted as cuttings), helianthemums, cistus; while among trees, shrubs easily raised from cuttings such as forsythia, ribes and cotoneaster may be used.

Propagate shrubs such as forsythia, ribes, kerria, ceanothus, hydrangea and jasmine from cuttings of dormant, hardwood shoots of the present year's growth, inserted in sandy soil in a sheltered part of the garden such as below a north wall. Cuttings should be 6 - 8 in. long, cut below a node or bud, and be placed with $\frac{1}{2}$ - $\frac{2}{3}$ their length well firmed in the soil.

Rake and collect fallen leaves: one of the modern leaf sweepers is invaluable for this. Only oak, beech or hornbeam are really suitable for making leaf-mould, and are worth gathering separately for this purpose. Stack in a moist condition in a wire netting enclosure; leave to rot for a year or more, until easily broken into flaky fragments. Use no activators, except those based on herbs (QR) or bacterial action (Fertosan). Good oak or beech leaf-mould is as valuable as peat for soil seed and potting composts. A mixture of leaves can be added to a compost heap, or composted together (see July notes)—all are valuable humus-forming materials if well rotted, including horse-chestnut, sycamore, etc. Pine needles, however, rot slowly, and if numerous they should be heaped separately to rot for two years or more, as they then make excellent material for strawberry and raspberry beds.

Mulch shrubs with leaves, if not composted, securing the leaves in position with a sprinkling of soil.

Roses: Plant new roses from now on until the end of March when the weather and soil conditions are congenial. Autumn or early winter planting is particularly helpful on light soils. Prepare planting stations by taking out enough soil the for roots to be spread out flat (as for shrubs: see preceding section). Prepare the rose for planting by cutting away any soft, weakly shoots, and shoots carrying forming hips or flowers; cut back hard any tap roots (roots growing straight down), and shorten to about 9 in. all thickish or long roots without much fibre. Do not let the roots dry out; a good trick is to dunk them in a thick 'soup' of soil and water, coating them with mud. Plant with the bud-union about an inch below the soil surface. Spread out the finer roots and fibrous rootlets evenly on the firmed, convex base of the planting hole, sift in soil to cover, firming it to the roots with the fingers, and then fill in the soil gradually, firming well—a bit of a palaver, perhaps, but only done once and worth doing well. In beds, plant strong-growing bush roses 3 ft. apart, others 2 - 2½ ft., and dwarf polyanthas 2 ft. Standards should be planted at least 3 ft. apart, and be staked at the time of planting; ramblers and climbers should be planted 8 - 10 ft. apart, with their roots placed away from walls or pillars up which they are to climb. Plant shrub roses 6 - 8 ft. apart.

Plant rose hedges. Selected forms of *Rosa canina* make good garden thicket hedges comparatively quickly, and are planted about 12 in. apart. Colourful summer hedges can be formed of strong-growing floribunda varieties—'Frensham', 'Queen Elizabeth', 'Masquerade', 'Donald Prior', 'Kirsten Poulsen'—planted 3 ft. apart, in a single row or double staggered formation, thus .·.·.·. For a tall hedge, the hybrid Penzance sweet briers—forms of *Rosa eglanteria* such as 'Amy Robsart', 'Lady Penzance', 'Lord Penzance', and 'Meg Merrilees'—are effective, up to 5 - 7 ft. Planting technique is as described for other roses. Possible drawback is the tendency for a hedge to be marred by disease in a season unfavourable to roses.

Remove forming seed heads of hips and weather-spoiled roses from established roses, and cut out weakly shoots which will not grow much more now. Gather leaves and, if it has been a bad year for black spot disease, give a final spraying with a captan or copper fungicide.

Lawns: Lay new lawns from turf on well-prepared sites. This can be done, given suitable weather and soil conditions, at any time during the next four months. Good drainage is essential. Prepare site by bastard trenching. If subsoil is heavy, lighten liberally with clinker, coarse sand and grit. Remove perennial weed roots completely. Firm and level.

Pre-fertilise before laying, raking in a mixture of 2 parts by weight bone-meal, 2 parts superphosphate, 2 parts fine hoof- and horn-meal, and 1 part sulphate of potash at 2 - 3 oz. per sq. yd. Lay turf from one side or one corner, moving forward in front of you. Pare each sod evenly to $1\frac{1}{4}$ - $1\frac{1}{2}$ in. thick in a turf box (a box made to take a sod, with sides at required thickness and one end open); remove weeds, then lay in bonded

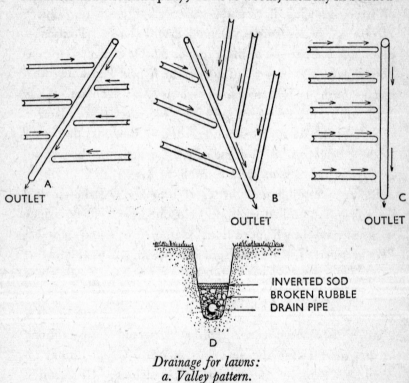

OUTLET

OUTLET

OUTLET

INVERTED SOD
BROKEN RUBBLE
DRAIN PIPE

Drainage for lawns:
a. Valley pattern.
b. Herring-bone pattern.
c. Grid pattern.
d. Section of drain.

formation like brickwork. Fit each sod in place, removing or adding soil underneath to level; check by means of a straight-edged board and spirit level. When complete, top-dress with sand liberally, and brush into the interstices. A lawn from turf is much dearer than one from seed. Seek suitable turf locally if possible to keep transport costs down.

Lawn hopelessly waterlogged? Install a proper drainage system. Dig narrow trenches 15 - 18 in. deep, for drains running to a major drain, with a fall of 1 in 200 from the higher point to the lower. Lay round clay, porous cement or plastic drainpipes in base of trenches, surround with broken clinker, brick or stone, topped with an inverted sod or layer of leaves, and replace soil. Use 3 in. pipes for subsidiary drains, 4 in. for the main drain, and let this empty into a ditch, land-drain or soak-away (a pit 4 - 6 ft. deep, 3 - 4½ ft. square, filled to just above the drain level with broken stone or rubble, and topped with inverted sods or a layer of leaves and soil).

Finish top-dressing established lawns for the winter before they become wet or affected by winter weather.

Give August sown lawns a cutting and a light top-dressing of sand if soil is inclined to be sticky.

Prepare loam for future top-dressings. The best loam consists of pasture or meadowland turf, cut in thick sods, 4 - 6 in. thick, and stacked upside-down to rot for at least twelve months. A little manure can be placed between layers for enrichment, and the sods dressed with flake naphthalene or aldrin insecticidal dust to control insect pests in the turf. Alternatively, the stripped top vegetation of weedy or neglected land can be stacked and rotted, but care will have to be taken to riddle and remove perennial weed roots, and sterilise the loam when it comes to be used.

Rock Garden: Coming into flower — *Erica carnea* 'King George'*; *E.* x *darleyensis**; *E. vagans grandiflora:* any other appeal will largely come from the presence of dwarf conifers, their form and foliage.

Complete planting of miniature flowering bulbs (see October notes). Construct new rock garden or walling, making sure that there is good drainage of the site.

Water Garden: Overhaul pumping equipment of waterfall gardens, and take the opportunity of overhauling fountains.

Place resilient material such as floating plastic sponge, boards of cork, or several rubber or plastic balls, in the garden pool to take the initial pressure of the ice when water freezes. Place near the sides, not in the middle, and do not stint on the material. Even so, it is wise to break any ice that forms as soon as possible—very gently if the pool contains fish, which are sensitive to vibrations and easily concussed by a blow transmitted through water.

Clear ice of snow soon after it has fallen, since lack of light will slow up plant activity underwater, and may lead to a dangerously low level of oxygen in the water for fish.

For coloured bark, insert cuttings of *Cornus alba* v. *atrosanguinea* and v. *spaethii*, and of *Salix vitellina* and its var. *britzensis*, in the bog garden.

* Continues flowering beyond the month.

Plant deciduous trees by the waterside or in wet soils that are tolerant of moist conditions, such as *Alnus glutinosa imperialis*, an alder with finely cut leaves; *A. incana aurea*, an alder with golden foliage; *Salix vitellina pendula (S. chrysocoma)*, the golden weeping willow; *Sorbus aucuparia asplenifolia*, a fine-leaved mountain ash; and *Taxodium distichum*, the pond cypress.

Fruit: Examine stored apples and pears periodically. If there is a sweetish smell in the air, give more ventilation and dampen the floor of the store, since it is chiefly ethylene from the fruit, which has the effect of speeding up the ripening or maturing of the fruit to the point of rottenness. Remove shrivelled and fungus-infected fruits and burn.

Plant fig trees early this month: 'Brown Turkey', 'Brunswick' or 'White Marseilles' varieties are suitable for outdoors. Root system must be curtailed. Most successfully grown on walls with southern, sunny aspect. Prepare planting space like a box, taking out the soil for an area of 12 - 16 sq. ft., to a depth of 3 ft. Pack the bottom with 12 in. of broken stone, brick or rubble. Build strong walls of brick, concrete, stone or asbestos sheeting to the surface. Fill with chopped turf, and a top 12 in. of loam mixed with rubble, shingle or coarse grit. Plant the fig in this. Train shoots in a fan.

Plant apples, pears, stone fruits and bush fruits from now on until February - March, when weather and soil conditions are suitable, though early November is probably the best planting time of all.

Choose apples budded or grafted on to rootstocks suited to the type of tree you wish to grow, and to your soil. Cordon and

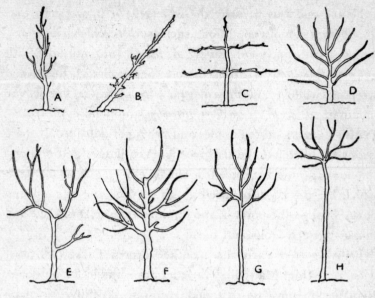

Types of fruit trees:

a. *Upright cordon.*
b. *Inclined cordon.*
c. *Espalier.*
d. *Fan-trained.*
e. *Bush.*
f. *Pyramid.*
g. *Half-standard.*
h. *Standard.*

trained trees (espaliers) and dwarf bush trees may be grafted on the most dwarfing rootstock—E. M. IX—on good soils (E. M. stands for East Malling Research Station where the rootstocks originated) but the semi-dwarfing E. M. VII or M. M. 106 is often better on the poorer soils. (M. M. stands for Malling-Merton, and designates rootstocks evolved and selected with the help of the John Innes Horticultural Research Station, at one time at Merton, now at Bayfordbury.) Bush, half-standard and

272

standard trees may be on rootstocks M. M. 104 or M. M. 111, while standards for large orchards are best on E. M. XXV. Pears are usually offered as cordon, espalier and bush trees on East Malling Quince A rootstock, and standards are only worth planting where one can afford the long time they take to come into bearing. There are no dwarfing rootstocks for stone fruits, and the rootstocks used—Brompton, Common Plum and St. Julien A—are the best available.

Plant in stations prepared as for ornamental shrubs and trees (see pp. 263 - 6). Trim torn or injured roots cleanly with a sloping cut on the underside, made with a sharp knife. For cordon and espalier trees, strong supporting wires on posts are necessary. Stake bush and pyramid trees on dwarfing rootstocks for the first year or two.

Plant black currant bushes by themselves or in association with culinary apple varieties, as they need similar manuring and feeding.

Plant red and white currants and gooseberries together or in association with dessert apples, so that they can receive similar manuring and feeding, high in potash.

Plant new raspberry beds this month, in ground liberally enriched with organic matter, spacing the parent canes 18 to 24 in. apart.

Plant loganberry, Himalaya berry, and cultivated blackberry on similar soil, to be trained on wires and with plants spaced 8 - 12 ft. apart.

Plant bush peaches out of doors, preferably on peach rootstocks (grown from seeds), or on Brompton as a poorer second choice. Peaches can be grown on bush trees in gardens fairly well sunned, and not too much given to late winter frosts.

Clean up the orchard floor of fallen leaves, and every third or fourth year give a dressing of basic slag (4 oz. per sq. yd.) to stone fruit trees, and one of bone-meal (4 oz. per sq. yd.) to other fruits.

Start winter pruning as soon as the leaves have fallen, as congenial days come along. Winter pruning of newly planted and young trees is largely concerned with stimulating wood growth to form a good framework of branches. Prune hard to provoke the reaction of strong shoot growth; prune lightly to provoke development in the buds along the shoot leading to flower and fruit formation. Simple general rules for trees in their early years are: cut back leaders or extension shoots of main branches by one- to two- thirds; then cut back lateral or side shoots according to vigour, pruning the weaker shoots harder. Once a good framework has been established and the tree has begun fruiting, the less winter pruning the better. On all trees remove dead or diseased wood entirely to base. Stone fruits are better pruned when in leaf, and no severe cuttings should be done in the winter.

Thin out older trees tending to become congested, and remove surplus branches to base. Then thin the fruiting spurs to ones or twos.

Cut out cankers on branches, cutting down to clean wood and painting the exposed wood with a tree antiseptic (Arbrex, Medo). Badly cankered growth is best removed entirely. Burn all prunings.

Prune newly planted black currants by cutting all shoots back to the nearest buds within 2 - 3 in. of their base. Prune established black currant bushes, if this has not already been done (see September notes), by removing a proportion of the oldest shoots.

Prune red and white currants to be trained as bushes by cutting back the central main leader to base, and shortening laterals to within 2 - 3 in. of their base. If to be trained as cordons, cut back the leader by one-half, and the laterals to within a bud or two of their base.

Prune gooseberries along the lines suggested for red and white currants when quality fruit is wanted—along the lines for black currants when fruit is wanted in quantity.

Begin winter spraying of fruit trees when pruning is finished, using a tar oil emulsion. Its purpose is mainly to destroy the eggs of aphides (greenfly) laid on the shoots of trees. It also has the effect of destroying moss and lichen growth on the trees, thereby improving their health and removing the potential hiding places of pests. For an initial spraying, use a $7\frac{1}{2}$ % dilution in water; for routine application, use a 5 % solution. Spray to wet and drench all exposed surfaces of the bush or tree, choosing a mild, still and dull day for the work. All pome fruits, stone fruits, currants and gooseberries benefit from this winter spray. Include ornamental trees of related species such as flowering crab apples, almonds, pears, cherries and peaches.

Vegetables: Cultivate ground now vacant in readiness for next year. It is wise to get the soil turned over before the end of the year, especially if heavy, so that it can weather and re-consolidate before sowing or planting time. Bastard-trench new ground or ground that has not been dug deeply for 4 years.

Organically manure the soil as you cultivate. It is usually best to spread the organic material on the surface and turn it in, mixing it thoroughly with the soil. There is no need to bury it, as then it rots only slowly. Animal manure, seaweed, spent hops (with a dusting of nitrogenous fertiliser), poultry manure and 'shoddy' may be incorporated fresh at this season. But compost, peat and leaf-soil can also be used. Organically manure for all crops except roots.

Leave clay soils roughly dug with clods exposed for the frost to act upon them. If a very sticky clay, dress with a soil conditioner after digging or ploughing. You can use gypsum, worked in while digging (it is quite compatible with organic matter or manures), or a seaweed derivative (sodium alginate). Lime later (if acid). Never let lime and manure come into contact outside the soil because chemical reaction will cause losses in plant nutrients.

Work all the organic matter you can into light sands, stony and chalk soils before winter, so that it may act as a 'sponge' and retain the winter rains, and impede leaching of soluble soil nutrients. 'Clay' such soils once—strewing the stickiest clay on the surface to weather—and this will give body to the soil for many years.

Apply marl (a mixture of clay and lime) to silt and peaty soils for a semi-permanent improvement.

Be hesitant about sowing broad beans or peas in autumn, except in the mildest localities on sheltered and well-sunned borders, or at least treat such sowings as experimental. A hard winter or a wet one often results in spoliage.

Plant thongs or roots of horse-radish if you want to, but take precautions to restrict it to its planting quarters, for it can become the most invasive and ineradicable of weeds!

Lift parsnips after frost, and store as for root vegetables (see October notes).

A cabbage infected by clubroot.

Take steps to eradicate clubroot if you are troubled by it. This is the fungus disease which causes the roots of cabbage, sprouts, cauliflower and related cruciferous plants to become swollen and knobbly. The cause is a slime fungus, *Plasmodiophora brassicae,* that lives in the soil. Remove infected plants with all roots as soon as possible to prevent the roots releasing more spores, and burn. Promote good drainage in infected soil. Lime to bring to *p*H 7. Stock with well-rotted organic matter. Crop with other vegetables than brassicas for at least 2 - 3 years. These measures help to reduce the parasite in the soil. Then when you do replant with susceptible crops, use 4 % calomel (mercuric chloride) dust at transplanting time.

Lift old clumps of rhubarb that are failing and divide into pieces, each with one or two buds; replant these on good soil, well enriched with organic matter. Discard the old centre of the clump.

Lift rhubarb roots for forcing and leave on top of the ground to be frosted before taking into greenhouse (see following section).

Plants Under Glass: Keep the air in the greenhouse on the dry side now. Maintain the night temperature at a minimum of 45°F. (7°C.). Give no water on dull, foggy days. This is when a mechanical fan ventilator can be of real service. Water growing plants sparingly, in the morning when necessary. Line walls of brick or wooden-based greenhouses with sheet aluminium foil, or sheet polystyrene to conserve and reflect heat back into the house.

Greenhouse plants you may have in bloom: plants marked with an asterisk* in October notes will still be flowering; *Cyclamen persicum*, *Primula malacoides*, *P. obconica*, and *P. sinensis*, grown from seed, will be coming into flower: plus *Parachetus communis*, the blue shamrock pea, *Amaryllis belladonna*, *Crinum moorei*, and *Lapageria rosea*. Potted plants of *Erica carnea* and its varieties will give colour even in the cold greenhouse.

Bring in the earliest of the bulbs potted in September, as they should be showing tip growth by now, and be ready for gentle forcing.

Feed indoor azaleas now showing bud with a liquid manure once every 7 - 10 days.

As chrysanthemums go out of flower, cut down and begin to take cuttings as they become available.

Bring in rhubarb for forcing; plant in a box of soil and place under staging, keeping moist.

Prune vines immediately after leaf-fall and harvest. Cut all lateral shoots to within the first strong bud of their base; dress soil with bone-meal and organic matter; bend the vine rods or main stems well down until new growth starts.

Plant new vines, placing where their growth can be best trained up to and along the roof of the greenhouse.

Plant new trained nectarine or peach trees in the border.

Lift and force sea kale. Lift the entire plants when the leaves wither. Cut the side roots off, retaining those of 4 - 6 in. long, straight and of little-finger thickness; bundle together and place them the same way up, as they have grown, in damp sand until spring when they are replanted out of doors. Now plant the crowns that remain in boxes 4 in. apart, or in pots, in old potting soil or moist peat, and place in darkness, with temperature of about 45° - 50°F. (7° - 10°C.). They take about 6 - 7 weeks to give produce. The spent crowns and roots are then discarded.

Beware of woodlice. Dust crevices and corners where the woodlice are likely to hide with a DDT insecticidal powder.

December

In a drear-nighted December,
Too Happy, happy tree,
Thy branches ne'er remember
Their green felicity.

JOHN KEATS

SHORT days and long nights not only curtail the activity of plants but of gardeners, and even then work out of doors is subject to the weather. December is a time for thinking rather than for doing, with future prospects in mind. Unlike Keats' happy tree, the gardener can not only remember and reflect on the green growing year behind him, but also make plans to improve on it in the year ahead.

An axiom of horticultural truth is that the key to saving labour is to do what has to be done at the right time, or a little in advance.

Make good use of congenial days to finish the winter pruning and spraying of fruit and ornamental trees and bushes.

On inclement days overhaul tools, sharpen cutting surfaces, get the lawn mower and the power cultivator overhauled; clean, sort and treat stakes and labels with preservative or paint. Treat wooden seed-boxes with an organic solvent preservative. Do not be tempted to use creosote for wood-work likely to come into contact with plants. When fresh, it is toxic to them; when dried and fumeless, it has lost much of its preservative power. Clean pots with the help of a solution of domestic bleach. Order replacements of pots, twine, etc. And in your leisure moments, read to enlarge your knowledge of plants, their botany and history, and of other gardeners' experiences.

Flowers: A blank month for flowers generally, though a note of colour could be introduced into borders by having a few clumps of the winter-flowering heaths—*Erica carnea* and its varieties. Anything else is either lingering on in a mild period or precocious.

Gamble with bulb-planting, if you must, but stick to the robust hardy kinds. Bargain offers are often made at this period, and where first-class results are not demanded, many bulbs and corms will give a show. Eschew those bulbs which have shrivelled, or which flower early in the new year. Your gamble is most likely to come off with the popular kinds of daffodils and narcissi, crocuses and tulips. Plant completely embraced in sand, if soil is at all wet.

Get the soil forked over in borders, and other flower beds renovated before the hard weather starts. Protect crowns of herbaceous plants likely to be damaged by hard frosts, with organic litter or a mulch of sawdust, chopped straw, bracken or peat. Welcome snow; there is no need to disturb it, except to shake it off plants that may break under its weight. Snow is insulating, and there is good evidence that it is beneficial to soil and plants when it melts.

Protect *Iris unguicularis*, now showing through the soil on warm borders, from slugs with a spraying of a metaldehyde emulsion, especially when a spell of mild weather brings it into bloom.

Christmas rose or hellebore, Helleborus niger var.

Place cloches or handlights over plants of the Christmas rose, *Helleborus niger*, to protect them from inclement weather and soiling of the blooms. Despite its common name, it may not flower before the month is out. The variety *H. n. altifolius* blooms earliest, and is the one to plant for any certainty of Christmas flowers.

Hedges: Continue planting of deciduous hedges in congenial weather and when the soil is nicely workable. Firm the soil to the roots well, and then top with a mulch of organic litter — invaluable for keeping the frost out of the soil.

Remove snow from coniferous or evergreen hedges where it

is weighing branches down, since it may break them when low temperatures tend to make growth more brittle.

Pollard trees such as poplars, willows and sycamores planted to form a screen, but becoming too high; cut to 6 - 9 ft. high.

Shrubs and Trees: Shrubs coming into flower, in addition to those asterisked* in November notes: *Viburnum grandiflorum**, *V.* x *bodnantense**, *V. tinus**; *Chimonanthus fragrans** (syn. *praecox*); *Lonicera fragrantissima**; *Erica carnea* 'Winter Beauty'*; *Clematis calycina**; *Erica* x 'Arthur Johnson'*, and *E.* x 'George Rendell'.

Continue planting deciduous shrubs and trees, given suitable weather conditions and workable soil. Do not be deterred by frost which has not penetrated the soil deeply. Simply lift the frozen soil on one side, plant in the friable soil beneath, give a covering of rotted manure, compost or peat, and put the frozen soil back on top. But do not plant in wet weather when the soil puddles easily and is sticky and difficult to manage. Put the plants as received in their wrappings in a frost-proof shed without unpacking. They are all right wrapped for up to three weeks. Alternatively, unpack to expose roots and put in tubs, boxes or containers, packed around with moist peat.

Prune deciduous trees such as beech, birch, chestnut, thorn, ash, hornbeam, poplar, oak, robinia, willow, elder, mountain ash and whitebeam before the turn of the year, if possible. In cutting off branches make two cuts, one on the underside

* Continues flowering beyond the month.

and one from the top, to avoid tearing the bark when the branch falls; finally cut branch flush with the older stem from which it has grown. Do not leave 'hat-pegs' or snags to die back and spread rot into the main stem. Prune to keep the growth habit and symmetry of the tree. Do not prune maples (*Acer* sp.), walnut or trees of the *Prunus* genus (cherries, plums, etc.) which are likely to 'bleed'; prune them when in leaf.

Tie cypresses and evergreen conifers with upright branching growth with raffia or tape to prevent snow breaking the branches down by its weight.

No berries on your holly? There won't be if you have only one plant. Hollies are usually unisexual, bearing male and female flowers on separate trees. Only female trees berry and they need at least one male companion near by for cross-pollination. Good female kinds are *Ilex aquifolium* vars. *camelliaefolia*, *fructu-luteo* (yellow berries), *hendersonii*, *hodginsii*, 'Golden King', 'Handsworth New Silver', 'Madame Briot'; and males, exceptional for their foliage merits are: *crispa picta*, 'Golden Queen' (misnamed), *argentea regina*.

Note the following for future planting, to enliven the winter garden scene: *Skimmia foremanii*, excellent smooth-leafed evergreen with berries that last the winter, with *S. japonica fragrans* for cross-pollination, and scented May flowers; *Cratageus* x *carrierei*, a fine thorn, with persistent orange-red haws; *Sorbus aria* v. *majestica*, giving autumn colour and bright red berries in clusters; *S. hupehensis* unusual for its persistent pink-tinted white berries, and *S. esserteauiana* with scarlet berries in clusters; *Pyracantha atalantioides*, best of the firethorns for its persistent berries; *Cotoneaster* x *cornubia*, evergreen with clusters of large red berries; *C. lactea* with reddish berries borne close to the stem; *C. rotundifolia* with berries along its shoots; *C. horizontalis*, the herring-bone cotoneaster, so magnificent on walls; and *Pernettya mucronata* in its hybrid forms ('Bell's Seedling', 'Donard Pink', 'Donard White') for lime-free soils.

Plant a specimen tree or two for winter bark beauty. Among the best are *Acer davidii*, with striated bark; *A. griseum*, with bark that flakes and is orange-russet; *Betula pendula* for its white and grey bark; *B. albosiensis septentrionalis*, with shining orange and brown bark; and *Prunus serrula* for its polished mahogany-red bark. None is difficult on reasonably well-drained soil, and all have other merits in their form and foliage.

Roses: Continue planting new roses in good weather and in well-conditioned soil. (See November notes for technique.)

Consider some of the shrub roses for planting in shrub and flower borders. True, they tend to flower only once in the year, but many of them make handsome specimens, with decorative foliage and colourful hips, and require much less attention that the more temperamental hybrids. Some suggestions are: *Rosa* x *alba* 'Amelia', fine scented pink; *R. gallica versicolor*, *R. centifolia muscosa*, the moss rose, in vars. 'Old Pink', 'Wm. Lobb' and 'Blanche Moreau'; *Rosa moyesii* in red 'Geranium' or white 'Nevada', with their persistent flagon fruits; *R. rugosa* in vars. 'Blanche de Coubert', 'F. J. Grootendorst', 'Pink Grootendorst' and 'Roseraie de L'Hay'; *R. moschata*, musk rose hybrids, in vars. *'Felicia'*, 'Cornelia' and 'Penelope';

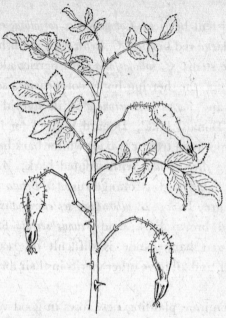

Rosa moyesii, carrying its bright red flagon-shaped hips.

and *Rosa spinosissima* in vars. 'Fruehlingsgold' and 'Fruehlings-morgen'.

Lawns: Turfing and drainage operations can be carried out in congenial weather, though it will be necessary to wait until the frost is out of the ground again if work is interrupted by a period of hard weather.

Keep dogs, especially bitches, from urinating on fine lawns. Train them to use waste ground or a sand-pit. Their urine is caustic, and damage to grasses is direct and immediate. Yellowing burnt patches will need taking up and replacing with new turf.

Aerate turf by slitting, spiking or forking when surface conditions permit, if not already done. Go over paths and areas subject to hard wear and pressure with a hollow-tine fork, and dress with coarse sand.

Rock Garden: Coming into flower — *Erica carnea* 'Winter Beauty', *E.* x *darleyensis* 'George Rendell', *E.* x *d.* 'Arthur Johnson'; *Iris unguicularis* (if weather is mild).

Keep a watch for damage done by mice or bank voles; not easily countered, unless the animals can be trapped, but mothballs pushed into all the holes that can be found are often effective as repellents.

Water Garden: Excavate site for a new pool, giving due consideration to its position. Obviously, pools belong naturally to the lower parts of the garden. On sloping sites, a waterfall cascading via pools at different levels to a large pool at the base is very effective. If concreting is done in chancy weather, use a quick-setting cement in the mix, and cover work with damp sacking and tarred paper at night.

Break ice on the pool gently as soon as it forms; do it daily in a freezing spell of weather.

Prevent herons taking fish from the pool by installing a nylon net, or a wire 4 in. high on sticks around the pool, since this stops them wading into it, as is their habit.

Fruit: Finish winter pruning of apples and pears and bush fruits, and winter-spraying with tar oil emulsion, on the first fine days that come along. If lack of opportunity or inclement weather prevent winter-spraying, spring measures will have to be taken against aphid pests.

Apply slow-acting fertilisers and manures not later than this month. Newly planted trees and bushes need nothing more than a top-dressing of organic manure or compost. Broadly speaking, dessert apples, gooseberries and red and white currants, need adequate potash in their feeding; culinary apples, pears and black currants respond to rather more nitrogen than the other fruits; and bramble fruits, raspberries and strawberries require nitrogen and potash in good balance, provided by good organic matter. A satisfactory plan is to furnish all fruits with phosphates in the winter, by applying bone-meal at 2 oz. per sq. yd., every other year; then give organic matter, reserving the heavier application of animal manure—pig, poultry, farmyard, etc.—for culinary apples and black currants. This winter manuring can be followed by balanced fertilisers in the spring (see March notes).

Prevent damage to tree bark by rabbits or hares by painting the stems with either tree-banding grease, or with a mixture of pure cow dung, clay and a proprietary repellent, to the height that the animals are likely to reach; or put trunk guards of wire netting collars round the base and lower 15 - 24 in. If a tree is barked by gnawing animals, it will recover, provided that the damage is only partial and does not extend completely round the tree. Pare the edges of ragged bark, dress the wounds with a tree antiseptic, and be prepared to feed through the leaves with foliar spraying in the summer. If a tree is girdled, with bark removed continuously right round the stem, it will die unless bridge-grafted in early spring—a somewhat delicate operation of inelegant tree surgery. If a tree is noted to be girdled, scions for grafting should be cut and stored right away; these consist of year-old shoots of the genus long enough to bridge the gap in the bark, inserted in moist soil or peat until grafting time.

Renovate old apple or pear trees that would appear to merit it. Begin by cutting out all the dead wood. Then remove branches that are ill-placed and ill-spaced, to open up the tree to air and light — especially those that cross and overlap others. Now remove 2 - 4 of the oldest branches right down to base to promote new growth. This cutting out of a proportion of the old growth can be repeated over a few years. Go over the branches and shoots left and thin the fruiting spurs. Give a thorough spraying with tar oil emulsion if encrusted with lichens and moss.

Dehorn old pear trees that have become too tall to manage easily; reduce the main stem and branches to manageable height for picking fruits and spraying. In the following year, during summer, thin the new shoots that tend to appear thickly near where the branches were cut, simply by bending and ripping them off, so that the base comes away with them and the likelihood of a rash of new shoots budding is avoided.

Why not plant a mulberry tree? The black mulberry (*Morus nigra*) makes a handsome bush, standard or wall-trained tree, with foliage that turns a lovely yellow before falling in autumn, and is very long-lived. Makes a good specimen tree for lawns, but in exposed and northerly gardens does best on a wall. Plant early this month as advised for other tree fruits (see November notes), but do not cut the long, rather fleshy roots at all, or they may 'bleed' and weaken the tree.

Plant outdoor vines this side of Christmas, if possible, as the sap begins to rise fairly early in the new year. Plant on sunny walls for best results, though they are being increasingly grown in the open, trained on wires for the making of wine. A most satisfactory variety for fruit is the 'Strawberry Grape'. Others are 'Brandt', 'Madeleine Royale', 'Royal Muscadine' and 'Chasselas Rose'.

Vegetables: Press on with digging and cultivation and organic manuring of vacant soil, along the lines indicated in November notes. When the ground is frozen, distribute organic manure or compost on the surface ready to be incorporated as soon as the frost goes. No real harm is done by walking on frosted ground; the time to avoid walking on the soil is when it is sticky and plastic, as the compressed clay tends to dry out hard and brick-like, and is very difficult to break down.

Go round and firm the roots of brassicas by treading the soil down during the frost, rather than wait until the ground has thawed and become soggy. Pick Brussels sprouts from the base of the plant upwards, as the sprouts attain usable size; use the head last. Protect broccoli and cauliflower heads from frost by means of cloches or even loose polythene bags tied over them. Gather up yellowing leaves and vegetable waste for composting.

Risk a sowing of broad beans, if you wish, when the weather is mild, choosing a warm, sheltered border and using the varieties 'Aquadulce Claudia' and 'Seville'. The seedlings have to run the gauntlet of February weather, however, and the crop is a gamble.

Prepare sea kale plants out of doors for forcing, covering the crowns of the plants with soil, and filling the shallow trenches from which the soil is taken between each pair of rows with manure, mixed with leaves, and placing sea kale pots or boxes over the crowns of the plants.

Plants Under Glass: Greenhouse management is much on the lines of those given under November notes, though more heat will be required to maintain temperatures as the weather grows colder. Since wind has much to do with the speed with which greenhouses lose heat, erect temporary wind-breaks of hurdles, chestnut paling, coir netting, or pea-sticks on the north and east sides on an exposed site.

Greenhouse plants you may have in bloom: these are much the same as in November, plus the early 'Indian' azaleas (*Azalea indicum*), late flowering chrysanthemums, cinerarias, *Erica gracilis, E. hyemalis, E. melanthera, Coronilla glauca variegata, Fuchsia* x 'Fanfare', *Jacobina* x *penrhosiensis, Abutilon insigne, Bouvardia jasminiflora, Camellia sasanqua, Zygocactus truncatus;* early flowering bulbs brought in for gentle forcing for Christmas, particularly Roman hyacinths, 'Paper White' and 'Soleil D'Or' narcisssi, and prepared hyacinths. Continue to bring in bulbs in succession and as they show robust growth.

291

Water plants in flower moderately, taking care not to let water lodge in the crowns. This is particularly important in the case of *Cyclamen persicum*.

Continue to cut down chrysanthemums as they finish flowering. Root cuttings for next year: try the technique of rooting in peat-wood fibre strip containers.

Make sowings of a dwarf variety of broad bean such as 'Beck's Gem', six seeds to a 9 in. pot, in J.I.P. 2 compost, to crop in spring.

Bring in chicory for forcing. Lift roots, cut top growth to within an inch of the crown, allow to dry for a few days in a cool place; then trim the roots, removing all side shoots and shortening to about 8 in.; pack in deep boxes in moist peat, compost or old potting soil, about 2 - 3 in. apart, and either cover with sand to a further depth of 6 in., or place in darkness, and force at 55°F. (13°C.).

Sterilise soil or loam for future propagation. There are two practical methods—by heat and by chemical treatment. The end in view is the destruction of all harmful organisms without impairing those that are beneficial or depressing the fertility of the soil. Actually it is a process of partial, not complete sterilisation that must be carried out.

Sterilisation by heat is the most efficient. To destroy fungi, viruses, parasitic insects, eelworms, weed seeds, and worms, it is desirable to heat all the soil to a minimum of 180°F. (82°C.) for ten minutes, but not to exceed 212°F. (100°C.). This can be done by steaming the soil, or by passing an electric current through it. Simple electrical apparatus is available on the market, and correctly used it gives excellent results. For those who must improvise, there are two simple ways of steaming without recourse to expensive apparatus: (1) cover a large saucepan with $\frac{1}{2}$ in. of water, bring to the boil, and pour in air-dry soil; cover and boil for about 20 minutes; empty the soil on to a clean surface to cool and lose surplus moisture; (2) place the soil, air-dry, in a perforated bucket or coarse sack, and suspend in a domestic boiler containing about 2 gallons of water, 2 - 3 in. above the water, and close; bring the water to the boil, and boil for 30 - 35 minutes; then empty the soil and spread on a clean surface to cool and dry. About two gallons of soil can be sterilised at a time.

To sterilise soil using chemicals: the soil is spread out on a clean surface, preferably in an airy place, and thoroughly watered by means of a fine-rosed watering-can with the chosen steriliser, using a gallon of solution to each bushel (8 gallons) of soil. The soil is then heaped, and covered with a tarpaulin or damp sacks, or sheet polythene, and left for 48 hours. The covering is then removed, and the soil spread out again to lose the fumes of the chemical. This usually takes up to 3 weeks. No chemical is so effective as heat. To control fungus diseases a 2 % solution of formalin (40 % formaldehyde) in water is used. To control parasitic insects, a $2\frac{1}{2}$ % solution of cresylic acid is used. Alternatively, a proprietary steriliser can be used in accordance with the maker's instructions.

To sterilise soil beds in the greenhouse, it is necessary to have the greenhouse empty of plants; apply 1 gallon of the chemical per sq. yd., cover with sheet polythene or damp sacks, and leave 48 hours, after which the greenhouse should be opened up and ventilated thoroughly. Planting may be done after 3 weeks.

Keep house plants thriving. The key to the successful cultivation of house plants is meeting their essential requirements. The choice of plants should be chiefly determined by the temperatures in which they will have to live, especially in winter. Some plants can stand fluctuations of temperature well; others require a steady temperature, such as is provided by central heating. Many of the plants brought indoors to flower require only cool conditions—temperatures between 45°F. and 55°F. (7°C. and 13°C.)—such as most hardy bulbs, indoor azaleas, *Cyclamen persicum*, and *Primula malacoides*, *obconica* and *sinensis*. All plants need light, since it is the regulator of their growth, but some tolerate shade better than others. When light and heat are diminished, watering needs are less. The following are some of the rules of house plant culture to be borne in mind.

Give most flowering plants ample light, without exposing to direct hot sun. Keep plants with variegated foliage in good light. Keep plants out of draughts. Plants are better off in light, open and porous composts, especially in winter. Avoid over-watering; too much is worse than too little. Keep atmosphere about plants moist, by standing pots in trays or saucers filled with gravel or pebbles or vermiculite, and keep this material moist. Alternatively, plunge pots in troughs or plant containers filled with moist peat. Keep leaves free of dust and dirt by sponging or brushing with a fine-hair brush.

Water plants that like their roots pot-bound—such as hydrangea, azalea, palms and other shrubs — by immersing their pots in a bath of water to soak, standing to drain thoroughly before replacing on their stands. Do not let plants stand with their pot bases in water. Watering needs vary according to growth activity—diminishing when plants are approaching their rest period, and in the short, dull days of winter, and increasing when in active growth and during the long, bright days of summer. Use soft water or rainwater for watering, if possible.

Select house plants according to the conditions under which they will have to grow. Here are some short lists.

(a) Plants which grow easily, and which are most likely to succeed under fluctuating temperatures—*Aralia elegantissima, Aechmea rhodocyanea, Cissus antartica, Ficus elastica, Hedera helix* in variety, *Peperomia* x 'Green Gold', *Philodendron scandens, Pilea nana, Sansevieria trifactiata laurentii, Aspidistra lurida, Tradescantia* in variety, *Zebrina pendula, Zygocactus truncata.*

(b) Plants likely to succeed with regular attention under central heating conditions—*Anthurium scherzerianum, Spathiphyllum wallsii, Croton pictum, Dracaena sanderiana, D. terminalis, Ficus benjamina, Maranta leuconeura, Monstera deliciosa, Peperomia caperata, P. sandersii, Philodendron hastatum, P. lacineatum, Scindapsus* x 'Marble Queen', and *Platycerium alcicorne.*

(c) Plants which are exacting in their requirements, though successful for a time, after which they often fail quickly—*Saintpaulia* (South African Violets) in variety, *Aphelandra squarrosa, Begonia* x 'Rex', *Caladium* sp., *Dieffenbachia* sp., *Eranthemum lindenii,* and *Fittonia verschaffeltii.*

295

INDEX